The Prose of Life

The Prose of Life
Sketches from Victorian Canada

Edited and Introduced by
Carole Gerson and Kathy Mezei

ECW PRESS

This book has been published with the help of a grant from the Canadian Federation for the Humanities, using funds provided by the Social Sciences and Humanities Research Council of Canada, and with grants from The Canada Council and the Ontario Arts Council.

Special thanks to Anne Yandle, Head, Special Collections, University of British Columbia Library, and to Charles Watt, Special Collections, Simon Fraser University Library.

Typeset by Trigraph and printed by University of Toronto Press

ECW PRESS
Stong College, York University
Downsview, Ontario M3J 1P3

The cover illustration, "Meet of the Snoe-Shoe Club," is from The Marquis of Lorne, K.T., *Canadian Pictures* (London: The Religious Tract Society, 1885), p. 91.

Canadian Cataloguing in Publication Data

Main entry under title:
The Prose of Life

ISBN 0-920802-27-3

1. Canadian essays (English) - 19th century.*
I. Gerson, Carole Fainstat, 1948-   II. Mezei, Kathy, 1947-

PS8369.P76   C814'.408   C82-094080-1
PR9197.7.P76

Contents

Preface

We have retained the spelling and syntax of the original sketches, making alterations only in the case of obvious typographical errors or confusing punctuation. All sketches are complete except P. T. S. Atty's "Law and Lawyers in Canada West," which has been abbreviated. We would also like to remind the reader that this collection is drawn from English-Canadian magazines, although some pieces describe life in Quebec. The selection of similar materials from French-Canadian magazines would constitute another collection. And, finally, the reader will notice that only some of the sketches are followed by biographical notes. This is because some authors were anonymous, while others left few traces behind them.

Illustrations

"Grandfathers," from Canniff Haight, *Country Life in Canada Fifty Years Ago* (Toronto: Hunter Rose, 1885), p.[11].

"Blackfeet Indians Crossing a River," from The Marquis of Lorne, K.T., *Canadian Pictures* (London: The Religious Tract Society, 1885), p. 152.

"Canadian Cow-Boy Life—Dinner in the Tent," from *The Dominion Illustrated Weekly*, 6 April 1889, p. 220.

"Night Fishing in the Creek," from Canniff Haight, *Country Life in Canada Fifty Years Ago* (Toronto: Hunter Rose, 1885), p.[43].

"From the Outside...," from Sara Jeannette Duncan, *An American Girl in London* (Toronto: Williamson, 1891), p. 34.

"The Market-Place, Quebec," from N. P. Willis, *Canadian Scenery*, Vol. II, Illus. W. H. Bartlett (London: George Virtue, 1842), p.[10].

"Ursuline Convent," from Alexander A. Boddy, *By Ocean, Prairie, and Peak* (London: Society for the Promotion of Christian Knowledge, 1896), p. 43.

"Canadian Farm Snowed-Up," from The Marquis of Lorne, K.T., *Canadian Pictures* (London: The Religious Tract Society, 1885), p. 20.

"The Medicine Man of 1790," from *The Dominion Illustrated Monthly*, ser. 2, 1 (April 1892), 140.

"Indian Medicine Men of to-day," from *The Dominion Illustrated Monthly*, ser. 2, 1 (April 1892), 141.

"Teepee and Red River Carts," from Captain "Mac" [MacAdam, J. I.], *Canada From The Atlantic To The Pacific* (Montreal: n.p., 1882), p. 285.

"Canoe Lake, Muskoka R., Ont.," from *The Dominion Illustrated Weekly*, 10 Nov. 1888, p. 301.

"Aunt Jane," from Canniff Haight, *Country Life in Canada Fifty Years Ago* (Toronto: Hunter Rose, 1885), p. 301.

"Cariboo Miners and Indians," from Captain "Mac" [MacAdam, J. I.], *Canada From The Atlantic To The Pacific* (Montreal: n.p., 1882), p. 325.

"A Coureur-De-Bois," *The Canadian Magazine*, 11 (Aug. 1898), 320.

Introduction

It was for want of other objects of interest that my attention
was first drawn to the natural productions of my adopted country, books I had none to assist me, all I could do was to note
facts, ask questions, and store up any information that I
chanced to obtain. Thus did I early become a forest gleaner.
— Catharine Parr Traill[1]

My father, when he married, bought a farm,—all woods, of
course; these were the only farms available for young folk to
commence life with in those days. There was a good deal of
romance in it, doubtless. Love in a cot; the smoke gracefully
curling; the wood-pecker tapping, and all that; very pretty; but
alas, in this work-a-day-world, particularly the new one upon
which my parents then entered, these silver linings were not
observed; they had too much of the prose of life.
— Canniff Haight[2]

IN THE NINETEENTH CENTURY, the sketch, a popular and accessible
literary form describing "the prose of life," frequently appeared in
Canadian magazines. More descriptive and episodic than the essay,
but less bound by plot and character development than the short
story, the sketch provided an appropriate medium for recording and

shaping noteworthy Canadian experiences. Some of our finest early books are collections of sketches and observations by travellers — Anna Jameson's *Winter Studies and Summer Rambles* (1838) — and by settlers — Catharine Parr Traill's *The Backwoods of Canada* (1836), and Susanna Moodie's *Roughing It in the Bush* (1852), subtitled "A Series of Canadian Sketches."

In nineteenth-century Canadian letters, the word "sketch" was commonly used as a catch-all term for descriptive prose pieces of varying lengths. As a genre, the sketch can be defined as an apparently personal anecdote or memoir which focusses on one particular place, person, or experience, and is usually intended for magazine publication. Colloquial in tone and informal in structure, it is related to the letter, itself a device allowing a writer to be personal. Traill's *The Backwoods of Canada* is composed of letters written home to her mother, and she addressed to her sister Agnes a sketch, included in this collection, describing a visit to the Chippewa Indians. Indeed, one of the essential characteristics of the sketch, the involvement of the reader with the scene, event, or character described, is appropriated from the letter. For example, in "A Visit to a Carmelite Convent," published in *The Week* in 1887, Sara Jeannette Duncan immediately engages her reader's attention with the invitation: "Let us walk awhile first."[3] While the sketch often takes the form of an eyewitness report, its primary focus is on the scene or event described. The use of anecdote and reported conversation further involves the reader, creates an ambiance of fiction, and increases the informality of tone.

These generalizations about the sketch as a genre are borne out by M. G. Parks in his introduction to the 1973 edition of Joseph Howe's travel sketches, *Western and Eastern Rambles*. Parks comments that due to the intimate nature of Howe's chosen form, "[his] sketches of Nova Scotia reveal considerably more of their author's distinctive qualities than do his correctly conventional poetry or even his magnificent speeches."[4] Combining "description and reflection,"[5] the two series of sketches, first published in the *Novascotian* from 1828 to 1831, document Howe's journeys and at the same time reveal much about his aesthetic temperament, breadth of knowledge, and sense of irony.

Occasionally there occur certain synonyms for the sketch and collections of sketches which illustrate the casual nature of the genre and the sense of personal observation: pen pictures, etchings, gleanings, maple leaves. Sketch writers themselves frequently call attention to the resemblance between verbal and pictorial processes of description. In her epigraph to *Roughing It in the Bush*, Susanna Moodie declares: "I sketch from Nature, and the picture's true."[6] Similarly, her sister, Catharine, interrupts a vivid descriptive passage in "A Visit to the Camp of the Chippewa Indians" with the comment that "A painter might have made a pretty sketch of the scene."[7] Such comparisons of the arts of writing and drawing emphasize the quality of realism characteristic of this form of prose.

In Canadian literature, the sketch can be regarded as a transitional genre that points towards the modern tradition of documentary writing—Barry Broadfoot's *Ten Lost Years*, Rudy Wiebe's *The Temptations of Big Bear*, Michael Ondaatje's *The Collected Works of Billy the Kid*, Daphne Marlatt's *Steveston*, and the recent proliferation of narrative poems about settlers and explorers: Don Gutteridge's two tetralogies, *Dreams and Visions* and *Time Is the Metaphor*; Gary Geddes' *Letter of the Master of Horse*; David Helwig's *Atlantic Crossings*; James Reaney's Donnelly trilogy. With its brevity and its emphasis on details of place or character, the nineteenth-century sketch also points towards the serial writing of Emily Carr, Stephen Leacock, Alice Munro, Clark Blaise, Jack Hodgins, and Hugh Hood, all of whom focus on the events, customs, and characters of a particular time and place. Hood has commented that "The connections between *Sunshine Sketches* and *Around the Mountain* are explicit and obvious and clear. They are both sketch books in the nineteenth-century tradition."[8] Another similarity appears in the fact that, like early Canadian sketches, parts of a number of these works were first published separately in magazines and then gathered into collections in which unity is loosely achieved through repetition of place, character, theme, or narrative voice.

The popularity of the sketch in Victorian Canada was partially due to the fact that newspapers and magazines, which were the main outlet for writers, demanded shorter literary forms. Moreover, because fiction was regarded as frivolous unless moral and instructive, the sketch provided light yet informative reading without being labelled as fanciful or corrupting, and without being intrusively didactic. For some authors, this genre served as a literary testing ground. Early in their careers, Susanna Moodie, Catharine Parr Traill, Sara Jeannette Duncan, and Archibald Lampman all wrote sketches; Duncan worked out her characteristic mixture of humour and realism, Lampman the precise and lyrical evocation of natural phenomena. In addition, this form of writing supplied some income and an outlet for creativity to budding authors, although many writers do not seem to have continued their literary careers. One such individual was Miss H. B. Macdonald, author of "Bush Scenery," included in this volume, whose entire output appears to consist of six items published in *The Literary Garland*.

Inspired by the drama of Confederation, editors of nineteenth-century Canadian periodicals encouraged writers to focus on local history, characters, places, and monuments. With its fine detailing of Canadian life, the sketch filled this patriotic need. In the 1880s and 1890s it also helped to satisfy and encourage the popular taste for local colour stories. Indeed, interest in recording and preserving Canadian scenery and experience dates from the early years of the century: in 1824, David Chisholme, editor of *The Canadian Review and Literary and Historical Journal* asked that writers

> apply themselves with assiduity to collect the scattered fragments of what may have happened in real life, and by combining them with those scenes of rural beauty of which nature has, almost, in every country been so profuse, present them to our view in the unassuming garb of facts which must inevitably lead to some moral deduction.[9]

Some of the pieces in this collection are by famous individuals; others are by anonymous, pseudonymous, or untraceable writers. This is a result of the reluctance of nineteenth-century Canadian periodicals to identify their writers. The periodicals which published interesting sketches range from the significant to the obscure. The best known sketches to appear in *The Literary Garland* (1839-52), Canada's most successful pre-Confederation periodical, were the pieces Susanna Moodie later collected in *Roughing It in the Bush*. Because these are available elsewhere, we have decided not to include them here. Instead, *The Literary Garland* is represented by a piece by Miss H. B. Macdonald. Other important pre-Confederation periodicals sampled here include Rev. MacGeorge's *Anglo-American Magazine* (1852-55) and the avowedly nationalistic *British American Magazine*, founded by Graeme Mercer Adam.

Post-Confederation Canada's growing concern with its own identity is reflected in the large proportion of pieces selected from periodicals of the 1870s and 1880s. The serious orientation towards realism and nationalism of both *The Canadian Monthly and National Review* (1872-78) and its successor, *Rose-Belford's Canadian Monthly*

(1878-82), is demonstrated by their inclusion of many sketches of local life. In Halifax and Saint John *The Maritime Monthly* (1873-75) likewise promoted harmony among the various regions of the new dominion by printing informative and entertaining descriptive and historical pieces. Sara Jeannette Duncan published many sketches in her columns in *The Week* and *The Globe*, as did Archibald Lampman, D. C. Scott, and W. W. Campbell in their *Globe* column, "At the Mermaid Inn"; during the last fifteen years of the century, sketches filled popular magazines such as *The Dominion Illustrated* (1883-95) and *The Canadian Magazine* (1893-1939).

The sketch not only described Canada to Canadians, but also presented pictures of the new world to the old. Sketches of Canadian life frequently appeared in English periodicals to which Moodie and Traill were two notable contributors. Several of the sketches Traill sent to *Sharpe's London Magazine* later reappeared in her incomplete series, "Forest Gleanings," published in Canada in the *Anglo-American Magazine*. She also contributed sketches to *Chambers' Edinburgh Journal*, while Moodie sent her writings to *Bentley's Miscellany*. Both *Blackwood's* and the *Edinburgh Review* occasionally published sketches of Canadian customs, activities, and scenery as well as reviews of books describing settlers' lives. (*Roughing It in the Bush* was reviewed under the title "Forest Life in Canada West" in *Blackwood's*, 71 [Jan.-June 1852], 355-65.)

The form of the sketch, while particularly appropriate to the realities of Canadian publishing and to the desire of Canadians to read entertaining and lifelike descriptions of themselves, arose from certain developments in British and American prose. Carl Ballstadt took the first important step in showing this connection when he pointed out that Susanna Moodie's sketches published in *The Literary Garland* were similar to some of her earlier work written in England. Her "Sketches from the Country" appeared in 1827-29 in *La Belle Assemblée*, a London periodical for ladies.[10] These were modelled on the work of Mary Russell Mitford, whose sketches of rural life, first published in the *New Monthly Magazine*, and later collected into several volumes as *Our Village* (1824-39), achieved great popularity. Identified by Harriet Martineau as the originator of "graphic description,"[11] Miss Mitford personally conducts her readers on rambles through the country-side during which she encounters quaint characters and scenes. The chattiness, informality, and humour of her prose, as well as her love of natural beauty and her delight in eccentric characters, became significant features of the sketch. At least two Canadian writers in addition to Susanna Moodie followed Mitford's example. In 1852-53 *The Provincial: or Halifax Monthly Magazine* published a series of eight anonymous pieces titled "Tales of Our Village," and in 1864 John Reade wrote a series of articles on "Our Canadian Village" for *The British American Magazine*.

Two other important sketchers of the early nineteenth century were Washington Irving and Nathaniel Hawthorne. Irving published his impressions of England and tales of American life in American periodicals. Their popularity was such that they were reprinted in English periodicals and finally collected in book form in 1819 as *The Sketchbook of Geoffrey Crayon, Gent.* Hawthorne contributed sketches to American magazines in the 1830s and 1840s. In addition to writing descriptive pieces, he entered into the realm of dreams, imaginary worlds, and religious ideas and feelings. The interest in rural beauty and local colour of sketchers such as Irving, Hawthorne, and Mitford generally reflected both the late eighteenth-century fascination with the picturesque and romantic attitudes towards nature. However, Canadian writers tended to focus on the harshness of the wilderness and on pioneer life rather than to inscribe elegies to a disappearing rural landscape, as did Mitford and Irving.

Certain characteristics of the eighteenth-century periodical essay carried over to the sketch — realistic description, humour, informality of style, the use of anecdotes, incidents, and reported conversations. Just as the clarity, simplicity, and informality of the periodical essays which appeared in the *Tatler* and the *Spectator* affected the prose style of the eighteenth and nineteenth centuries, Canadian sketches, with their evocation of the wilderness, have influenced later Canadian writing. Consider the hold of Susanna Moodie and Catharine Parr Traill upon the imaginations of modern writers such as Margaret Atwood, Carol Shields, Robertson Davies, and Margaret Laurence.

In the wide spectrum of Canadian life covered by the sketches in this volume, there are certain recurring features. In the earliest piece we have selected, "Streams and Rural Places in Nova Scotia" (1842), the anonymous author discusses the importance of establishing a sense of locality in the new land:

There is something not unpleasing in the idea of being natives of a small and remote province of a great empire, rather than of the central portion and immediate seat of power. It is grateful to those feelings of *locality*, by which we are ten-fold more attached to the small and obscure neighbourhood, with every spot of which we are acquainted, than if we be denizens of a city....There is a *unity*, the oneness of thought, feeling, opinion, and information....Now, very similar to this is the position of Nova Scotia relatively to the great centre of the British Empire....[T]here is something gratifying in the reflection, that we are not a mite lost to sight in the magnitude around us, —that though only a speck, the speck is distinct and perfect, standing forth boldly in relief, and not pictured faintly in the back-ground.[12]

Other writers seldom overtly mention this process, yet its importance is implicit in the way they repeatedly commence their pieces by describing the scene which forms the background to their subject, often comparing the Canadian setting to rural England.

Their opening descriptions of landscape frequently set the mood of the ensuing narratives. In "Fishing in Rice Lake" (1882), Archibald Lampman begins his account of an idyllic day on the water by likening Rice Lake to "a little patch of dreamland."[13] In contrast, the first paragraph of "The Castaways of Gull Island" (1873), Reverend Moses Harvey's report on an incident of shipwreck and cannibalism, accentuates the "dreary and repulsive appearance" of the Newfoundland coast:

Dark, frowning cliffs, lofty headlands, miles on miles of rocky walls, from two to three hundred feet in height, with little verdure, even in summer, crowning their summits; bold promontories sculptured into grim, fantastic shapes by the blows of Atlantic billows—these are what greet the eyes of the voyager as he sails along the eastern coast. The iron-bound shores present no pebbly beaches on which the summer waves break, in softened music; but rugged, precipitous cliffs frown defiance on the stormy Atlantic, and not unfrequently shape themselves into forms of stern, majestic beauty.[14]

In other sketches, the opening description of the landscape contrasts with what follows. This is most striking in "A Horrible Night" (1892), where George Brooks begins by praising the "pastoral loveliness" of the Frog Lake Settlement:

> In that land of clear skies and magnificent distances which is bounded on the south by the north branch of the Saskatchewan river, and which stretches northward to the region of eternal ice and snow, there is, perhaps, no lovelier spot than that known at one time as the Frog Lake Settlement. Beautiful as the landscape generally is in that particular portion of the Dominion, nature seems to have redoubled her efforts in some localities, and to have made one supreme exertion to excel herself about the lake and settlement with the somewhat uneuphonious name. Grander scenery, more magnificent views, can be seen in hundreds of places in Canada, but it is doubtful, if anywhere else—even in beautiful Prince Edward Island—can be seen more pastoral loveliness, more of that charming landscape which so reminds the traveller of rural England. There is the same hill and dale, the same refreshing greenness of leaf and blade, the same park-like beauty, the same wealth of fern, bracken and wild flowers: all that is wanting to make the visitor believe himself in Devonshire or Kent is the villages with their ivy covered churches and thatched cottages.[15]

Here the description of the landscape is part of the dramatic development of the narrative, leading to the author's eyewitness account of the utter desecration of this paradise by the 1885 massacre.

Another recurring feature of Canadian sketches is the use of the journey as an organizing structure. This may derive from the models available to the writers: Sara Jeanette Duncan, for example, begins "A Visit to a Carmelite Convent" in the Mary Russell Mitford fashion of conducting her readers on a walk. However, there are distinctively new world elements in some of the journeys. One of these is the way the visit or journey provides opportunities for the author to compare Canada to Britain or continental Europe. Another is the way the Canadian sketch often describes a personal conflict between expectations of order and the apparent disorder of the new land. This discrepancy can distract the writer from his main subject, the form of the sketch appropriately reflecting the meandering, loose structure of the journey itself. In *The Rural Tradition*, W. J. Keith notes that "Rural writing is successful in so far as it reproduces the effects of experiencing the random sights and sounds of the countryside."[16]

In some sketches describing short trips, the writers record how the romantic notions with which they had originally approached the land are dispelled by their personal experiences. Miss H. B. Macdonald begins her piece, "Bush Scenery" (1849), with the question "What emigrated European is there amongst us, who had ever formed a correct preconceived idea of an American forest?"[17] — and then recounts two hikes through the wilderness which corrected her own inaccurate preconceptions. In "A Visit to the Mineral Spring, East Bay, Cape Breton" (1873), W. D. Dimock describes his disappointing discovery that purportedly health-restoring waters are nothing more than a "filthy bog-hole."[18] Occasionally, the journey is of greater interest than the destination. In Thomas C. Birnie's "A Trip After Bark in Northern Ontario" (1893), we are never told about the actual cutting of the birchbark, the ostensible purpose of the expedition, but instead are treated to a detailed view of Ojibway customs and folklore. One senses that for some writers, the writing of the sketch became itself a voyage of discovery, in the course of which they learned about the new land and brought it under imaginative control. This is especially true of "A Trip After Bark," in which Birnie describes the fascination of "coasting around a wild lake which the eyes of the white man have never seen before."[19] He then actively participates in the process of taming the "wild" landscape when he rechristens this lake. Its Indian name, Min-e-gob-e-shing, "the place of the big eyes," "did not suggest pleasant memories, for the 'big eyes' were the frozen, swollen eyes of an unfortunate hunter, who perished here from exhaustion and cold." Birnie rejects both the danger of the new land and its Indian history when he selects the meek name, "Pretty Lake," for what "hereafter would be 'our lake.'"[20] Like Birnie, other authors describe voyages of discovery which they make in canoes or sleighs. Because it is indigenous to North America, the canoe provides an appropriate vehicle and image for a voyage which is inner as well as outer. This motif recurs in Margaret Atwood's *Surfacing*, Wayland Drew's *The Wabeno Feast*, and Douglas LePan's poem "Country without a Mythology."

Not surprisingly, sketches wholly or partially comic appeared frequently in Canadian periodicals, for humour was another means of taming the land. "Streams and Rural Places" concludes with an anecdote which reduces the menacing wilderness to the harmless setting of

9

a rather crude ethnic joke: An Irishman, lost and presumed eaten by bears or drowned in a waterfall, is discovered alive and well after overindulging in "a flask of his darling liquor."[21] In a similar fashion, the late nineteenth-century sketch describing the terror of being "Buried Under an Avalanche" in British Columbia modulates to an ironic tale. The narrator spends thirty-five dreadful days incarcerated in his cabin, running out of food and fuel, only to learn that the snow under which he had presumed himself to be trapped was largely a figment of his imagination. Tired of hearing exaggerated tales of "the tenderfoot and the avalanche,"[22] he ships out for Peru. Adventures in the wilderness were not the only source of humour; in 1872 *The Canadian Monthly and National Review* published the lively, pseudonymous "The Proctors. A Sketch of Canadian University Life" (presumably set at the University of Toronto) describing an elaborate prank played by senior students on a pair of pretentious but gullible freshmen.[23]

An interest in history lies behind many other nineteenth-century Canadian sketches whose authors were motivated by a desire to record their personal contact with momentous historical events, and to preserve their perspectives for posterity. One such individual was George B. Brooks; in 1885 he responded to the Dominion Government's call to arms by joining the "91st Regiment or Manitoba Light Infantry"[24] as a commissioned officer. His essay, "A Horrible Night. An Historical Sketch of the North-West Rebellion" (1892), recounts the details of his shattering experience as a member of the "first party of white men" to reach the Frog Lake settlement after the massacre. Similarly, Captain E. D. Clark of the North-West Mounted Police was inspired to his first literary effort by his role in Canada's negotiations with Sitting Bull.[25] Pioneer life was the concern of other writers, such as Canniff Haight[26] and Archibald MacMechan,[27] whose memoirs are tinged with considerable nostalgia for the good old days, as is P. T. S. Atty's description[28] of setting up his law practice. That the past was less than perfect is revealed by the trials of W. W. S., whose unadorned sketch of his struggles as a settler, published in *The British American Magazine* in 1863,[29] echoes many of Susanna Moodie's experiences.

Less personal treatments of history appear in sketches like Reverend Harvey's chilling account of the shipwrecked passengers of the *Queen*, who in December, 1867, suffered miserably from hunger, thirst, and cold as they waited in vain to be rescued from a rocky little island only three miles off the Newfoundland shore.[30] The most moving parts of his sketch are not the actual details he has pieced together, but the pitiful letters written by the dying castaways. Nearly the opposite approach to facts was taken by William McLennan in "The Coureur-de-Bois," published in *The Canadian Magazine* in 1898.[31] McLennan spins a fictional sketch out of documented history, adding dialogue and incident. This wide variety of approaches to history, both personal and national, shows that the sketchers were keenly aware of their importance as participants in the process of nation-building. Despite (or perhaps because of) the rawness of the new land, they felt moved to preserve its past by whatever means best suited their topic and talent—anecdote, documentation, memoir, or fiction.

Another subject which attracted nineteenth-century writers was Indians. In their sketches, even the most sympathetic writers reveal their condescension to a people whom they cannot refrain from perceiving as savages, either still noble or in a state of decline from their noble past. This attitude is not unexpected in the work of Catharine Parr Traill, but is more startling to encounter in "Indian Medicine Men and Their Magic,"[32] a sketch by Pauline Johnson, who founded a literary career on her public image as spokeswoman for the Indians' cause. However, once the reader gets past her first paragraphs, he discovers in her description of past and present shamanic practices a vivid memoir which could only have been written by a person with Johnson's native heritage. The author of "Early Provincial Settlers," an account of the capture of the Payzant children by Indians in Nova Scotia, reminds the reader in closing that "there is another side to these stories": "acts of cruelty on the part of the white man."[33]

Nineteenth-century sketches about Indians should be read as historical documents which reveal both a degree of sympathy and the ingrained prejudices which prevent that sympathy from growing into true acceptance of the Indians as equal human beings. It is at the level of description that this condescension is most evident to us, even if unconscious on the part of the writer. For example, Capt. E. D. Clark's patronizing attitude permeates his self-laudatory account of the Mounties' dealings with the Indians, and is reinforced by his frequent use of the word "savage" and his insistence on enclosing Sitting Bull's name in quotation marks. He describes Sitting Bull's willingness to negotiate peacefully as "a worthy tribute, if only from a savage, to the glorious colour which is the pride of every Englishman, and which has won respect in all quarters of the globe."[34]

11

More modern in attitude are a number of sketches about women, in particular those by Sara Jeannette Duncan, published in her columns in *The Week* and *The Globe*. One we have selected is a witty account of her attempt to buy accident insurance: she deflates the pompous sexism of the masculine business world by pointing out the absurdities of their assumptions about women. In another piece, "A Visit to a Carmelite Convent," she again opens in a witty, almost flippant, fashion as she looks at Montreal through the eyes of a visitor from Ontario. But when she actually meets the Carmelite nuns who have chosen to renounce the world completely, her light-heartedness mutes to awe at such severe self-denial.

Other kinds of sketches which appealed to Canadian writers were character studies — represented here by Campbell's " 'General' Bain of Sandy Beach" — and descriptions of hunting and fishing adventures, such as "My First Cariboo" by Hubert Humber and "Fishing in Rice Lake," by Archibald Lampman. These are rather conventional topics, common in English and American as well as Canadian periodicals.

The value of the sketches in this volume lies in the insight they provide into the taste and manners of Victorian Canada. Susanna Moodie, avid sketcher of characters and incidents, noted that "The real character of a people can be more truly gathered from . . . seemingly trifling incidents than from any ideas that we may form of them from the great facts in their history, and this is my reason for detailing events which might otherwise appear insignificant and unimportant."[35] And, in his iconoclastic approach to the Victorian era, Lytton Strachey remarked that

> It is not by the direct method of scrupulous narration that the explorer of the past can hope to depict that singular epoch. If he is wise, he will adopt a subtler strategy. . . . He will row out over that great ocean of material, and lower down into it, here and there, a little bucket, which will bring up to the light of day some characteristic specimen, from those far depths, to be examined with a careful curiosity.[36]

Like Strachey's studies, the sketches in this book therefore should be read as "characteristic specimens" which contribute to our knowledge and understanding of our cultural ancestors not by the "direct method of scrupulous narration" but by "detailing events which might otherwise appear insignificant and unimportant."

Although sketches continue to be written, the form as we have discussed it flourished during the latter half of the nineteenth century. In the 1890s writers like Duncan Campbell Scott, Charles G. D. Roberts and E. W. Thomson incorporated the local colour characteristic of the sketch into their fiction. After the First World War, with the emergence of realistic fiction and changes in the magazine markets, the sketch ceased to dominate the pages of magazines. However, many of its features, particularly the desire to document experiences in an imaginative way, have been adopted by the modern novel, serial stories, and documentary poems.

1 "Forest Gleanings, VI," *The Anglo-American Magazine*, Feb. 1853, p. 183.

2 "Canadian Life in the Country Fifty Years Ago," *Rose-Belford's Canadian Monthly*, 4 (Jan. 1880), 2.

3 "A Visit to a Carmelite Convent," *The Week*, 4 (10 Nov. 1887), 800.

4 "Joseph Howe, *Western and Eastern Rambles: Travel Sketches of Nova Scotia*, ed. M. G. Parks (Toronto: Univ. of Toronto Press, 1973), p. 31.

5 Howe, p. 32.

6 Susanna Moodie, *Roughing It in the Bush; or, Life in Canada*, 1 (London: Bentley, 1852), title page.

7 "A Visit to the Camp of the Chippewa Indians," *Sharpe's London Magazine*, 7 (1848), 116.

8 Hugh Hood, "An Interview with Hugh Hood," by J. R. (Tim) Struthers, *Essays on Canadian Writing*, Nos. 13-14 (Winter-Spring 1978-79), p. 51. Haliburton's *The Old Judge* (1849) is also in this tradition.

9 *The Canadian Review and Literary and Historical Journal*, 51 (July 1824), 50.

10 Carl Ballstadt, "Susanna Moodie and the English Sketch," *Canadian Literature*, No. 51 (Winter 1972), pp. 32-38.

11 *Harriet Martineau's Autobiography* (London: Smith, Elder, 1877), 1, p. 418.

12 "Streams and Rural Places in Nova Scotia," *Nova Scotia New Monthly Magazine*, March 1842, 33.

13 Archibald Lampman, "Fishing in Rice Lake," *Forest and Stream*, 19 (10 Aug. 1882), 28.

14 Rev. Moses Harvey, "The Castaways of Gull Island," *The Maritime Monthly*, May 1873, p. 435.

15 George B. Brooks, "A Horrible Night. An Historical Sketch of the North-West Rebellion," *The Lake Magazine*, 1 (Oct. 1892), 165.

16 W. J. Keith, *The Rural Tradition: A Study of the Non-Fiction Prose Writers of the English Countryside* (Toronto: Univ. of Toronto Press, 1974), pp. 20-21.

17 Miss H. B. Macdonald, "Bush Scenery," *The Literary Garland*, n.s. 7 (April 1849), 182.

18 W. D. Dimock, A. B., "A Visit to the Mineral Spring, East Bay, Cape Breton," *The Maritime Monthly*, July 1873, p. 67.

19 Thomas C. Birnie, "A Trip after Bark in Northern Ontario," *The Canadian Magazine*, May 1893, p. 213.

20 Birnie, p. 214.

21 Anon., "Streams and Rural Places in Nova Scotia," *The Nova Scotia New Monthly Magazine*, March 1842, p. 35.

22 John C. Werner, "Buried Under an Avalanche: An Experience in British Columbia," *The Canadian Magazine*, March 1895, p. 457.

23 Allan A'Dale, "The Proctors. A Sketch of Canadian University Life," *The Canadian Monthly and National Review*, Oct. 1872, pp. 362-66.

24 George B. Brooks, "A Horrible Night. An Historical Sketch of the North-West Rebellion," *The Lake Magazine*, Oct. 1892, p. 166.

25 Captain E. D. Clark, "In the North-West with 'Sitting Bull,'" *Rose-Belford's Canadian Monthly*, July 1880, pp. 66-73.

26 Canniff Haight, "Canadian Life in the Country Fifty Years Ago," *Rose-Belford's Canadian Monthly*, Jan. 1880, pp. 2-12.

27 Archibald MacMechan, "The Last of the Hostelries," *The Dominion Illustrated*, 5 July 1890, p. 10.

28 P. T. S. Atty, Esq., "Law and Lawyers in Canada West," *The Anglo-American Magazine*, April 1854, pp. 392-99.

29 W. W. S., "In the Bush. A Settler's Own Tale," *The British American Magazine*, June 1863, pp. 185-94.

30 Reverend M. Harvey, "The Castaways of Gull Island," *The Maritime Monthly*, May 1873, pp. 435-47.

31 William McLennan, "The Coureur-de-Bois. (A Sketch)," *The Canadian Magazine*, Aug. 1898, pp. 321-25.
   One year later, McLennan included this piece in *In Old France and New* (New York: Harper, 1899), which he dedicated to

W. D. Howells in gratitude for the latter's "early encouragement of my treatment of these French-Canadian sketches."

[32] Pauline Johnson, "Indian Medicine Men and Their Magic," *Dominion Illustrated*, ser. 2, vol. 1 (1892), 140-41.

[33] "Early Provincial Settlers. An Indian Tale," *The Provincial: or Halifax Monthly Magazine*, Aug. 1852, p. 306.

[34] Capt. E. D. Clark, "In the North-West with 'Sitting Bull,'" *Rose-Belford's Canadian Monthly*, July 1880, p. 69.

[35] Susanna Moodie, II, 39.

[36] Lytton Strachey, *Eminent Victorians* (1918; rpt. Harmondsworth, Eng.: Penguin, 1980), p. 9.

ABOVE MONTMORENCY FALLS.

Anonymous

"Streams and Rural Places in Nova Scotia"*

THERE IS SOMETHING NOT UNPLEASING in the idea of being natives of a small and remote province of a great empire, rather than of the central portion and immediate seat of power. It is grateful to those feelings of *locality*, by which we are ten-fold more attached to the small and obscure neighbourhood, with every spot of which we are acquainted, than if we be denizens of a city. It is true, that the man who spends his life in the crowded streets, or the dull brick houses, of the latter, may have become warmly attached to them: but this has required years. On the contrary, in the village the circumference of which might be half that of a town-square,—its inhabitants about as numerous as the inmates of a London hotel,—with one little church to which every body goes,—one little coterie, of which all the members are the best friends in the world, you soon feel an affection for every foot of the road you tread,—you would draw a limit between your vicinage and the world without, and feel, in short, as snug and as comfortable as if you sat all day in your own chimney-corner, the fragrant weed in your mouth, and a glass of—whatever you'll take (tee-total or otherwise) beside you. There is a *unity*, the oneness of thought, feeling, opinion, and information, which renders your neighbours and yourself like a pair of lovers, or rather perhaps, like tried

The Nova Scotia New Monthly Magazine, March 1842, pp. 33-35.

17

friends who have, passed the hey-day of youth, and with whom, from long intercourse and familiarity, the possessions of each—the valued dog or the treasured curiosity—have become equally dear. Now, very similar to this is the position of Nova Scotia relatively to the great centre of the British Empire. The latter (it hath pleasant nooks, but they have not the charm which *remoteness* gives) seems like a huge sea constantly convulsed, now rising high from its native level with tumultuous fury, now falling precipitously into a valley presently to mount anew. Faintly the murmur seems to be borne to us across the bosom of the broad Atlantic, as the fisherman reposes safely in his storm-shaken hut, and hears the roaring surge that dashes on the rocks below. But this is not the only portion of the pleasure to which we allude. It is not alone the quiet, the remoteness from the turmoil which agitates the great empire of which we are a portion; but there is something gratifying in the reflection, that we are not a mite lost to sight in the magnitude around us,—that though only a speck, the speck is distinct and perfect, standing forth boldly in relief, and not pictured faintly in the back-ground. Now this *locality* neither injures, nor is injured by, our nationality. We are equally loyal, equal compatriots of the inhabitants of Britain, and it is only as provincials, that we feel and are proud of our *unique* position.

The province of Nova Scotia is far from being destitute of rural beauty. The native lover of nature sees a thousand picturesque scenes in this—the land of his birth. True it is that he who has wandered beneath the unsullied skies of enchanting and romantic Italy, or by the banks of the majestic Rhine, can meet with no landscape in this country to attract his attention; but still there are scenes in Nova Scotia presenting a rich extent of prospect, and some which, we have often thought, would bring strikingly to the remembrance of the wanderer from our father-land some long-familiar spot. There is little attractive scenery in Nova Scotia in which water does not form a very prominent point. Those sequestered nooks, in which a cottage, a prominent tree, a close circumference of wood, a distant spire, are sufficient to be marked by a quiet and bewitching beauty, are but rarely to be met with here. The prospect is in general wide, and the very *soul* of it, at all times, seems to be the bay, harbour, river or lake which forms a portion of it. Indeed, in water scenery Nova Scotia has nothing to fear in a comparison with many more celebrated acquatic places. The harbour of Halifax is excelled by few, if any, in the United Kingdom, while the three principal rivers, as we presume we may term the

Annapolis River, the Avon and the Shubenacadie, are all beautiful. The Annapolis River takes its rise in the eastern part of King's Country, and flows through King's and Annapolis Counties with very little variation in its course, into a harbour formed by the Bay of Fundy, and which is one of the most beautiful sheets of water, of the same extent, in North America. The Avon is short, but wide, and runs in a northerly direction. The beauty of its appearance below Windsor is, however, somewhat spoilt by the tide which, at lower water, leaves the banks of a muddy hue. The third river, which is known by the Indian name of Shubenacadie, (river of Acadia), has its source in the well-known chain of lakes near Dartmouth,—and, flowing to the north, with an easterly inclination, runs a distance of some twenty miles by the side of the great eastern road, from which the traveller may now catch a glimpse of its extremely picturesque waters, and now lose sight of them as they take a more circuitous route and pass on unseen amidst the dense and majestic forest. The unfortunate issue of the attempt to connect, by a canal, this river, the lakes, and Halifax harbour, and which would have been of immense advantage in opening an inland navigation through the centre of the province, is a subject with which every one is acquainted. The timber on the banks of the Shubenacadie is by it made highly profitable. It is transported to the mouth of the stream in the Cobequid Bay, which is a portion of the Bason of Minas,—and, being of a large growth and otherwise valuable, ship-building is carried on to advantage. At the mouth of the river, the harbour, or rather bason, formed by its waters and those of the adjacent stream, is, at higher water, very beautiful, and, on a fine evening in the time of the Salmon-fishery, there is not a more pleasant sight than the boats of the fishermen dropping up slowly with the flood, unimpelled by oars, while their occupants are securing that delicious fish which Mrs. Hemans should have enumerated among the treasures of the deep. The sun in the west, sinks below the waters of the Bay of Fundy, and leaves twilight to rest softly and not less pleasantly upon the scene.

At the head of the Cobequid Bay we find the little river of Truro. This is a fine stream for trouting, but besides being small, it is too deficient in any particular attraction to merit attention, save that it runs through a place which is said somewhat to resemble in appearance an English Village. The village of Truro lies in a valley nearly surrounded by hills, for the most part, of no great height. Though its appearance is pleasing, it would be difficult to say in what the similar-

19

ity spoken of consists. The hawthorn hedge, the thatched cottage, are wanting; but that in which it more peculiarly differs from English villages is the extent of prospect, Truro being wide and diffuse, on a uniform level. It is however one of the prettiest places in the Province. The hills on one side are covered with spruce, fir, birch &c. and in the course of a stream which flows amongst these, there is a waterfall—small, indeed, but of no mean beauty. The partridge shooting was very good at the place we speak of, a few years ago. We remember, on one occasion, being with a party who dived into the recesses of these woods on a shooting excursion. The day proved extremely fine, and the sport ditto; but a few drops of rain having fallen towards evening, and the sky beginning to look dark and lowering, it was determined to return at once, although we had before resolved to remain out during the night. On mustering our party accordingly, an Irishman who had accompanied it was found to be missing. In vain we hallooed with our utmost strength—the echoes of the forest were the only reply. Loading our guns, we separated into five bands, each composed of three persons. One of these parties was left on the ground at which we divided, and the rest took different routes, intending to make a circuit of about six miles. The missing man had not been seen since two o'clock, at which time he had, with several others, made a halt, and refreshed himself with the creature comforts. Various surmises were, of course, hazarded as to his fate. Two or three large bears had been seen in the neighbourhood shortly before, but it was very unlikely that they should have remained near so large a shooting party during the day, or that, if they had, no tracks should have been discovered. Stories were related by some of wildcats, and other fierce animals; large numbers of which had once been inhabitants of these woods. The night was dark and drizzly, and towards morning we all became completely disheartened. At length some one suggested that, as the waterfall (which we before mentioned) was but half a mile from the place of halt, and the banks high and precipitous, poor Tim Collins might have wandered thither and fallen over. When persons are thus at bay, an opinion possessing any degree of plausibility is generally concurred in. Such was the case in the present instance, and the whole party immediately set off for the falls. The weather cleared up as we were on the way, and the sun shining brilliantly was received as an omen that Tim would be found, if not with a whole skin, at least "in the land of the living." We reached the bank, therefore, in comparatively good spirits. It was a spot which seemed only to want a connection with some legend of death to render it a place of pilgrimage to travellers. The stream was narrow, but the noise of the fall was sufficient to prevent any other sound from being heard. The high and very steep banks were, in most places, covered all the way up with tall spruce and birch, with which were here and there mingled a few trees of other kinds. The course of the stream, both above and below the fall, immediately changed,—and the banks, with their lofty trees, appeared, to form the circumference of a circle, the centre of which was the fall, with the bason into which the water fell. At the very steepest part of the bank there were but few trees. To this place one of the party went, and having looked over, came back to the rest, who were on their way down, with the information that there was a man stretched out near the edge of the water below. Between the bottom of the bank and the stream was a space of about twenty feet, perfectly level. Here we found the body of the Irishman, with the face downwards. His clothes were torn,—but as the bank, though steep, was not rough, his body had not been lacerated. At first we thought him dead, but a slight movement of the arm convinced us of the contrary. Having sprinkled his face with the clear water of the brook, he somewhat revived. We then placed him on a litter hastily constructed, and bore him towards home. As we got beyond the noise of the falling water we found to our amazement that Tim's tongue was going at a more voluble rate,—and presently he leaped from his high position, and wished to know "if we hadn't a dhrop of the craythur to give a feifer, instid of brakin' his bones in that rampageous fashion." Greatly astonished at this undignified conduct in a man whom we had really supposed near his end, an explanation was demanded, and we were, *of course*, highly delighted to learn that the cause of our having made a night journey of some twenty miles, was Tim's having secured a flask of his darling liquor, with which, being of an unobtrusive nature, he retired to this "sweet sequestered spot" to regale himself, and so—fell asleep. Poor Tim! he has since taken the pledge, and assures us that he never intends to *lose* himself again. We have heard, however, that he cannot refrain from relating this adventure, and generally concludes by boasting that—"Fifteen of the best gintry in the counthry were in purshuit of me, but none of 'em could find me but meeself."

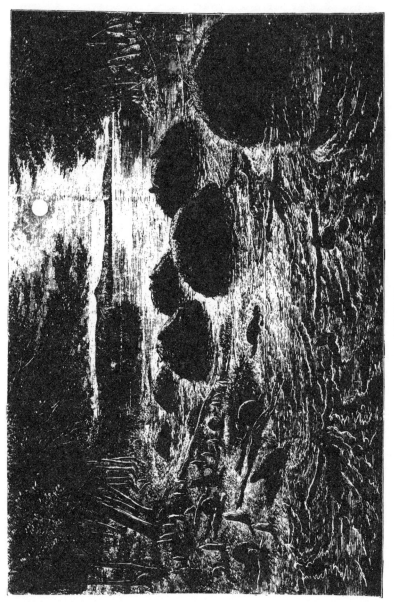

A Beaver Village.

22

Miss H. B. Macdonald

"Bush Scenery"*

WHAT EMIGRATED EUROPEAN is there amongst us, who had ever formed a correct preconceived idea of an American forest?

I can well recall my own ideas on the subject, namely: of vast, huge-trunked, spreading-boughed, patriarchs of the woods, extending gigantic arms over vast plains of green turf, chequered by their shadows with light and shade;—a vision of an English forest of the olden time described to the ears of our childhood in ballads of Chevy Chase, and tales of Robin Hood,—with glades, and lawns and sunny spots, and nooks of shade under interlaced arbours, where the glancing horn of a deer, or the yellow gleam of a squirrel appeared to give life to the scene. How very absurd and irrational these ideas proved. If one could have but afforded oneself the trouble of a little correct reflection, after experience, as the vision resolved itself into an eternal, unvaried plain of long, straight sticks, of trunks standing thickly together, each with a shapeless bush at the top—more resembling a forest of gigantic mops than respectable specimens of the vegetable genus; with eternal night, and a wilderness beneath them, where nothing flourishes but dark fungi and crawling parasites, interlaced so impenetrably, that only wild beasts of the forest and creeping things can pierce them. And, perchance there may be the gleam of a sluggish

*The Literary Garland, April 1849, pp. 182-85.

23

river, making its way among fallen trunks, rotting branches and sedges, among which it loses itself at its shores, for no bank, in most instances, can be discerned. Or where cultivation, with its axe and ploughshare has admitted some of the light of heaven on these dreary wildernesses—we discover a landscape of rough, wooden-fenced fields, plentifully dotted with stumps and logs, with a few rickety wooden sheds clustered here and there, and the whole surrounded as with a shore by the eternal outline of the primeval forest—and we have what is denominated "a clearing." Yet has "the bush" its sunny places and its charms; and I retain few more pleasant impressions of any scene in the Old World or the New, than of a visit paid in the back-wood township of Beckwith, in Upper Canada, to a place bearing in that district, the designation of

THE BEAVER MEADOW.

There are few townships rejoicing in a more plentiful allowance of swamp, than this of Beckwith. There is no admission into its bounds without a traverse of the "Long Swamp," a process accomplished over five miles of "corduroy," which, for those who have not the heart to dispense with the rough waggons of the country in the stead of their own good limbs, is about as sad an affair as the situation of Dr. Colman's German culprit, exclaiming:

"Aint I pon de wheel,
      "D'ye tink my blot, and bones, and nerfs can't feel!"

Having attained Beckwith through this delectable pathway, on a visit of a few days to an exiled friend, I began to enquire on the third day after my arrival, just when on the point of a threatening of *ennui*, whether there was anything to be seen in the district, or any direction where one might enjoy a pleasurable walk, or anything at all, beyond this dreary waste of swamp, larches and cedars, which, like some wicked magic circle, seemed to environ our eyes and our footsteps, and irreparably to bar them from the world beyond.

"I know of nothing worth visiting," was the reply, "but the Lake Mississippi, and that is ten miles off—and perhaps the Beaver Meadow."

The designation took my fancy, directly—"Oh! by all means let us go then to the Beaver Meadow!"

"But how you are ever to reach it, is the question," said my friend; "it is barely two miles distant, but every step is through the swamp, and half the way more wading than stepping; and then the mosquitoes —they are in full force at present, and more like a vision of African locusts in this locality, than an ordinary pest of Canadian insects."

24

Difficulties are naught, when the mind is bent upon its whim, and accordingly, after dinner, equipping ourselves each in a pair of extraordinary leathern boots, and a branch of foliage to wave off the mosquitoes, we set out, a party of three, for the Beaver Meadow. Now I had not the remotest idea of what sort of place this Beaver Meadow was; but the difficulties of the path which led to it, gave promise of a paradise. It seemed the very mockery of a pathway, being anon a place of mire ankle deep, at one time a series of slippery logs, whose distance from each other, suggested the idea of very ungraceful strides; at times a bridge of frail reeds laid crosswise, and not unfrequently a puddle of muddy water. After walking for a considerable distance through this path of gloom, the tall trees almost meeting above us, we came all at once, after a sudden turn in the forest, on a wide opening of light and verdure. I uttered an exclamation of delight.

"This!" said my friend, "is the Beaver Meadow."

There it lay, a large space of emerald, level as the ocean, winding for thousands of acres into the forest like a lovely lake, indenting itself into the form of bays, round promontories and undulating coasts, into the sombre outline of the forest that surrounded it with its dark evergreen shores. A clear stream ran through its centre, whose many curves the wide space of the meadow appeared to follow as it extended itself into the forest, and bright green clumps of hazel and alder and other shrubs appeared here and there on its surface, like islands of the blest; just some such spot of magic as we would have expected, in Fairy Tales or Arabian Romances, to have blessed some travel-toiled hero after long wanderings in weary deserts—a vista of light and shade offering unknown haunts, as it wound its length endlessly into the forest, and secluded nooks for the imagination to rove in, with solitude and silence and stillness over it, like the witchery of a fairy vision! It appeared to me like the very spot for an enchanter's wand to touch and dissolve into nothing; and I could do naught but stand in silence in the opening by which our pathway had conducted us into it through the woods, and gaze. And then it was in a perfect blush of wild flowers, while ever and anon came the clear, short, though inexpressibly sweet trill of the Canadian robin, that haunted the spot like the genuine voice of some spirit of the solitude. As I wandered through the meadow alone, for I left my companions resting on the green grass, I was carried back to old Indian times, and would half expect to see some old dreaming child of the forest start from behind some of these alder clumps, with the lofty look and free mien of these lords of the wilderness, ere they knew of another race

25

to turn them from their old customs and their ancient homes. I thought of this romantic imaginative race, with all their wild traditions and poetical beliefs, till, shall I confess it, in brooding over the present dreary transition state of this western world, where there is neither the grandeur of savage life nor the beauty of civilization, I half regretted the old days of the wilderness, when a vast forest extended from sea to sea, offering a vision perchance of a solitary canoe on silent waters—a wigwam in some sequestered nook—a hunter on some tangled deer path, or on some spreading meadow under the trees,—a council of grave and venerable sages. Most of all did I regret the loss of those old traditions in which the new race have no part, and which are dying away with the departure and extinction of the old. And not one of the least beautiful of them is that which regarded such spots as this, which are numerous on the continent, as a sort of Indian Elysian Fields. Surrounded as they usually are by frightful swamps, and only in certain seasons of the year at all accessible, it was natural that the Indians, only seeing them rarely and by glimpses through the woods, should imagine them, with their quiet hues and verdant tracts, paradises of rest for the souls of their departed warriors. To increase the sacredness of the associations, it was supposed death to the living to have viewed or discovered one of these places. True they always vanished, and at a near approach faded into mist; but the doom of the rash discoverer was regarded as sealed. "Woe to the hunter!" says the tradition, "who may catch a glimpse in his wanderings of these far off and shining spots. He returns to his wigwam an altered man—he languishes in the chase, and soon the green haunts of the forest shall know him no more!"

"You will scarcely credit," said my companions as I rejoined them, "that all this is the work of the beavers. Ages ago it was one vast beaver dam which the little creatures formed by blocking up the stream. In process of time the trees rotted, through the influence of the water, and fell—were covered with herbage, and we have now this rich and beautiful meadow which you see. Being the greater part of the year under water, no larger trees will flourish than those clumps of alders and water shrubs, that add such a charming variety to the landscape."

"But where are the beavers?" said I.

"Oh! they are fled far away—vanished before the approaching civilization. There is indeed an old inhabitant of the district who remembers two or three solitary animals—the last of their race—haunting the spot, as if mourning like human creatures over the desolation of the scene which had once, with its thousands of little huts and active, stirring population, been such a flourishing and busy colony.

"If I could but accomplish the drainage of this place," added he, "and deepen the channel of the river a foot or two, what a splendid farm should I not have here in a few seasons."

"And destroy the beaver meadow?—oh! you utilitarian monster, you would never be so barbarous!"

"All very fine!" returned he, "but the age of romance is past; and if you talk and think in this way about beaver meadows and such places, you will only get laughed at. Since you have been so gratified to-day, however, I shall reward you to-morrow by a visit in another direction, —our poor 'bush' may possess greater treasures in your line than you wot of."

"Oh! certainly. Whither are you about to conduct us?"

"To a solitary piece of water in the midst of the woods, rejoicing in the designation of

LAKE MISSISSIPPI."

The next morning dawned, an agreeable summer day, with just enough of wind and cloud in the firmament, to moderate the intense heat of a Canadian June. Our party was increased by one, since the Beaver Meadow excursion of the previous afternoon, and we set out two ladies and two gentlemen—a pleasant square number for all purposes of conversation and politeness—in what is called a "lumber waggon," a conveyance always more remarkable for strength and convenience than for elegance or lightness. After being indulged with a drive of a mile over the mail road, we suddenly turned into the forest.

"Whither under the sun are you about to conduct us?" exclaimed I; "I see no road."

"It is the best you shall have to-day, nevertheless," said our *cicerone*; "and what fault do you find?"

There was nothing but a sort of *claire obscure* opening through the forest, where might be discerned a glimpse of a track occasionally, caused by former unhappy waggons, bestrewn with logs, rotting branches and stumps, standing so thickly that no skill in the world seemed sufficient to charioteer us safely through. But nothing dismayed, the driver urged on his cattle, and they, like animals quite at home amongst such obstructions, worked their way through with infinite intelligence till after one, as I thought, hair-breadth escape from overthrow followed closely by another, I began to breathe freely

27

and imagined there might be a bare possibility of reaching Lake Mississippi with unbroken bones after all. As might be expected, our speed had in it nothing akin to that of a railway, and it was not till nearly two o'clock, after being most painfully tried with mosquitoes and jolting, that emerging from the woods upon a gentle eminence, we saw Lake Mississippi with its islands spread out before us. A perfect lake of the woods was Lake Mississippi, extending like a vast expanse of silver amidst the dark of the environing forest; now lost to the eye behind some vast wooded promontory or island — again appearing in the far off distance like a river or some lesser lake, till stretching beyond the boundary of view, it was lost in the horizon, where its azure waters appeared to blend with the kindred azure of the skies.

I longed to launch myself in a canoe and sail amongst these numerously and fantastically formed islands, which rose like patches of emerald on its silver surface, and cast such splendid fringes of shadow, as well as its surrounding edges, wherever their dark green shores met the surface of the mirroring waters. A magnificent diversity of light and shade, of woods and waters, of silence and solitude, did this vast surface now before us present, just as it might have looked hundreds of years before, ere the art of man began to deface the wild savage beauty of uncultivated nature. We dismounted from our car and quickly found ourselves in a canoe. One of our party, who was of a more adventurous or romantic disposition than the rest, got into a canoe by himself and launched forth on the waters alone. But being rather a novice in the art of paddling, after permitting his bark to transport itself a considerable distance into the lake, our adventurer appeared disposed to leave it to the freedom of its own will, and seemed to enjoy himself amazingly, like another Alastor basking amid the beauties of an enchanted lake. But apparently getting tired of this, we observed the canoe making extraordinary gyrations towards different parts of the shore which it was seemingly destined never to attain; as no sooner did it appear on the point of landing, than by some invisible influence it was wafted back again.

"So — ho! What is the matter with your boat?" was exclaimed from ours, as we swept past with two skilful paddlers, on our way to an island that we were intending to visit.

Our friend made no reply, but we began to entertain strong suspicions that he did not know how to effect a landing, a paddle being a most obstreperous instrument in unskilful hands; and that he was doomed like a modern Ulysses to be a wanderer of the waters in search of a port, from which one envious Fate ever appeared to deter him.

Meanwhile our canoe swept on towards the Island, and I, whom my friends consider a little wrong headed on the subject of the classics, began, as we swept under its green shadows and towards its enamelled turf, incongruously enough to think of Calypso's Isle in the Grecian Seas; — that precisely so might it have looked with its green turf that inclined to the waters, and serpentine path which we discerned now leading from the landing, arboured over with wild vines and creeping plants as they stretched from tree to tree. I began to think of this pathway, starred as it was with wild flowers and bordered with wood strawberries — as perchance leading to some grotto of the nymphs, inhabited by forms of superhuman beauty, with celestial grace in their motions and immortality in their eyes. And so, as we swept through a bed of water lilies cradled like stars amid their broad green leaves upon the rocking waters, I was awakened from my reverie by the canoe grounding on the shore. We were received by a nymph, a native of the Island, who, however, did not look at all like the goddess Calypso, but presented a sturdy pair of rustic unsandalled feet, with curtailed skirts, and welcomed us in a most unmistakeable Doric, which was none of the Greek, towards her island domain. We followed to her bower, by the path aforementioned, and found a long shanty with a bedstead, "bunk," and sundry other household articles, in the single apartment of which it consisted; and for nectar and ambrosia were regaled with oaten cakes and whiskey. After a long talk regarding old Scotland, of which our nymph was a native, "and the hills and the glens and the bonnie braes," our entertainer, as is customary, expressing her longings for the old country, and anathematizing every thing in the new, "whar the vary bit oaten bread itsel'," as she said, "hadna the same sweetness under the tongue as it used to hae at hume," we took our way to the other side of the island to view the lake from another point of view.

To our surprise we found the sky overcast, and a storm rising; and by the time we reached our destination the wind had amounted to a hurricane, with a suddenness, as we were told, common to the inland waters. The lake looked like a beauty in a storm, the spray driving like mist along its surface which, blackened and agitated, dashed up against the many islands in a thousand tumultuous waves. The rush and roar of the wind among the woods was tremendous, while the crash of falling trees was heard like the crack of sharp rifles above the noise of the storm! More beautiful in storm than in calm, thought I, — oh! sleeping beauty — then sleeping so softly, as if a breath could dissolve thee away like a mirage vision; now so strong and stern in thy wrath, which none of the boldest of us would dare encounter, with black, wrinkled scowls, and patches of turbulence and foam —

> "Drives like tears thy spray along!
> And the light of strong emotion
> Glimmers in thy dark blue eyes!"

We began to look blank at each other, and to think about home, and the angry lake that lay between us and its shelter, as well as the dreary ten mile drive through inhospitable woods. We made our way back to the "shanty," and were pressed by our Calypso, with all the blandishments of which her nature was capable, including a renewed offer of cakes and whiskey, to partake of her hospitality for the night. But the beds looked very unpromising, and that was not to be thought of — so making our way down to the landing, we resolved to see if we should not attempt our fortune on the angry waters. The waves were by no means so high on this side of the island as on that from which we had just returned; still our canoes were not to be thought of. But our Calypso, who was by no means of such a monopolizing disposition as the Homeric one, to our great surprise appeared presently rounding a small promontory with a stout boat, which she rowed, accompanied by a male assistant. Having undertaken to convey us to the mainland, we stepped in, some of us very loath, and were soon rocking and tossing on the lake. A most unenviable position was ours, for the boat was a perfect shell, and toppled and reeled to such a degree that we appeared as if every moment on the point of being swamped. The oars seemed none of the stoutest — nor our crew of the most skilful, and ever as the fierce winds came in an intenser gust, we heeled and bent over to it as it hissed past us, until it seemed impossible that the boat could ever recover her balance. Though splashed and wetted to the skin, we all maintained a remarkably silent resignation, which I afterwards attributed to the dread of worse evils. There never was such a silent party under the circumstances; the ladies of us even never ventured upon a shriek or scream. After we landed, which we did happily without accident, we were all as bold and brave as lions, and of course none of us had been in the least degree frightened, yet none could help being witty on the subject of his neighbour's late anxiety of feature. I must say, for the credit of the gentlemen, that they seemed quite as anxious and careful on the subject of their lives as the ladies had been; yet one, who quizzed me particularly regarding my terrified face, on being retorted upon, on account of his own, which presented as unmistakeable a picture of dismay as one could fancy of a caricature, insisted, as he still does to this day, that his fears were not at all for himself, but, listen, oh! ye contemners of Mammon! amid the splashing of the spray, mainly for the safety of his *gold watch*.

We returned homewards through the forest by the same road as we had travelled in the former part of the day, and after a late dinner enjoyed a profounder and more comfortable night's rest than I, at least, experienced for many months.

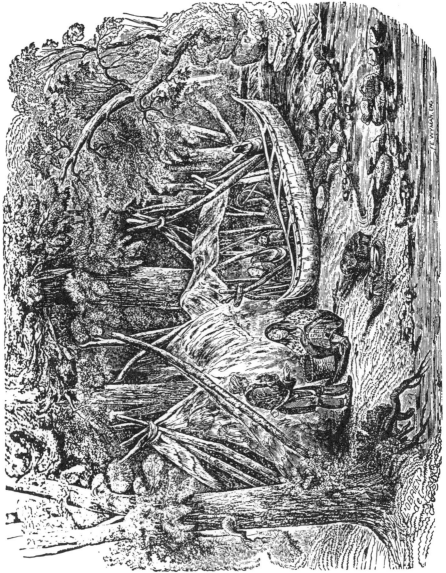

INDIAN VILLAGE.

Catharine Parr Traill

"A Visit to the Camp of the Chippewa Indians"[1]*

YOU ASK ME if I have seen anything of the Indians lately. I am glad you were interested in my former accounts of them, and will supply you with any little anecdotes I may collect, from time to time, for your amusement. I have not seen old Peter, the hunter, or his good-tempered squaw, since the death of poor Jane, the pretty Indian girl I told you of: she had been married about six weeks, when she fell ill with a bilious epidemic, which proved fatal to her and many other of the Indian village.

Last harvest Tom Noggan (old Peter's brother), his squaw, and their children, came to our neighbourhood, and encamped on the opposite shore, near one of my brother's little islands. The squaws came frequently to get pork and flour from me, and garden vegetables, in exchange for fish, venison, or baskets. For a few pounds of salt pork they will freely give you a haunch of venison, or dried salmon trouts. They are fond of peas, Indian corn, melons, pumpkins, or indeed any vegetables; sometimes they will follow me into the garden, and beg "*onion*," or "*herb*," to put in soup: potatoes they never refuse. They often beg for the shells of green peas, to boil in their soups and pottage, and will eat them by handfuls.

Mrs. Tom Noggan is sister to Mrs. Peter, and was once reckoned an

Sharpe's London Magazine, 7 (1848), 114-18.

Indian beauty—but no trace of comeliness remains; but their notions of beauty possibly differ somewhat from ours, for her brother, who bears the appellation of "Handsome Jack," is, to European eyes, a sad ill-looking savage. But, to return to my squaw. When she first came she was in very ill health, and had a poor, sick, brown baby with her, about whom she seemed very uneasy. The poor babe was suffering under the effects of a slow fever, that seemed to be wasting and withering up its weakly frame. Its tiny hand hung listlessly beside it, its skin was hot and damp, and its tongue deeply furred and ulcerated. The sorrowful mother besought me, in the most intelligible manner she could, to give it medicine to cure it. I first petitioned to have the poor thing unbound from its wooden cradle, and suffered to have the free use of its limbs, unrestrained by the close swathing bands that confined its narrow chest. I then administered to it, as the safest and readiest remedy, a dose of castor oil, and, in spite of my compassion for the poor little sufferer, I could not help being amused by the original plan the mother adopted to make the papouse swallow the medicine. As soon as I had put it into the child's mouth with a tea-spoon, she gently shook its head from side to side, till she fairly got it down the poor thing's throat, reversing the old joke of "Before taken to be well shaken."

Mrs. Tom was very thankful for some white bread and rusks, and a bottle of new milk, with which I supplied her, from time to time, for the sick child. She generally came every day to show me the little patient, and I gave her some rhubarb and magnesia for it. Whether they were the proper medicines for its case I cannot say, or if it was the better food it got, and the release from its cradle, that agreed so well with it; but I had the satisfaction of seeing a wonderful improvement take place in a short time, and before the Indians moved their camp, little Moses was quite brisk, and as lively as a kitten.

When Mrs. Tom was so poorly, and came to trade for meal or flour, and I asked for baskets, she used to shake her head, and answer in a plaintive tone, "Got-a none," "Go Mut-a-Lake," or "Buckhorn-a-Lake," meaning she had got none till she went to Mud Lake or Buckhorn Lake. The former place is where the Indian village is situated at present; but, on account of the unhealthiness of the site, it has been judged expedient to remove them to Buckhorn Lake—one of the largest of our beautiful chain of Otonabee lakes. This sheet of water takes its name from the singular indentations of its bays and peninsulas, which they say resemble the horns of a deer.

34

The Indian women manufacture their baskets from the inner tough rind of the bass, which you know is a large species of the lime or linden, and from the blue beech; having stripped off the hard or outer bark, they then divide the inner or white rind into strips, and beat it with a tomahawk to render it pliable, keeping it wetted frequently whilst they are at work; these they dye black, or red, green, blue, or yellow, to fancy, with indigo, logwood, butternut, hickory, blue beech, redwood, and other dyes, with the uses of which they are intimately acquainted; but they are not very communicative on the subject, and will not tell you how they give those bright hues to the porcupine quills.

The winter and spring passed over without our seeing anything more of the Indians, with the exception of three squaws, who came in one cold day; and though I showed them some attention, they were apparently very insensible to it, and on my declining to purchase some ill-wrought baskets, they rose simultaneously, and wrapping their black mantles about them, walked forth without saying another word. They were very uninteresting squaws.

A few days ago, I received a friendly visit from Mrs. Tom and little Moses, with half a score more squaws and papouses, and after most affectionately greeting me, and bartering some fine fish for flour and bread, they all expressed a desire for us to visit the wigwam, which was situated on Strawberry Island, the largest of the three islands in our lake. But a difficulty arose; they had only one birch canoe, and that was deeply laden, as you may suppose, when I tell you it had conveyed ashore Mrs. Tom, her really pretty sister, the widow, Nancy Boland, Mary Anne Fron, and Mrs. Muskrat, with two little Noggans, two little Bolands, and six Muskrats; you may imagine there could be little stowage for Jane and me, and little James; however, as the squaws had set their hearts on our company, they managed to overcome the apparent difficulty of the transport. An old leaky birch canoe lay on the shore; the lively widow set herself to work, and heating some gum, such as they use in stopping the seams and cracks of these frail vessels, she soon made it as safe as the other, and invited Jane and little James to take a seat at the bottom of it, while Mrs. Tom directed me to step in beside her among the papouses and the other squaws. With that genuine politeness which is taught in nature's own school, the good creature gathered together some cedar boughs, which formed a smooth and fragrant matting at the bottom of the canoe; over these she cast her black cloth shawl, and then with a face radiant with

35

benevolent smiles, that made ample display of a set of pearly teeth of unrivalled colour and shape, she beckoned to me to take my place. The sky was so exquisitely blue above, and the water so clear below, with all the richly wooded banks reflected in its depths, that I enjoyed my short voyage exceedingly, and could hear the rapturous shouts of my little boy from the other canoe, as it cut through the great beds of water-lilies, which were just rising to the surface and displaying their full fragrant silken cups and broad floating leaves, gemmed with the sparkling insects that rested on them. Hundreds of blue, purple, green, scarlet, and bronze dragon flies, just emerged from the pupa state, were to be seen at rest, or just fluttering their newly expanded wings; the neat deer-fly, that torment to cattle, and even to man, with its angular spotted wings and bright gilded green head, and many others; while the surface of the water, where it was quite glassy and smooth, was gay with the splendid blue shining water-beetle, and others of a brilliant scarlet, dancing their gleesome circles upon the watery mirror. Sometimes the eye was enlivened by the transient flash of the splendid scarlet tanager, or blackwinged summer red bird, a living glory among the feathered tribes, which now and then was seen darting swiftly among the trees of the islands, while the ear was greeted with the full melody of the Canadian robin, or migratory thrush, and the sweet clear note of the little song-sparrow, flitting gaily from bush to bush, and pausing at intervals to cheer you with its pretty songs. These sounds were blended with the light dip of the paddle, and the hoarse rush of the rapids, as the waters gurgled and eddied round the fallen cedars and huge blocks of stone that obstructed their passage downwards.

A painter might have made a pretty sketch of the scene. The broad expanse of tranquil water, bounded on either side by the dense mass of forest, varying from the gigantic pine to the dwarf-silver-leaved willow that trembled beneath the swell of the mimic waves that undulated beneath them. The line of trees broken only by our clearing, with the little loghouse and adjoining buildings, the green turf sloping down in emerald verdure to the brink of the lake. Higher up might be seen the islands with the rapids between them; at the head of one of these, on a little green platform above a steep bank, clothed with roses and other low flowering shrubs, might be seen the white canvass tents of the Indians; the thin blue smoke rising in light vapoury mist, and spreading among the young aspens and birch that crested the summit of the bank on either side; below, just rocking in the shallow water, lay two empty birch canoes; our own, freighted with the women and children, making for the island, completed the picture.

While I was dwelling with delighted eye on all before me, a temporary disturbance was caused by the rude behaviour of one of the papouses, an ugly ill-favoured imp, who persisted in leaning over the side of the canoe and snatching at the broad floating leaves of the water lilies, or paddling with his brown hands in the water, to the imminent peril of overturning the frail boat. Mrs. Tom, who was steering with her paddle, gently remonstrated against his wilful behaviour, but to no purpose; the urchin only raised a pair of broad shoulders with a significant grumble indicative of his determination to persist. The squaws expostulated with him by turns, but without raising an angry voice or menace. I do not remember ever hearing an Indian woman scold; the peculiar intonation of their voices rather sinks into a plaintive whine when they are displeased, and instead of speaking more rapidly, they seem to give force to their words by a slow and deliberate style of utterance.

At the first outbreak of the forward child the good-humoured mother only laughed, and seemed inclined to jest at the anger of the boy, till, losing all command of himself, he proceeded to acts of violence, and taking up handfuls of water dashed them in his mother's face. This undutiful conduct caused a burst of indignation from Mrs. Muskrat and Mary Anne Fron, while the now offended mother held up her finger and pointed upwards, as if warning the little fellow that God looked down upon his sinful conduct; but passion held the mastery over the rebellious child and he became yet more ungovernable, and even struck his mother and flung more water in her face. Any one but an Indian mother would have boxed the delinquent's ear soundly, and poured forth a torrent of words; but she suited her punishment to the nature of the offence, by taking up in her turn large handfuls of water and pouring upon his thick black hair, patting it down as she did so, till he looked like a fierce drowned rat. He screamed with fury, and struggled in vain to escape from her grasp, but she gently laid him sprawling at our feet in the bottom of the canoe, foaming with impotent rage. I was not a little amused by the cool deliberate way in which the squaw conducted herself, and inwardly congratulated her on her command of temper, and the victory she had gained; but obstinate perserverance is a distinguishing trait of the Indian character, and no sooner was the refractory imp released from thraldom than he darted up and reseated himself, casting looks of defiance on his mother, whose heart had already begun to relent at her severity, for she gently drew forth a gay handkerchief and softly wiped his streaming hair and face, patting his head with soothing accents. The ungrateful child took advantage of his mother's advances towards reconciliation, but disdained her overtures, and, with an expression almost of malignant triumph, snatched the handkerchief from his head and flung it into the water. The squaw now seemed to think further opposition useless; the handkerchief was rescued at the end of the paddle, and the disobedient urchin continued to dabble in the water till the canoe touched the bank.

I must tell you that in the middle of the fray a nice brown girl, Anne Muskrat, fell asleep with her head on my lap; so the mother removed her gently to her own knee, and I took the opportunity of taking up the relinquished paddle, and made a pretty successful essay in the art of propelling the canoe up the rapids, to the great admiration of the whole party. For my own part, I enjoy the motion of a birch-bark canoe far more than a boat or a skiff; it is so gentle and gliding, no noise nor shocks from the effort used in rowing; the paddles are so slight and short, that a child may use them, and, provided the canoe be in good order and well balanced, and persons sit quiet in it, there is no danger. The chief care required is in shallow water to avoid sunken rocks and fallen trees. These last often fall along the edge of the water, projecting far into the stream and forming eddies, and are dangerous for such light craft unless shunned in time, for the branches are apt to injure the frail material of which they are formed.

Some of the old massy cedars that have lain for years in the water, become the depot for all sorts of loose floating matter; sticks, rushes, reeds, grass, and all sorts of water weeds, in tangled masses, find a lodging among the immersed branches; a variety of ferns, fungi, mosses, and small plants cover it with deceitful verdure, while the work of decay is rapidly proceeding beneath. You often see a flourishing growth of young pine, hemlocks, swamp elm, and other seedling trees on these trunks. Quietly, but surely, does Nature carry on her grand operations by the simplest and most insignificant agents. Corruption and decay become the foundation for life and renovation, and we wonder and admire the economy displayed in the works of an Almighty Creator as much as his wisdom and power, as if to set forth an example to his children. He is in no one thing wasteful or prodigal of the materials of the visible world, but has ordained that something should indeed "gather up all fragments, that nothing may be lost."

But while I am philosophizing I am wandering from my party. You must suppose us all safely landed, and, after a good scramble up the steep face of the bank just in front of the encampment, which consisted of two nice white canvass tents, the floor strewn with cedar boughs according to custom. The fragrance of this rural carpet, with the delicious odour of some bunches of the wampum grass, of which the Indians braid belts and necklaces and other ornaments, was sufficiently powerful to overcome the smell of the venison, that hung in an unsightly manner along the front of the tent, drying in the blaze of a July sun. A large piece of the same meat was roasting over a fire of brands outside; it was suspended by two cross sticks, much after the fashion the gipsies manage their roasts; three or four deer hounds lay stretched at their ease, lazily eyeing the meat, and snapping angrily at the flies that were buzzing about them.

The two men, Tom Noggan and Joe Muskrat, had been left at home to cook the dinner; but, from the black aspect of the viands, methought they had not been over faithful in the discharge of their office; indeed, when we arrived, the two men were fast asleep, covered up to their chins with great blankets, though the thermometer stood at eighty degrees in the shade. Muskrat did rouse himself, and taking out a well-thumbed Bible, began to read; but Tom, whose laziness is proverbial, just opened one sleepy eye, and, having examined the party with apathetic indifference, turned on his side, and only gave token of his being awake by sometimes pointing with a significant grunt to one of the children to bring him any thing he required.

The squaws soon disposed of the sleepy, weary children, and all were asleep in a few minutes, excepting one nice neat little gipsy-looking girl, Rachel Muskrat, who hung fondly about her father, caressing him with quiet tenderness; her black hair was all curiously woven, the ends into a braid with the sweet grass, and formed a sort of border, or cap, round her head; it looked neat enough, but must have cost great time and patience to have arranged it so cleverly. On her father expressing a desire for drink, the little dark-eyed maid snatched from the ground a square sheet of birch-bark, which she gathered up at the corners, and quickly returned, bearing a full draught of water from the lake in this novel and simple vessel. Surely here was a proof how few are the wants of man in a savage state, and how easily supplied. Here was a vessel capable of containing liquid, formed without toil or trouble. This valuable material supplies the want of all sorts of earthenware utensils; divided into thin sheets, it makes no contemptible substitute for writing-paper, and can be rendered as fine as the most delicate tinted note-paper. When cast into the fire, it curls and writhes like parchment, but quickly ignites, and then bursts into a most brilliant and gaseous looking flame, emitting a highly aromatic perfume, that I am sure might be made from it.

Whilst sitting under the tent I took notice of the perfumed grass, and the widow soon employed herself in weaving a chain of it, which she linked together very prettily with bands of coloured quills. When she had completed it she placed it about my neck, and said, with a most agreeable smile, "Present for you; wear it for me."

I was delighted with its fragrance, and ordered several more of the same kind to be made, for which I paid her in some trifling articles; and send them to you, for they are far sweeter than lavender, to lay among your linen, for I know you, like myself, used to practise that sweet but now old-fashioned custom.

The squaws told me they got the sweet grass, or wampum, on an island in Stoney Lake, and that none of it grew anywhere hereabout; it is very long and rather harsh, but smells delightfully.

The only article I have been able to procure of their work for you, is a pair of bracelets, which I really think are very neat; the coloured quills, you may perceive, are cut as small as beads, and strung in a sort of antique pattern, something like what we used to call the Grecian scroll,—these, with a little canoe and a knife-case are all I could procure worth sending home. They make some things neatly enough, and others as carelessly. It is a mere chance your getting anything well made by them, and never if you order it. They invariably give me the same brief answer if I ask for anything pretty that I want to send home,—"Got-a-none," "Village," or "Go Mud-a-Lake" or "Stoney Lake," or some other place, and that old excuse of "By-and-by," or "To-morrow," which means some day or other.

[1]Letter from Mrs. Traill, Authoress of "The Backwoods of Canada," to her sister, Miss Agnes Strickland.

CATHARINE PARR STRICKLAND TRAILL was born in 1802 in London, England, and died in 1899 at Lakefield, Ontario. The sister of Susanna Moodie, she came from a large literary family. After immigrating to Canada in 1832, Traill published *The Backwoods of Canada* (1836) both to warn prospective settlers of the hardships to be encountered in Canada and to teach them to use the new land to its best advantage. Unlike Moodie, Traill generally remained optimistic, even when facing the often harsh trials of a gentlewoman in the backwoods. Her second survival manual for prospective settlers, *The Canadian Settlers' Guide* (1854), illustrates the difficulties of pioneer life. Both books include recipes adapted to Canadian vegetation and reflect their author's strong interest in nature study. Always careful in her attention to detail, Traill became a recognized authority on the plants and flowers of Canada, publishing *Canadian Wild Flowers* (1868) and *Studies of Plant Life in Canada* (1906).

Both sketches in this volume were published in *Sharpe's London Magazine*, "A Visit to the Camp of the Chippewa Indians" in 1848, "Female Trials in the Bush" in 1852. The latter also appeared in Canada in 1853 as one of the items in Traill's series of "Forest Gleanings," in *The Anglo-American Magazine*.

SPINNING.

Catharine Parr Traill

"Female Trials in the Bush"*

IT HAS BEEN REMARKED how much more prone to discontent, the wives of the emigrants are than their husbands; and it generally is the fact, but why is it so? A little reflection will show the cause. It is generally allowed that woman is by nature and habit more strongly attached to home and all those domestic ties and associations that form her sources of happiness, than man. She is accustomed to limit her enjoyments within a narrow circle; she scarcely receives the same pleasures that man does from travelling and exchange of place; her little world is *home*, it is or should be her sphere of action, her centre of enjoyment, the severing her at once forever from it makes it dearer in her eyes, and causes her the severest pangs.

It is long before she forms a home of comfort to herself like that she has left behind her, in a country that is rough, hard and strange; and though a sense of duty will, and does, operate upon the few to arm them with patience to bear, and power to act, the larger proportion of emigrant wives sink into a state of hopeless apathy, or pining discontent, at least for a season, till time, that softener of all human woes, has smoothed, in some measure, the roughness of the colonists' path, and the spirit of conformity begins to dispose faithful wives to the endeavor to create a new home of comfort, within the forest solitudes.

*The Anglo-American Magazine, April 1853, pp. 426-30.

43

There is another excuse for the unhappy despondency too frequently noticed among the families of the higher class of emigrants; and as according to an old saying, "prevention is better than cure," I shall not hesitate to plead the cause of my sex, and point out the origin of the domestic misery to which I allude.

There is nothing more common than for a young settler of the better class, when he has been a year or two in the colony, and made some little progress in clearing land and building, to go to England for a wife. He is not quite satisfied with the paucity of accomplishments and intellectual acquirements among the daughters of the Canadians, he is ambitious of bringing out a young lady, fit to be the companion of a man of sense and taste, and thoughtlessly induces some young person of delicate and refined habits to unite her fate to his. Misled by his sanguine description of his forest home and his hopes of future independence, she listens with infinite satisfaction to his account of a large number of acres, which may be valuable or nearly worthless, according to the local advantages they possess; of this, she of course knows nothing, excepting from the impressions she receives from her lover.

He may in a general way tell her that as a bush settler's wife, she must expect to put up with some privations at first, and the absence of a few of those elegant refinements of life which she has been accustomed to enjoy; but these evils are often represented as temporary, for he has rarely the candour to tell her the truth, the whole truth and nothing but the truth.

Deceived by her lover and deceiving herself into the fond belief that her love for him will smooth every difficulty, she marries, and is launched upon a life for which she is totally unfitted by habits, education and inclination, without due warning of the actual trials she is destined to encounter.

There is not only cruelty but even want of worldly wisdom in these marriages. The wife finds she has been deceived, and becomes fretful, listless and discontented; and the husband, when too late, discovers that he has transplanted a tender exotic, to perish beneath the withering influence of an ungenial atmosphere, without benefitting by its sweetness or beauty. I need hardly dwell on the domestic evils arising from this state of things, but I would hold such marriages up as a warning to both parties.

Some will say, but are these things so? and is the change really so striking between a life in England and one in the colonies? I speak that which I have seen, and testify that which I do know. Even under the

44

fairest and most favorable circumstances, the difference must necessarily be great between a rich fertile country, full of resources, and one where all has to be created or supplied at the expense of time and money. But I speak more especially of those, who, living in the less cultivated and populous portions of the colony, are of course exposed to greater privations and disadvantages, as settlers in the bush must be.

In towns and populous districts these hardships are less remarkable.

I remember among many instances that have fallen under my notice, one somewhat remarkable for the energetic trials of female fortitude that were called forth by a train of circumstances, most adverse and unexpected.

A young man residing in our neighbourhood, of sanguine disposition and slender property, had contrived by means of credit and a little money to start a large concern, a saw mill, a store, tavern, and other buildings, which were to form the germ of a large village. Full of hopes of the most extravagant kind, if he deceived others, I believe he also deceived himself into the vain belief that all his various castles, were destined to make his individual fortune, and confer a lasting benefit on the country where they were situated. Under this delusion, and finding moreover that it was absolutely necessary to raise resources for carrying on his schemes, he went home, and was not long in forming an acquaintance with an accomplished young lady of some fortune. She was an orphan, and charmed with the novelty of the life he described, she consented to marry him and become the queen of the village of which he gave her so glowing a picture. Perhaps at that period he was not fully aware of the fact, that the property of the young lady was under the control of trustees, and that the interest only was at her command, and fortunate it was for her that the guardians were inflexible in their principles, and resisted every solicitation to resign any part of the capital.

The young bride, accustomed to the domestic beauties and comforts of the mother country, beheld with dismay the long tract of gloomy pine wood through which she journeyed to her forest home, and the still more unseemly fields, blackened by charred pine and cedar stumps, in the midst of which rose the village, whose new and half finished buildings failed to excite any feeling in the breast but bitter disappointment and aversion; and she wept and sighed for all that was fair and beautiful in her own beloved country, rendered now ten times more lovely by the contrast with all she beheld around her;

45

yet though she was miserable and discontented, she clung with passionate love to her husband, and, with womanly fondness, made every sort of excuse for him—even to herself, and always to others. It was this love which, as it increased, upheld her as the sad reality of ruin arrived. Misfortune, as an armed man, came fast upon the devoted pair—every fair and flattering prospect vanished. Unable to provide for the satisfaction of his importunate creditors as he had expected to do from his wife's property, they would no longer be put off and he became a perfect prisoner in his own house. The land, buildings, all, faded as it were from his grasp; even the yearly income arising from her money, had been forestalled, and all her costly clothing went by degrees, all her pretty ornaments and little household business were disposed of piece-meal, to supply their daily wants. All, all were gone, and with fresh trials, fresh privations, came unwonted courage and energy to do and to bear. She was now a mother, and the trials of maternity were added to her other arduous duties. She often lamented her want of knowledge and ability in the management of her infant, for she had been totally unaccustomed to the trouble of young children. To add to her sorrows, sickness seized her husband, he who had been used to a life of activity and bustle, scarcely caring to rest within doors, unless at meal-times was sunk under the effects of confinement, chagrin and altered diet, and a long obstinate intermittent ensued.

Though to some persons it might appear a trifling evil, there was nothing in all her sad reverse of condition that seemed so much to annoy my poor friend as the discolouring of her beautiful hands; she would often sigh as she looked down on them and say, "I used to be so vain of them, and never thought to employ them in menial offices, such as necessity has driven us to."

Poor thing! she had not been trained to such servile tasks as I have seen her occupied in, and I pitied her the more because I saw her bearing up so bravely under such overwhelming trials; she who had come out to our woods, not two years before, a bride, a proud fastidious woman, unable and unwilling to take part in the best household labour, who would sit on the side of her bed while a servant drew the silk stocking and satin slippers on her tiny white feet, and dressed her from head to foot—who despised the least fare that could be set before her by any of her neighbors—who must despatch a messenger almost daily to the distant town for fresh meat and biscuits—and new white bread, was now compelled to clothe herself and her babe, to eat

46

the coarsest fare, black tea unsweetened and only softened with milk, instead of rich cream which she walked twice or thrice a week to fetch from my house or that of my sister-in-law, bearing her stone pitcher in one hand, with the additional weight of her baby on her arm. So strange a thing is woman's love, that she, whom I had been wont to consider decidedly selfish, now showed a generous and heroic devotion towards the man whose thoughtlessness had reduced her to that state of poverty and privation that seemed to make her regardless of poverty. What personal sacrifices did she not make, what fatigues undergo? I have met her coming from a small field where oats had been sown, with a sheaf on her back, which she had cut with her own fair hands to feed an old ox—the only remnant of stock that escaped the creditors, and which was destined to supply the household with beef the ensuing fall. Yet she was quite cheerful and almost laughed at her unusual occupation. There was a poor Irish girl who staid with her to the last and never forsook her in her adverse fortune, but she had been kind and considerate to her when many mistresses would have turned her out of their house, and now she staid with her and helped her in her time of need.

One day I came to visit her, fearing from her unusual absence, that something was amiss with the child or herself. I found her lying on a rude sort of sofa, which she had very ingeniously made, by nailing some boards together, and covered with chintz, after having stuffed it with hay,—for she was full of contrivances; "they amused her, and kept her from thinking of her troubles," she said. She looked very pale, her fair hair being neglected, and there was an air of great languor and fatigue visible in her frame. But when I expressed my apprehension that she, too, had fallen a prey to ague or fever, she eagerly replied,—"Oh, no, I am only dreadfully tired. Do you know, I was wandering in the woods a great part of the night!"

"On what errand?" I inquired, in some surprise,—on which she related her adventures, in these words:—

"I had reason to suppose that English letters of some consequence had arrived by post, and as I had no one to send for them, to whom I dared trust them, I made up my mind, yesterday morning, to walk down for them myself. I left my little boy to the care of Jane and his father, for, carrying him a distance of so many miles, and through such roads, was quite beyond my strength. Well, I got my letters and a few necessary articles that I wanted, at the store; but what with my long walk, and the delay one always meets with in town, it was nearly sunset before I began to turn my steps homeward. I then found, to my great distress, that I had lost my faithful 'Nelson' [a great Newfoundland dog that accompanied her wherever she went]. I lingered a good while in the hope that my brave dog would find me out, but concluding, at last, that he had been shut up in one of the stores, I hurried on, afraid of the moon setting before I should be out of the dark wood. I thought, too, of my boy, and wondered if his father would waken and attend to him if he cried or wanted feeding. My mind was full of busy and anxious thoughts, as I pursued my solitary way through these lonely woods, where everything was so death-like in its solemn silence, that I could hear my own footsteps, or the fall of a withered leaf, as it parted from the little boughs above my head and dropped on the path before me. I was so deeply absorbed with my own perplexing thoughts that I did not at first notice that I had reached where two paths branched off in nearly parallel directions, so that I was greatly puzzled which of the two was my road. When I had walked a few yards down one, my mind misgave me that I was wrong, and I retraced my steps without being at all satisfied that the other was the right one. At last I decided upon the wrong, as it afterwards turned out, and I now hurried on, hoping to make up, by renewed speed, for the time I had lost by my indecision. The increasing gloom of the road thickly shaded with hemlocks and cedars, now convinced me I was drawing near swampy ground, which I did not remember to have traversed in my morning walk. My heart thrilled with terror, for I heard the long-drawn yell of wolves, as I imagined in the distance. My first impulse was to turn and flee for my life, but my strength suddenly failed, and I was compelled to sit down upon a pine log by the side of the path to recover myself. 'Alas! alas!' said I, half-aloud, 'alone, lost in these lonely woods, perhaps to perish miserably, to be torn by wild beasts, or starved with hunger and cold, as many have been in this savage country! Oh my God! forsake me not, but look upon the poor wanderer with the eyes of mercy!' Such was my prayer when I heard the rapid gallop of some animal fast approaching—the sudden crashing of dry boughs, as the creature forced his way through them, convinced me it was too near for escape to be possible. All I could do was to start to my feet, and I stood straining my eyes in the direction of the sound, while my heart beat so audibly that I seemed to hear nothing else. You may judge of the heartfelt relief I experienced when I beheld my dear old dog, my faithful Nelson, rush bounding to my side, almost as breathless as his poor terror-stricken mistress.

"You know that I don't often indulge in tears, even when overwhelmed with trouble, but this time I actually cried for joy, and lifted up my heart in fervent thankfulness to Him who had guided my dumb protector through the tangled bush to my side that night. 'Come, Nelson,' I said, aloud, 'you have made a man of me.' 'Richard is himself again, dear fellow, I shall fear neither wolf nor bear while you are with me.' I then fastened my bundle about his neck for my arm ached with carrying it, and on we trudged. At first I thought it would be best to retrace my steps, but I fancied I saw light like a clearing breaking through the trees, and conjectured that this bye-road led in all likelihood to some of the bush farms or lumberer's shanties. I resolved to pursue my way straight onwards; nor was I mistaken, for some minutes after brought me to the edge of a newly burnt fallow, and I heard the baying of dogs, which no doubt were the same sounds, I, in my fright, had taken for wolves.

"The moon was now nearly set, and I judged it must be between one and two o'clock. I peeped into the curtainless window of the shanty, the glimmering light from a few burning brands and the red embers of the huge back-log in the wide clay-built chimney showed the inmates were all asleep, and as the barking and growling of the dogs, who, frightened by Nelson's great size, had retreated to a respectful distance, had failed to rouse them, I took bush-leave, opened the door, and stepped in without further ceremony. On a rude bed of cedar sticks slept two females, the elder of whom was not undressed but lay sleeping on the outside of the coverlet, and it was with great difficulty that I managed to rouse her to a consciousness of my presence and my request for a guide to the mills. 'Och! och! och! my dear crayter' she said, raising herself at last upon her brawny arm and eyeing me from under her black and tangled locks with a cunning and curious look, 'what should a young thing like yourself be doing up and abroad at sich a time of night as this?'

'Good mother,' I said, 'I have lost my way in the bush, and want a lad or some one to show me the way to the mills.'

'Sure,' said the old woman, 'this is not a time to be asking the boys to leave their beds, but sit down there, and I will speak with the master.' She then pushed a rude seat in front of the fire, and roused up the logs with a huge handspike, which she wielded with strength of arm that proved she was no stranger to the work of closing in log-heaps, and even chopping, and then proceeded to wake her partner, who, with three or four big boys, occupied another bed at the farthest end of the shanty.

After some parleying with the man it was agreed that at day-break

49

one of the elder boys should be sent to guide me home, but not sooner. 'There Mistress' said the man, 'you may just lie down on my old woman's bed, the girl has the ague, but she is as quiet as a lamb, and will not disturb you.' I preferred sitting on my rude seat before the now blazing fire, to sharing the girl's couch, and as to a refreshment of fried pork and potatoes which my hostess offered to get ready for me, I had no appetite for it, and was glad when my host of the shanty and his partner retired to bed, and left me to my own cogitations and mute companionship of Nelson. One feeling was uppermost in my mind — gratitude to God for my present shelter, rude as it was; the novelty of my situation almost amused me, and then graver thoughts came over me as I cast my eyes curiously around upon smoke-stained walls and unbarked rafters from whence moss and grey lichens waved in a sort of fancied drapery above my head. I thought of my former life of pride and luxury. What a singular contrast did it present to my situation at that moment. The red flashing glare of the now fiercely burning logs illumined every corner of the shanty, and showed the faces of the sleepers in their humble beds. There lay close beside me on her rude pallet, the poor sick girl, whose pale visage and labouring breath excited my commiseration, for what comfort could she have, either mental or bodily, I asked myself. The chinking in many parts, had been displaced, and the spaces stuffed with rags, straw, moss, wool and a mass of heterogeneous matter, that would have plainly told from what part of the world the inmates had come, if their strong South of Ireland brogue had not declared it past all disputing. Few and scanty were the articles of furniture and convenience. Two or three unplaned pinewood shelves, on which were arranged some tinware and a little coarse delf, a block of wood sawn from the butt end of a large timber tree, and a rude ricketty table, with a pork and flour barrel, some implements of husbandry, among which gleamed brightly the Irish spade, an instrument peculiar to the Irish laborers' cabin, and a gun which was supported against the log walls by two carved wooden hooks, or rests, such was the interior of the shanty. I amused myself with making a sort of mental inventory of its internal economy, till by degrees weariness overcame me, and leaning my back against the frame of the poor sick girl's bed, I fell sound asleep, and might have slept on till broad day, had not my slumbers been suddenly broken by the rolling of one of the big logs on the hearth, and looking over, I almost started at the sight of the small, sinister-looking eyes of my host, which were bent upon me with so penetrating a glance, that I shrank from before them. In good truth more stout-hearted persons might have been justified in the indulgence of a cowardly feeling, if they had been placed in a similar situation, so utterly helpless and alone; but my courage quickly returned. I thought it wisest not to show distrust, and addressed the uncouth-looking personage before me with a cheerful air, laughing at his having caught me napping. Yet I remember the time, when I was a youthful romance reader, I should have fancied myself into a heroine, and my old Irishman into a brigand; but in my intercourse with the lower class of Irish emigrants, I have learnt that there is little cause for fear in reality. Their wild passions are often roused to a fearful degree of violence by insult, either against their religion or their nation, to acts of vengence; but such a thing as murdering or robbing a helpless, unoffending stranger, seeking the hospitable shelter of their roofs, I never yet heard of, nor do I believe them capable of an act of covetousness or cruelty so unprovoked. While I thought on these things my confidence returned, so that I would not have hesitated to take the man for my guide through the lone woods I had to pass, trusting to this impression of the Irish character, which, with many defects, has many virtues, while that of hospitality is certainly one of the most prominent.

"The first streak of daylight saw the old woman stirring, to prepare their morning meal of pork and potatoes, of which I was glad to partake.

"One by one came stealing sleepily from their nests four ragged urchins, whose garments I verily believe were never removed for weeks, either by day or night. They all had the same peculiar smoke-dried complexion, a sort of dusky greyish tint, grey eyes, with thick black lashes, and broad black eyebrows, with a squareness of head and a length of chin which I have not unfrequently noticed as a characteristic feature in the less comely inhabitants of the Irish cabins. The boys stole looks of wonder and curiosity at me, but no one spoke or ventured to ask a question; however, they bestowed great marks of attention on Nelson, and many were the bits of meat and potatoes with which they strove to seduce him from my feet.

"When our meal was ended, I gave the old woman a small piece of silver, and, accompanied by Master Michael, the biggest boy, I left the shanty, and was glad enough to seek my own home, and find all as well as when I had left them, though some anxiety had been felt for my unusual absence."

Such were the midnight adventures of my poor friend. It was only one of many trials that she afterwards underwent before she once more regained her native land. She used often to say to me, "I think, if you ever write another book on the backwoods, some of my adventures might furnish you with matter for its pages."

I would not have it inferred from these pages that, because some young men have erred in bringing out wives, unsuited by their former state of life, to endure the hardships of a bush-settling life, there are no exceptions. I would warn all who go home for British wives, to act openly, and use no deception, and to choose wisely such as are by habits and constitution able to struggle with the trials that may await them. It is not many who have the mental courage that was displayed by her whose adventures I have just narrated.

AN INDIAN WIG-WAM.

R.

"Early Provincial Settlers.   An Indian Story"*

THE THIRTEENTH DAY OF SEPTEMBER marks a memorable period in the history of North America. It is the anniversary of an event which told powerfully upon the kingdoms of England and France, at the time of its occurrence, and whose effects are felt to the present day. The scene of it was the City of Quebec. On the morning of the day, in the year 1759, several boys had climbed upon that part of the wall of the city which overlooked the Plains of Abraham, and were gazing with intense interest upon a novel and striking object. They were discovered by the military guard, who immediately ordered them down. One of them refused to obey, and the attention of the guard being immediately directed to matters of more importance, the refractory youth was suffered to remain in quiet possession of his post. The object at which he was gazing with so much eagerness was a battle. Two hostile armies were engaged in fierce and dreadful encounter upon the Plains of Abraham. It was the day of the taking of Quebec by General Wolfe. The youth who looked in despite of the danger of his position and the order of the guard, was well known many years afterwards throughout Nova Scotia, as a minister of the Gospel of peace. He went to the grave in a good old age, like 'a shock of corn fully ripe;' but still lives in the hearts of many who sat under his

*The Provincial: or Halifax Monthly Magazine, Aug. 1852, pp. 300-06.

ministry. He was the Rev. John Payzant, of Liverpool, who died in 1834. When Quebec was taken he was in that city a British prisoner. The events of that memorable day set him free, together with his mother, two brothers, and two sisters. They had all been taken by the Indians. The history of their capture and captivity, as related to the writer a few years ago by one of the number then in his ninety-sixth year, cannot fail to interest the reader, though related without any attempt at embellishment.

On the southern coast of Nova Scotia, between Chester and Liverpool, are scattered grotesquely groups of beautiful islands. It is said that in all, they number as many as the days of the year. One of them at the mouth of Mahone Bay is celebrated as the scene of the tragical event about to be related. This Island, at the time that Lunenburg was settled, was granted to the father of the late Rev. J. Payzant. He was a merchant of some wealth, whose father had fled from France during the stormy times which followed upon the revocation of the edict of Nantes. The city of Caen, in the Department of Normandy, was his native place. Thence he had fled to the Island of Jersey, whence he afterwards removed with his family and effects to Halifax.

Why he afterwards chose this Island as his place of residence is not known. He had lived there about a year. The brushwood cabin—the wigwam—first erected for the accommodation of those employed in clearing the ground, had been superseded by a comfortable log hut, in which the family resided. Boxes and bales of valuable merchandize occupied no small portion of the room preparatory to entering upon business on an enlarged scale. A large two story house was advancing rapidly to its completion. A field of wheat had been sown, and our informant, the late Lewis Payzant, Esq., of Falmouth, distinctly remembered that at the time they were taken by the Indians, the wheat had sprung up, for the field was green.

It was in the month of May, 1754. The week had closed. The laborers and the mechanics who were employed had retired to their several homes. The darkness of night had gathered around this lonely dwelling. The family were preparing to retire, when an unusual noise alarmed them. There were evidently some evil minded persons about the house. It was a time of trouble among the Colonists. Lunenburg was then recently settled, chiefly by Germans and Swiss. Their expectations had been raised high by the inducements to emigrate, held out to them by the British authorities. They had expected to find 'easy times,' a sort of Paradise, in the land to which they had come. It would, no doubt, they supposed, abound in 'corn and wine,' and 'flow with milk and money;' and they would be far removed from danger, and could sit every man 'under his own vine and under his own fig-tree,' where none would make him afraid. Instead of the realization of these golden dreams, however, they found a cold climate, an untried soil, and a waste howling wilderness, where roamed the savage beast and the more cruel and more to be dreaded savage man. Filled at length with disappointment and vexation, they rose in open rebellion. They were not subdued without much trouble, nor without the aid of a strong military force sent from Halifax for that purpose. The Governor had told Mr. Payzant that if they should offer to disturb him, to fire upon them. Supposing that some of those malcontents were now about the house, he seized his musket, and went out to oppose them. Imagining, no doubt, a slight demonstration in the 'line of battle,' would frighten them, he discharged his piece. Alas! he had mistaken the danger that threatened him, and the mistake was fatal! The harmless flash of his gun revealed his position. It was answered by a volley from the assailants. The terrified wife and mother rushed out just in time to throw her arms around her fainting husband. She begged him to come in. Death choked his utterance as he exclaimed, 'my heart is growing cold! — the Indians!' and he fell lifeless at her feet. The terrific 'war-whoop,' and the rush of the Indians confirmed her worst forebodings. Resistance was out of the question. She retreated to the house, she barred the door; but when baffled in their attempts to force it, she saw the Indians deliberately beginning to carry their threat into execution of burning the house over her head, and that of her helpless little ones, she resigned herself to her fate. She desired her oldest son to open the door. They rushed in like so many tigers.

Nearly a century had passed away when Mr. Payzant told us the story. He was literally bending under the weight of years. Both mind and body were enfeebled by age. It was some time before we could get him fully roused. But he well remembered the scene. As he dwelt upon it and related particular after particular, in answer to various enquiries, it came up more and more vividly to his recollection. We shall not easily forget the excitement of his manner as he reverted, on one occasion, to the rush of the savages into the house when the door was opened. He drew up his bent and contracted form into an erect position. He raised his voice, and his eyes flashed. 'O,' said he, 'I hear them now! I see them! Hewing down the boxes! Hewing down the boxes! Seizing and securing every valuable article as fast as they could!' He remembered too that his oldest brother gave battle. That he sprang upon the table, and attempted resistance, shaking his fist and giving expression to his anger, and he was only dissuaded by the entreaties of his mother. He remembered the screams of a poor servant woman, who with her infant child occupied an apartment to which access was had by a different door. They had killed the poor woman, and dashed out the brains of the babe, before they had succeeded in entering Mrs. P.'s apartment. And he remembered how they afterwards mimicked her cries in their sports, and called out, as she had done, 'Mr. Payzant, Mr. Payzant.' And the old gentleman imitated, in turn, *their* voice and manner, as he related the story.

A young man had been taken by the party in the neighbourhood. They had promised to spare his life and give him his liberty, in case he would conduct them to a rich prize. He had promised to do so. That promise had now been fulfilled. They had obtained five prisoners, and a large amount of plunder. Their ends were answered, and they fulfilled their part of the agreement by killing the hapless young man and adding his scalp to the booty. One deed remained to be done, the one which usually concludes the scene in the horrid tragedy of war. The house must be fired. When the captives were secured — when the plunder had been placed in the canoes and they were ready to push away from the Island, the torch was applied. High into the air shot up the flame, shedding its lurid glare far over the waters. The wretched captives turned a last sad look towards their late happy home. Sudden and awful was the change. They glided away rapidly into the dense gloom. Darker and more gloomy was the prospect before them. Many a cup of affliction had that sorrow-stricken woman tasted before. There were others still in reserve for her. But so deep was her grief on this occasion, that tears would not come to her relief. There was but one arm that could afford relief, and surely it was extended to her in this time of need.

The party landed at Chester and travelled across the country, through the pathless woods, about twelve miles, to the head of the St. Croix River, which empties into the Avon, just below Windsor. They passed this latter place on the following night. The night was clear, and they could distinctly see the sentry as he walked his rounds. The canoes drew in close under the shore, and moved noiselessly along, while the captives were terrified into silence by the flourishing of a tomahawk over their heads. The first place at which they landed was Cape Chignecto, where was a French settlement at the time. Thence they were hurried on to what is now Fredericton, then called St. Ann's, the name by which it still goes among the Indians. There the French Governor resided, and there the Indians expected to obtain the promised reward for prisoners and scalps. During the terrible voyage Mrs. P. espied among the plunder her wedding shoes. It may be easily imagined that having preserved them with so much care, she would be anxious to regain possession of them. But they were worthless in the eyes of the Indians, and the only answer made to her entreaties that they might be restored to her, was a loud insulting laugh, and the shoes were thrown overboard.

'And upon what did they feed you' we asked. 'Feed us upon,' was the reply, 'why sometimes they fed us upon berries; sometimes upon bread; and sometimes upon *nothing!*' Mr. P. remembered that the Indian to whom he was assigned on the division of the spoil, had a son, a small boy about his own age and size. During their travel through the woods, they were carried alternately upon the old Indian's back. 'He would take me by the shoulders,' said he, 'and swing me round upon his back.' Mr. P. thought that the Indians did not ordinarily subject them to any ill-treatment, beyond what would naturally arise from the circumstances of the case. He recollected one exception. The piece of bread, given to him one night for his supper, was so bad that he could not eat it, and he threw it away. For this offence he was sentenced to go without food for the night. As it happened, a larger portion than was necessary for the time being, had fallen to the lot of his tawny companion. As the latter fell asleep it fell out of his hand, and was eagerly appropriated by the hungry white boy. The little Indian awoke in the morning, and looked for his bread. It was gone. Lewis had taken it. A complaint was lodged against him. The old Indian was just starting upon a fishing excursion. He seemed greatly enraged, and threatened in a tone which left little doubt on the child's mind that it would be carried into execution, that he would sacrifice him on his return. Whether he really intended to do so or not, could never be known. The Indian got drunk that day, fell out of his canoe, and was drowned. He was brought back a corpse.

On their way to Fredericton, the Indians murdered two young Frenchmen and took their scalps. They had discernment sufficient to perceive that the scalp of a Frenchman could not be distinguished from that of an Englishman. How often may such acts have been perpetrated, and how often may a fearful retribution in this way have been visited upon those 'enlightened' nations, who could descend to

59

the barbarity of hiring the savages to wage this horrid species of warfare. Oh war! Thou art dreadful in all thy forms. When, oh when shall the sword be put up into its scabbard? When will the long looked for period arrive, when the 'nations shall learn war no more?' When the pure principles of the gospel shall exert their benign influence so extensively, that 'swords shall be beaten into plowshares, and spears into pruning hooks,' and the 'knowledge of the Lord cover the earth as the waters the channel of the deep.'

Mrs. Payzant was separated from her children at Fredericton, and sent on to Quebec. She left them in the hands of the Indians. Months passed — months of suspense and anxiety, before she heard from them. News at length arrived that two of them were in the hands of the French, but that the other two — the oldest son and only daughter,[1] were still retained by the Indians, who refused to give them up on any terms. They had probably been adopted, after their manner, in the place of some who had been killed by the English. What were the feelings of the sorrowing mother when this painful intelligence arrived, may be better conceived then described. She went to the Roman Catholic Bishop and implored his aid. He instructed the Priest at Fredericton to demand the children, and to refuse absolution to the Indians in whose hands they were, unless they were given up. This was effectual. The children were forthcoming at once. At the end of seven months they arrived, among other British prisoners, at Quebec. Hearing of their arrival, the mother was, as may naturally be supposed, transported with joy, and eager to rush forth to meet them. This was, however, denied her. A military guard obliged her to remain at the door of her lodgings, until a group of children were brought up — she, alas! had only been one among many who suffered in a similar way — and she was directed to select her own little ones. It was easy to do that. Thank heaven! there they were! The marks of their long captivity upon them; but they were her own precious little ones, and she pressed them to her bosom, covered them with kisses, and bathed them with her tears.

Probably owing to the fact of their being of French descent, they were allowed all the indulgence that could be allotted to prisoners. The taking of Quebec, of course, gave them their liberty. They returned to Nova Scotia, but Mrs. P., naturally enough, could never think of returning to the place of her former troubles, and selected a different locality for a residence.

Such is a brief and unvarnished statement of incidents illustrative of the hardships and trials of the early settlers of Nova Scotia. It is a portion of our history, and the public has a right to a knowledge of it. It were easy to comment, to embellish, and to moralize, but we choose to present the story in the simple garb of truth. Thanks to a merciful Providence, these days of trouble with the Indians of the Provinces have passed away, never to return. The white man has nothing to fear now from the Indian. The fear and terror is, alas! the other way. It is not the sword; it is not captivity, that these children of the forest dread in their present defenceless condition, and their wretched homes; it is outrage and wrong. But 'the poor shall not always be forgotten;' their Father in Heaven will remember them, and he will plead their cause. It is not for us to visit the sins of the fathers upon their children. We should rather confess and forsake our own and the sins of *our* fathers. Let no one exclaim against the red man because of such scenes in former times, as are here related. Be it remembered that there is another side to these stories — that they can tell of acts of cruelty on the part of the white man, co-equally outrageous as any which has been recorded against them. But let the atrocities formerly committed on both sides be forgotten in efforts to civilize, enlighten, and save, the present remnant of a once mighty people.

[1] A second daughter was born after she arrived at Quebec.

THE RESIDENCE OF JUDGE HALIBURTON

P. T. S. Atty, Esq.

From "Law and Lawyers in Canada West"*

MY INTENTION...in these memoranda of my early days was to give some idea of the practice of the profession in Upper Canada. I cannot say that I am enabled to do so from having had an extensive one; but I think I may say I have met with almost every variety of client, which a general practitioner can do in a country practice, from the rich merchant whose periodical visits to his distant customers, strikes terror into their unprepared cash accounts, down to the litigious yeoman who, of course, deprecates law, and satisfies his propensity by suing his neighbor for half a day's use of an ox sled. It was one of the latter class who gave me by earliest employment, as a counsellor; and so, without further preface, I will endeavor to give an account of

"MY FIRST CASE."

'Tom Touchy is famous for taking the *law* of everybody.'

Spectator.

After I had been established in my chambers, or rather chamber, about a week, and was beginning to feel that business prospects were not very bright, I came to my office, as usual, about ten A. M. I hold a regular attendance at your office conducive to success, and I was thinking of some way by which I could emulate Mr. Bob Sawyer, in the Pickwick papers, and delude the public by a series of clever

The Anglo-American Magazine, April 1854, pp. 392-99.

artifices, into the belief that I was enjoying an excellent practice, and that my continual engagements were very likely to disappoint my intended clients, unless they took strenuous measure to ensure a consultation with me upon their several affairs. I have observed in sundry towns, (and not excepting the metropolis), hurried announcements on the doors of lawyers' offices, such as "Gone to Crown Office"—"On consultation"—"Back in half an hour"—and to the uninitiated they have held out inducements for them to become "dwellers on the threshold," as Bulwer Lytton hath it; but to young aspirants to the woolsack they are more suggestive of a sederunt at a saloon, or a temporary absence in ascertaining the nautical position of the solar luminary. I had never yet resorted to any such devices since I had been a barrister; and on this occasion, after taking a view of the exterior of my office, and ascertaining that my friend the grocer had not entirely excluded my brilliant sign by the "delicacies of the season," I took my seat in my office chair at the critical moment when the harmonious cordwainers were announcing that the heroine of their lyric had assumed masculine attire for the sole object of being near her erratic true love. I began to smoke—yes smoke! (and not a cigar either—but a clay pipe which was beginning to approach a luxurious state of narcotic perfection)—very disagreeable, I admit, on many accounts, occasionally so to your lady friends, and at times nauseating to yourself; but, after all, many celebrated men have smoked, and still do smoke, and young barristers smoke, of course, from sympathy. Under the soothing influence of the pipe, I was studying attentively the celebrated case of Bardell vs. Pickwick, 2 Dicken's Reports, when my attention was withdrawn from my book by the sudden and rather unexpected entrance of a visitor, whom I hoped was a client, and therefore in my excess of hospitality, I jerked my feet from the table, where they had been resting, and discomposed the "set" of my Toronto pantaloons, in order to receive him with becoming ceremony. He wanted to be polite, and certainly was, so far as he knew how. His appearance, however, was not attractive; but I mentally resolved that, notwithstanding appearances, in the event of his requiring my services, I would consider, in the language of Lord Brougham, "my sacred duty to my client." He looked thin and wiry, rather above the middle height, with what phrenologists would call a sanguine bilious temperament which seemed, somehow or other, to impart an influence to his habiliments. His hair was light and wiry, and his head was covered with an old flattened dyed musk-rat cap, with a straight forward peak. His great coat was of a remote age, being coarse, well worn, and of a yellowish drab color, and matched with his hair. It was very long, and reached nearly to his ankles, and the lapels extended up to the back to two faded mother of pearl buttons, close together, and with a foot of the old fashioned six-inch rolling collar. His boots were stogys, and his trowsers of the homemade butternut variety; and before he spoke he seemed exactly the sort of man who "never wanted any more than what's right;" but, at the same time would prefer having a lawsuit in its acquisition.

"Squire," says he, "how goes the times? I've been thinking to call on you before; but aint had no chance till now. Hows'ever, time enough I guess. I've got a kind of a little case that bothers me some, and I was thinking if it didn't cost too much, I'd get you to work it out for me, and pettifog a spell."

I was half inclined to be angry when I heard our noble profession slandered, albeit ignorantly; but when I came to think about board, lodging, tailors' bills, and office rent, I pocketed the affront, in expectation of a fee, and assured him my charge should correspond with the importance of the case.

"Well," he continued, "it aint no great account, after all; but it's the principle's the thing,—when a man calc'lates to be ugly, he ort to be stopped,—that's it,—I don't calc'late to gouge anybody, *and* I don't mean to be gouged;" and using this lucid exordium, fortunately for all parties in an allegorical sense, he sat down on a chair, indicated the absence of a pocket handkerchief, nursed one of his feet upon the other knee, and proceeded, as I anticipated, to a more particular and deliberate explanation.

"You see, the business of the story's this,—me and the man I'm going to tell you about's neighbors, and more'n a year ago he got put out with me, cause I dogged his hogs outen my pertater patch, and one on 'em went home chawed up considerable. Well, he gin out around that my dog was wicked, and used to kill sheep, and byemby, after a spell, my dog come limping like as though h'd bin caught in a trap, and I allus suspicioned who done it. Well, that aint what I'm going to tell you about, and I dunno as it has anything to do with what I *am* going to tell you; but I thought I'd let you see what kind of a man he was anyway. Hows'ever, things went along, and byemby, about a week ago, I was coming along home, and middlin' close up to his fence, ('twas a little after sundown, and getting a kinder dusklike,) *I* found a log chain. Well—seeing it right there in the road, I picked it up and shouldered it home—hadn't no more thought of its being hissen more'n a child, and so I commenced right to using it, as a body might nat'rally, and one day a long spell arterwards, when my boy was snaking up some drags o' firewood, along *he* comes, and claims the chain. Well, I warn't to home jest then. I was off tending court in a suit I had about some flour, and so my boy wouldn't let him have the chain. Well, first and foremost, he goes to work and abuses *me* to kill; told how me and my family was a thieving breed, and not satisfied with that, down he puts hot foot to the squire, and swars my boy *stole* the chain! and byemby a constable comes along and takes him up for the robbery. Well, I kind of mistrusted how it was going to be, and I told the squire I was bound to defend the case anyhow, and so he put off the case for a spell, and the hearings is going to be tried right here in town to-day,—I guess you can onsuit him, if you're smart, *and* I want you to flail him *if you kin*. I *don't* like law any way, and don't want no more than my rights; but the business of the matter's this, that when a man goes to cutting up his rustys in that way—why, then, I jest want to teach him, he's got to look out."

As I was totally inexperienced in receiving retainers, I did not demand payment of a fee as a necessary preliminary, and after hearing numberless details of the outrage under consideration, and many aggravating instances of prior impositions, I inquired the place and time of attending the sessions of the justice, and, dismissing my client with repeated injunctions to be prepared with his witnesses, with all the enthusiasm and energy of a strong sympathy for the cause of my much injured friend (and with far from mercenary feelings so far,) I proceeded to look up the case with all the research my library afforded, and in the interval charged my mind with a confused mass of information respecting crime and its punishment in the abstract, as well as of every species of larceny and felony known to the courts of Oyer and Terminer, and General Gaol Delivery.

In due time I attended at the magistrate's room, and found the case about ready to proceed. My client appeared triumphant as I entered with him, and encouraged his son, the prisoner, by informing him that he was "bound to see him through." Being late in the autumn, there was a fire in the stove in the room where the justice, a worthy yeoman of the neighborhood, was sitting. He was seated at a table with some stationery, &c., on which also lay the information and papers already taken in the case. All parties were sitting down, and for some time the conversation turned calmly upon general matters not at all bearing

66

upon the case in hand, and the constable, totally unmindful of the presence of the magistrate, had his chair tilted aginst the wall, at an angle of fifty-five, chewing tobacco sedately, and digesting, with all deliberation, the contents of the local newspaper. I don't think the prosecutor cordially approved of my presence; but I was profoundly polite to him, which rather tended to our mutual embarrassment. The prosecutor was a short clumsy man, at present of rather morose aspect and uncleanly appearance. He was attended by his wife, a lady evidently of a strong minded turn, one of the description who could figuratively "hold her own" in every sense but her tongue;—his daughter, who appeared to dislike her present position, and two of his young boys, who, it was easy to see, stood in more fear of their parents' displeasure than of a little obligatory perjury. The "logging chain scrape," as it was termed, attracted an increasing audience, whose presence the heat of the stove and limited dimensions of the room rendered unpleasant and inconvenient, almost enough to defeat the ends of justice; but his worship proceeded to try the case with the additional discomfort of an utter absence of elbow room, with several gaping boors intently gazing over his shoulder upon the evidence he was taking down; but of which they were unable to read a word. Add to this, there was a density of confined and heated air enough to mystify the clearest brain, and to make the position of administrative authority anything but a sinecure.

The information was, however, read, stating, of course, among other things, that the prisoner feloniously stole the article in question; that it had been found in his possession, seemed apparent; and the prosecutor seemed to consider this as a sufficient substantiation of his complaint. With frequent promptings from his wife (who informed the court in a loud voice, sufficiently energetic and exacting conviction, that she knew all about the chain—where she bought it—who cut it off—the blacksmith who put the hooks to it, &c. &c.,) the prosecutor identified the chain to be his—that the chain was on his premises just before he missed it ("I see it close by the bob-sled *myself*," the wife interrupted.) The rest of the evidence was very vague as to whether it was on the prosecutor's premises the night it was missed, or whether it had been left near the bob-sled, or in the road or out of the road. As to proof of the felonious abstraction there was default of evidence on oath. The strong minded woman offered to swear that she believed the prisoner was mean enough to do it, or at all events, if he, the prisoner, wasn't, his father was, but this did not seem to satisfy the worthy magistrate as to the felony. It must not be supposed that the prosecutor and his party had been allowed to give their evidence without interruption from their opponents, as during its progression all sorts of variations of the lie direct and the lie collusive, had been actively exchanged. The magistrate threatened several times to commit the parties, unless more order was observed; but it had very little effect; and the introduction by the hostile parties of irrelevant matters tending to mutual criminations, generally succeeded a temporary lull. "I should like to know who stole that side of pork?" was answered by "I should like to know how *you* came by that buffalo robe?" My good opinion of my client was by no means increased. I began to see that both parties were in a state of feud, and were gratified by any frivolous opportunity of annoying each other, and I really could not feel much triumph when the justice dismissed the case, and recommended the prosecutor to seek his remedy in *trover*. "Trover" to the prosecutor seemed unintelligible, and in its nature, as a civil action, not sufficiently annoying; therefore, the decision was unsatisfactory. My client, too, appeared dissatisfied, and wanted to know from the justice "whether he was goin' to get any costs for being dragged up here with his witnesses, and losing so much time just for nothing." But he received a severe lecture from the magistrate, in an upright, homespun way, recommending him to be less litigious, and foment fewer quarrels among neighbors. The prisoner was released from custody, very much to his satisfaction, and the court broke up without being terminated by a committal to the county jail, which, as the amiable partner of the prosecutor hoped would have taken place. She told the ungainly lad who had been in custody, in her valedictory address to him, that she "hoped to see some of 'em yet where the dogs wouldn't bark at 'em, and if every body had their own, 'some folks' would be in the 'jug' at this present moment."

My client seemed disposed to avoid me; perhaps he had discovered the absence of any sympathy with his fortunes since the dismissal of the case; but more probably he did not wish to have any allusion made to the retaining fee which he knew I expected. I allowed myself to overcome my native modesty, and with sundry misgivings, but with a placid countenance, I adverted to my recompense. The artful litigant said, "Oh, I'd like to forgot all about it. How much do you charge?" I replied, that my services, if worth anything at all, were worth five dollars. "Five dollars!" said he. "Well, you do earn your money easy— why, that's an awful sight to earn so quick. You warn't more'n two hours there altogether—and it's a considerable spell to night yet. I've got a dollar about me which you *kin* have, if you say so; but I won't have any money to go home with, if you take it. Like as not I'll have some more business some time, and I'll call and settle it up altogether." My first client and I parted. I began to wish him in the "jug" for the manner in which he had used me; and although I really wanted the ridiculously small sum of one dollar, I should have spurned it had I had an opportunity of taking it on this occasion, which I had not. This was the first disagreeable blow I had had. After all, I did not care so much for the absence of the fee, as to feel that I had been fooled by my first client. Since then I have made a resolution, in taking up cases, and that is, to receive my fee before proceeding. If a man have a fair cause of action or defence, and prepays for your attention, he has a right to demand your best services thus secured. If he endeavor to make bargains with you dependent on the result, he is the sort of character who is neither generous in success, nor just in failure.

I must, however, again introduce my first client. About a week after our first interview, he again called at my office, and strenuously endeavored to induce me to bring an action for false imprisonment against the owner of the logging chain, grounded on the prosecution I have endeavored to detail, and promising me that whatever damages were recovered, I should have a moiety for my services. I declined the action; but my client was not satisfied. He, however, retained a professional rival, who was my senior in the Law Society, but junior to me in his arrival in our town. By the good management of my learned friend, however, and by those wonderful freaks which sometimes inexplicably influence juries, at the trial of the cause for false imprisonment, at the next assizes, my quondam client obtained a verdict for fifteen pounds damages! I being for the defence; and as for the costs of such defence, as well as for my aforesaid services before the magistrate, they remain unpaid by both parties to this day, and I have long looked upon them as bad debts; but as being associated with useful warnings to avoid litigious characters of the calibre of "my first client."

SUGAR MAKING.

W. W. S.

"In the Bush. A Settler's Own Tale"*

IN THE YEAR 1835 I emigrated to Canada. I was advised to come by the way of New York, as offering, at that time, better facilities for reaching the Upper Province, and, meeting with some Scottish friends, I remained there two or three months, hoping to fall into some employment to better my situation. Not succeeding according to my wishes, I proceeded to Upper Canada; having in the meantime considerably reduced my little purse of ready money, which represented all I had of fortune. Again I erred; for instead of accepting employment as a farm laborer for a year or two, I was impatient while my money yet lasted, to get a farm of my own. Of course, I was only able to buy a bush farm. I obtained in the north-eastern part of the Gore District, which is now a beautiful farming country, but was then a rude wilderness, a very good hundred acres of land. The timber, which covered every part of it, was very heavy; immense maples, basswoods, beeches and elms interlaced their branches above and their roots below, in undisturbed possession. There were no saw-mills within reach, at which lumber could be obtained for house building; and as I knew that the axe, in skilful hands, could supply that want, I engaged two men for a month to assist me in putting up a house. It was in the month of September when I first began my bush life. Delightful

*The British American Magazine, June 1863, pp. 185-94.

sunny days, with no oppressive heat, and cool, breezy nights, gave freshness and vigour to my frame; for my health was impaired from the heat of the last two months. Perhaps a nervous anxiety about my family and prospects, had tended to increase my ailments. Now, I was in high spirits. Was I not the *bona fide* owner of a hundred acres? Should I not be able to make a comfortable living for my wife, my little ones, and myself? It is well for us we do not know the future. I should have shrunk from the prospect had I known *all* that awaited me. I left my family in a little village that has since changed its name and become an incorporated town. A log house of two rooms, for a dollar a month, seemed not only most suitable to our wants and condition but was at the time the only house to be rented in the place. So kissing "good bye" to wife and weans (I like the old-world expression yet, Canadian as I have become) and returning over and over again the caresses of little Jeanie—poor dear, lost Jeanie!—I started with my two assistants one Monday morning, to travel fifteen miles into the bush, to "hew out a home." It would lengthen this part of my story too much to particularize the incidents of the month we passed in the woods. Suffice it to say that my two friends (for such they proved themselves to be,) pronounced my "lot" to be a good one, and prophesied that I should "do well on it"; basing this prediction on my seeming "to get the *hang of things* first-rate, for an old countryman"; praise which Canadians and old settlers do not always accord to new beginners. We slashed down an acre or more of the wood; finished the house, such as it was; "underbrushed" about two acres or more, and made a beginning towards opening out the road for a mile or two from my lot. Then we returned; and with the aid of one of these men (and his oxen) we managed to get ourselves settled down in our own home, on the 15th day of October. It was on a Wednesday, and it was my wife's birthday. Seven years before we had spent the day together, beside the burn and among the knolls of our native place; and now, wandering over a portion of our "domain," while our two children gathered beechnuts and crimson maple leaves, or watched the squirrels aloft among the branches, and the third, the youngest, crowed and danced in his mother's arms, we named the stream and the farm after some of the old haunting memories of home. But the name would never *stick* to it; and even we ourselves, in after years, almost forgot that the farm had any other name than "Mr. Wood's place." But I am anticipating; for at the time there was not a living being within several miles. My wife had always had a dread of wild Indians. She had read old and highly coloured stories of their outrages; and it was certainly much to the satisfaction of us both that we learned that we should not probably see an Indian thrice in a year, and that they were perfectly harmless. I myself had always had a feeling of insecurity with respect to wild beasts; and I had been informing myself on that subject. An occasional wolf was found in that part of the country, but generally kept at a respectful distance from any dwelling; though not all to be trusted in the matter of sheep (which were always securely folded at night). Bears were also known to exist, but I was cautioned that it was probable I should never have an opportunity of seeing one. Foxes were more numerous in the old settlements than in the new. There were said to be no poisonous serpents near us. Game was scarce. Wild pigeons for a few weeks in summer, a few partridges, quails, &c., in the autumn, and an occasional deer in winter, and, in some places, a considerable number of wild ducks in the spring, made up the most important page of our natural history.

Winter set in about the fifteenth of November. That is to say, the snow first fell then, and never quite went away again. By the beginning of December, it was settled wintry weather. The cold did not strike me at all as severe. I had been prepared to expect a greater extreme. The dryness of the air, and the absence of wind (the latter peculiarity more observable in the woods than in the "old settlements"), tempered the severity of the winter so much that I had no complaints to make of it, except its length.

Our house, which has long been replaced by a better, was very snug, though now we would think it extremely small. It was eighteen feet square. Of course it was all in one apartment; but we had a chamber, above, which we found very useful. The floors, both above and below, were of cedar and basswood, hewn into planks, with a rough dressing with the jackplane. The door creaked on wooden hinges, and was fastened with a wooden latch; locks we had none. The chimney was made of clay, upon a frame work of sticks; the back of the fireplace contained the only stones in the whole building. The roof was of cedar shingles about three feet long, each course of which was held down by a heavy pole, laid across the roof, and fastened at the ends. We had but one window of six small panes below, and one of two panes above. The spaces between the logs were plastered with well wrought clay; and if we could have got enough lime to whitewash the inside of our house, my wife would have been quite proud of her little home. I dwell with the more pleasure on this part of our experience,

73

for our troubles had not then begun. My days were spent in hard chopping, within sight and hearing of the little cabin; and our evenings, round the fire, high blazing with "fat pine," were seasons of happy content. My eldest, little Jeanie, was six years old; and with her golden hair, which she inherited from her mother, laid upon my shoulder, she would look up into my face, and wile me into relating some old tale that I had read or heard; or if I had neither read nor heard it, 'twould be all the better! Willie would be on the other knee, and sound asleep, in the meantime; and when gently removed by his mother, would always be sure to wake up enough to hold up his mouth for a good-night kiss, and to murmur his little prayer, ending with "God bless father and mother, and little brother and sister, and make Willie a good boy!" I may say we saw nobody through the winter; — only twice any strangers came to the door — once, two hunters after deer; and once three young fellows who were returning from finishing a "chopping" two or three miles beyond us. I myself was only absent from home one night. When Spring came, I was still busier than ever. I had logging and burning to do, and I had no oxen with which to log. So I "changed work" with the nearest neighbour — more than two miles away. When my turn came to have his oxen, I managed to get about four acres logged. I had previously burned the "brush," though I had not a good "burn" — it was damp weather. This waiting on my neighbour's convenience was unfortunate for me; for it was a very bad season for crops, and many fields of spring wheat, put in late, as mine was, never ripened at all, but rotted during the fall rains. Had I depended altogether upon potatoes and other green crops, I should have done better; but I was a little ambitious to have a crop of wheat of my own raising, and devoted nearly all my ground to it. I waited wearily on my crop, and when at last I cut it, and carried it all in on my own back, to a little shed I had put up to serve the purposes of a barn, I found that not only was its bulk exceedingly small, but the "sample" was so miserably shrunken, that our year's bread could not possibly be got out of it. This was a serious business for us, for I had now no money left. However, with brave hearts we prepared to face our second winter in the bush, — I hoped, for the children's sakes, to have got a cow this summer; but I dared not face the responsibility of running into debt without the prospect of paying. Besides, I did not seem to have fodder enough to keep her over the winter. The only live stock we had were a few hens.

Were such noble trees as surrounded my house and covered my

land, in Britain, they would be greatly admired and valued; and had I not been obliged to win my children's bread out of the land (and only as fast as I destroyed the trees) I should have admired them too. They were very grand in winter, when their naked arms were hanging in icicles, or piled up with narrow ridges of soft snow. But there was nothing in sympathy with my circumstances — all was hard, stern, and unrelenting. I threshed out my crop, and winnowed and suited it by a makeshift process, and found I had twenty bushels of very poor wheat. Six or eight bushels of this I must keep for seed till Spring, and the remainder we might eat. I took it, before the snow was too deep, to my nearest neighbour's, and he kindly allowed me to have his oxen to take it to the mill. This took two days; and I was glad to accomplish it without any necessity for ready money, which was not now to be thought of in my case. My wheat was so poor that, though I took twelve bushels to the mill, it was not anything like twelve bushels to the standard weight of 60 lbs.; and so I made the miller separate the coarsest of the bran, and put all the rest together as "flour." It was coarse, but made wholesome bread.

I worked harder than ever this winter. It seemed to be "the darkest hour before day." I hoped for a short winter and a mild Spring, and that I should be able to get out of all my difficulties. But I never had the faculty of "taking things easy." When March came, and no signs of Spring, my prospects were gloomy indeed.

We made a little maple sugar this spring, which was of benefit to us. Had we possessed a large kettle we should have had a great deal more. We could only make 20 lbs. Though it seemed as if the Spring was *never* going to come, it came at last; and with it a repetition of the process of the former season, I got into the ground, and in somewhat better season, my eight bushels of wheat. I also planted five bushels of potatoes, and a little corn; and when the time came, I sowed half-a-pound of turnip seed. So late was the season (1837) that when first of June arrived, I had, by incredible exertions, just got my sowing over.

I had been revolving in my mind for some time, the possibility of leaving home for a month, to earn some money to get provisions; but I gave it up. I dared not be away so long, especially now that little Jeanie seemed to labour under ill health. I could not tell what ailed the child; but she seemed to get weak and puny — her eyes grew larger and brighter, and her voice softer and more tender — and yet she did not complain of any actual pain. Could it be that she had divined the

75

sorrow and trouble in the house? She often asked me "When I got my supper?" and when once I told her I should get it with her mother—after she was in bed—she looked at me with such a glance that I had to turn away; and returning a few minutes after, I found her sobbing as if her little heart would break. I could but press her in my arms, and then rush out to the shelter of the woods. Another reason against going out to work, was the great uncertainty of getting it. People were trying to manage as best they could; for there was neither money nor money's equivalent in the country, with which to pay labourers.

In coming to America, away beyond all game-laws, I had promised myself much sport in gunning, and brought a fowling piece with me. But I had done little or nothing with it; and now I determined to turn it into bread if possible. On the 16th June I took a survey of our stores. A very few poor potatoes, not more than 10 lbs. inferior flour, and a very little maple sugar—and that was all. We had sacrificed some of the laying hens for Jeanie, but thought it good policy to leave three, for the sake of an egg each for the children. I had turned botanist and herbalist in my extremity. Cow-cabbage, docks, and dandelion leaves, furnished us with limited quantities of very wholesome greens; but these could never take the place of bread, and it would be more than a month before we could expect to have any new potatoes. So, a day or two afterward, I started off early one morning, without waking little Jeanie, who knew nothing of my intention. I promised my wife I should be back at the end of five days, and shouldered my gun and all the paraphernalia belonging to it, and took my journey southward. Two or three hard cakes of brown flour were my stock of food for the journey. I knew the way, and with a heavy heart pursued it. By night I was twenty-five miles from home, and in the midst of a prosperous settlement: that is, prosperous in good times; but people were looking at each other in blank despair, which was not much removed by the appearance of the season. Rain almost every day; the hay crop would be immense, but the wheat! In low situations, it would lodge as soon as headed, and probably before, and never fill; and if the rains continued long, it would neither ripen well, nor could it possibly be secured. I got lodgings without much trouble, in a settler's house (hospitality will never die out, I hope, in Canada); but when I learned the exact state of affairs, I could not accept this hospitality for nothing. I gave the eldest boy, who owned a ricketty gun, my shot-pouch and powder-flask. In return they loaded me with thanks, and made me promise to stay over night on my return. "For," said the settler, "we're nearer *help*, if we should get quite run out, than you are; and I trust we will now get the 'daily bread' we pray for."

Before the second night, I got a country storekeeper to take my gun for eight dollars "in trade." Flour was worth twelve dollars a barrel in the towns, and so I got something less than half a barrel for six dollars — about eighty pounds — and "took out" the rest in other things. I had been fond of a pipe of tobacco; but in famine times a man has something else to do with money than to smoke it away; and although the struggle (such creatures of habit are we!) was a severe one, I remembered my little pining one at home, and mastered the longing. I have never gone back to it. I got some tea, and a little rice and oatmeal, and two or three little articles of drugs we could not well do without; tied them and the flour all securely up in one bag, and started. I found I was very heavily laden. The perspiration was pouring down my face, when, after several rests, I got back to my lodgings of the previous night. It was some time after dark. The days were at the very longest. I had been accustomed, in Scotland, to find the twilight last, sufficient to read by, till half-past nine; but in Canada, I found the darkness came on an hour sooner. I passed a pleasant night with the man who, from henceforth, was my friend. A community of suffering, makes a community of feeling. 'Twas only last month, as we were sitting together in the County Council, we talked these old times over again; and his son, now the Reeve of a neighbouring township, was sitting opposite to us, and I am sure he guessed our conversation. In the morning, Mr. G—— insisted that his son should take "the old mare," and carry my flour just as far as he could get back from before night. As this was rather indefinite, and I knew that the lad's good-will would take him further north than he could retrace again, it was arranged that he should accompany me as far as Mr. S——'s — turn out the mare for two hour's pasturage, and then return. So John mounted, with the bag of flour before him, and I walked. John wanted to change places; but I did not like to oppress the poor beast. Indeed I was secretly very much pleased to see John dismount before we had gone two miles — declaring that "old Nell had quite enough to do to carry the flour!" and he would walk. He said he could ride going home. We had one shower on the way. We took shelter under a beech, and did not get much of it; but the roads were execrable. I had not so much observed it when coming down alone; but when I saw the poor beast struggling through great sloughs of mud, and getting her feet fast among the roots, and the flour reeling on her back — only kept in its place by a girth about her—I thought, indeed, "These *are* Canadian roads!" However, about midday we got to the house of Mr. S——. He too, like everybody else, was pinched for everything like food for man or beast—except that for the latter he had plenty of grass. As that was the extent of our demand, we fared not so badly. We had bread with us; and while the beast was baiting, we gathered some handfuls of fine strawberries. They were very early ones. It was only on one stony knoll any were ripe. I made a little paper bag, put some cool basswood leaves inside, and saved a handful to take home. Parting with John, and shouldering my heavy burden, I pressed on. I rested every quarter of a mile. It did not seem to be always thus requisite; but I thought it best to husband my strength. The fact was (though I did not think of it before), I was weak for the want of sufficient food; and the better providing of the last two days had not yet made much difference in my strength. About three miles, as I afterwards found, from my nearest neighbours, and six miles from my own house, night began to come on, and I had to make provision for "camping." I was not quite unprepared for it, for I had a small hatchet, such as hunters carry, and flint and frizzel. I had seen friction matches, but they did not get into common use in the backwoods for about five years after. A good sound, lying tree, to build my fire against, seemed the first requisite; and that was soon found. Then, despite damp tinder, a fire was soon crackling against it. It was not necessary to build my booth very near the fire, as the night was warm—only to be near enough to it for protection. Nothing prowling about on four feet will come near a fire; and mosquitoes never venture on the smoky side of a fire, so on that side I raised my tent. I placed a layer of hemlock twigs for my bag of flour, and covered it (quite rain-proof) with bark. Then a bed of the hemlock for myself; and as much of shelter from rain and dews as I could manage in half an hour. Having taken a good draught from a little stream trickling near by, and discussed the last crust of bread I carried, I gathered a few more sticks for night fuel, and prepared to seek repose.

Ah, that sleeping in the woods! I have slept in the woods three or four times since, but I always most vividly remember that first night I slept thus, *alone*. The woods are so solemn. 'Twas only three days ago, a young man from Australia told me, that there you are deafened by the noise of insects and paraquets, and I don't know how many creatures—but in Canada there is a solemn stillness prevailing. You will, in the day time, hear an occasional thrush, or bullfinch, or song sparrow, or a robin; but (dear little warblers!) they like best to be near our little fields and cottages, and to see "how we do?" about the settlements, and so the wild woods are drained. And at night, when these have rolled themselves up into little balls of feathers, and are fast asleep, there is not the voice of any creature heard but the ever-present mosquito, and now and again a solitary owl or whip-poor-will. And as you lie on your back, and look through the openings of your wigwam, and of the interlaced branches, up to the starry sky, you feel yourself an *atom* in the lone creation—insignificant as one of the withered leaves you press beneath you.

A hasty toilet by the side of the little stream; a handful or two of dry oatmeal, washed down by a few laps of the clear water, and I was "homeward bound." There seemed to be less need of rest than on the previous day. Perhaps it was excitement. As my neighbour's house was right on the path I was to take, I took a rest there for half an hour, and went on again. They were not expecting me home that day, being only the fourth. But who could ever deceive the instinct of affection? As far as I could be seen (and much further than any step could be heard) through the wood, my wife had her eye on me; and soon I saw my children coming. Jeanie, weak as she was, could far have outstripped Willie, but with a noble self-control she put out all her little strength to pull him along, and they came bounding hand in hand. I threw off my burden and sat down with outstretched arms. In a moment Jeanie was in my arms, and her little mouth close to my ear,—"Father, father, mother did, not eat a bit all yesterday; I watched her, and when I asked her if we'd ever have bread again, she just lay down and opened her eyes wide, and did not speak for ever so long!" I knew that she had fainted—fainted for want of bread. "God be praised, your mother shall not faint again!" I exclaimed, as I picked up both the children and ran toward home. She knew that bread was found, for she had seen me lay down my burden; and in a moment more she was weeping on my breast. "I know it all Mary!" I said, "But the worst is now past I hope!" She raised her head, and shook it mournfully. Neither of us had voice to speak. After running back and picking up the bag, I opened out my treasure—we should have a good meal this time! I made Mary sit down, and Jeanie beside her—pale, both of them, as lilies. The two boys had a *carte blanche* to do as they pleased, I had learned a little homely cooking in the school of necessity on board ship, and now I put it to use. A good bowl of gruel seemed the best thing for them all; and if ever oatmeal, salt, and sugar, were artistically metamorphosed into the most delicious of gruels, it was on that occasion. For bread, I had some cakes baked in the ashes. It was not that I loved to hear myself praised but because I wanted them to eat, that I extolled the dish, and pressed more upon them; and although I had never been in the habit of "returning thanks" after meals (I don't know why) I did so that day, and every day after. It seemed to be so sweet to thank the Father for daily bread secured.

We had no more trouble about bread. The practical sort of botany I had practised still furnished me with further spoils as the season advanced; and by the first of August we began to use new potatoes. The harvest was not very late, but miserably wet. I cannot remember so wet a harvest since, as was that of 1837. There was a thunderstorm almost every afternoon, and it did seem well nigh impossible to get wheat sheaves dry enough to take in. And then everybody was flailing out a bushel or two to take to the mill for bread, drying it for days on sheets in the sun, to get it hard enough for grinding. I had to do the same with my small "grist"; and to "back" it for three miles, before I obtained the privilege of tying it on a *sled* and driving off through the mud, and over the roots and stones, to G——, to get it ground. And when, after waiting two nights and a day (for the mill was full of bags) I got it, I could hardly tell which was flour and which was bran; for, from the rawness of the wheat, the bran would not separate, and was nearly as heavy as the flour. On this occasion I sold some of the flour and all the bran, and bought a dried ham—the first "meat" in our house for a twelvemonth.

Next year "I got up a barn, and I kept on clearing a little every year." Ten years from that date I was out of the reach of actual poverty, owning a good farm, cleared, and paid for. Now (I don't know why I should say it) I am considered one of the pillars of the township —there being about a dozen of such "pillars." Willie is living on a farm of his own; and a younger "Willie" runs to meet me when I go there — a wonderful boy for feretting in pockets. And Johnnie, who has run some danger of being an old bachelor, is likely to leave me too, if I may believe certain hints I got, and a pair of blushing cheeks I met yesterday. And a younger boy and girl, you are not acquainted with, dear reader, are still at my fireside; and according to the custom (not exactly *law*) of the country, this youngest son, in the course of events, is sure to be the heir. You see the elder sons are always portioned off; and so, much to the "puzzlement" of old country people, the youngest son becomes "The Laird," as the Scotch would say.

"But what of Jeanie?" ah! I wish my tale ended here. Go back softly with me over the furrows of five and twenty years, and step with hallowed tread around a little grave, where lies the dust of one too sweet to linger here. From the day you last caught a glimpse of her, she faded away, like a flower in the presence of frost. She got thinner and weaker, and more spiritual in expression, day by day. No murmur, no forgetfulness of the present; as ready to suggest plans of easing her mother's cares, as if she were twice the age and in good health. Willie could not understand it, and it was well for him. But it was over-powering beyond expression to hear the little fellow pleading with his sister to "come out and play." And she would not break his heart by telling him she was too sick and could never play again, but would put him off; "Not just now, Willie," "Some other time, maybe"; and once, when either she had said she was too tired to walk, or he had under-stood her so, the little fellow discovered she was almost as light as air (though he had no idea of the cause) and picked her up in his strong arms, and ran out to the sunshine with her. We smoothed her passage to the tomb, and she smoothed the rough path that lay between her tomb and ours. From the day when the light of those dear eyes was quenched, a new light sprung up in the hearts of the parents, and though it was some time ere nature would cease her convulsive sigh-ing, yet the peace came, and remains.

We had not a soul at the burial but ourselves. My nearest neighbour had fled the woods, and the man who was to succeed him had not arrived. And so, on a little sunny bank, where I afterwards planted a bower of wild roses, we laid our darling down. I have often remarked, in emigrant families, *one* dropping away during the first years of their residence; and I never yet knew it but the verdict in the heart of the survivors was, "The best of all our family is gone!" I believe everyone thinks so, who mourns a lost one. I know not how true it may be in other families, but in my own case my heart has never disputed it for twenty-five years, and never will!

A FIRST SETTLEMENT

82

Hubert Humber

"My First Cariboo"*

LOOKING NORTHWARD FROM QUEBEC one sees a range of low mountains extending all along the north shore of the St. Lawrence away to
Anticosti, and behind this range of hills for hundreds of miles lies a
wild land of mountain, lake and river—the home of the moose and
cariboo deer. The cariboo, unlike the moose, is a great runner, seldom
staying long in one place; and, being very wary, and of prodigious
powers of endurance, even after receiving a mortal wound, its pursuit
is justly considered the most exciting of all our Canadian sports. When
the cold of early winter has driven the deer from their far northern
haunts into the mountains in the immediate vicinity of Quebec, there
are always to be found those who are willing to encounter the privations and dangers of that inhospitable region for the chance of a
successful stalk after such noble game.

"Cariboo not like moose, no for sure."

These words were spoken to me by my Indian hunter, Michel, as I
sat looking ruefully at the carcass of a huge bull moose which lay
before me half buried in the snow; and when Michel added, "no get
cariboo easy like dat," I resolved that my last shot had been fired at
moose, and that the next season—it was too late that year—I would
try my hand at cariboo: so a few days after, when parting with Michel

*The Canadian Monthly and National Review, June 1872, pp. 509-18.

at the village, I made a compact with him that when the time came we should hunt cariboo together.

The summer had come and passed; the fall snipe shooting was over; the long arrow-shaped flocks of wild geese had passed with noisy flight to the southward, and the long Canadian winter was setting in with great severity when I sent word to Michel to come in and see me. We met, and the result was an engagement to start on the 15th of December, and a specific estimate of our wants in the shape of powder, shot, biscuits, pork, &c.

As the weather continued very favourable, that is to say, intensely cold with not too much snow, I went early to bed on the fourteenth fully assured that the next morning would bring Michel. The thickly frosted windows told me, when I awoke, that the thermometer was very low even in my room, and it required some consideration before I could take a leap into my bath, the water in which was almost ice. How comfortable the coal-fire looks when I get down stairs and I am all right, when my old housekeeper, looking severely over her spectacles, says, "your savage has been down stairs speerin' aboot this hour." "All right, send him up, Mrs. Bruce."

A light, almost noiseless, step comes along the passage and Michel glides quietly into the room—a man about forty years of age, of middle height, broad shoulders and deep chest, with rather bow legs, clad in a dark blanket coat, his thick waist girt by a crimson sash from which hangs a heavy hilted hunting knife in a sheath of deer skin, gaily worked with beads and porcupine quills. His feet and hands are small, and his swarthy face has the haggard look which I have noticed in many of these men, the result, I fancy, of the great privations and hardships which they sometimes have to endure. His keen eyes are small and black, and over the collar of his coat, a plentiful supply of jet black hair falls down, coarse as a horse's mane. In manner, the man is quiet, easy and self-possessed.

While we are at breakfast, Michel quietly unfolds his budget of news. The chances for a successful *chasse* are good—his brother-in-law, Antoine, has been out looking after some traps and shooting grouse and hares for the market, and reports many cariboo tracks—the lakes and rivers were all frozen two weeks ago—the snow is not too deep and the cold is on the increase—Antoine would have finished marketing and all his small purchases made by eleven o'clock and then we would start—we should reach Madame Lachance's at about three o'clock, sleep there that night and take to the forest on our snow-shoes early the next morning—a long day's march, a night in the snow, and then another tramp for half a day would bring us to the grounds we intended to hunt. A morning pipe is scarcely smoked when Antoine drives up to the door; the dark coat of his famous mare is covered with frost; and as he flings a buffalo robe over her, she puts back her ears and paws the snow impatiently eager to get home.

How unlike the two men are: Antoine, a little dark French Canadian, has all the vivacity and small talk of his race, and when I succeed in getting him to sit by the fire and take a cup of hot coffee and a bit of steak, dear me, how he does talk and how he laughs; what a contrast to the quiet sombre man who is going about my room superintending the final preparations for our departure! The men are very courteous to each other; but I notice that Antoine always defers at once to Michel. At last all is ready and Antoine having stowed away the provisions in his comfortable box sleigh, the guns, snow-shoes and Indian sleighs are also packed, and then we all jump in. We descend the narrow steep hills leading out from the old town, and are soon on the Lorette road then we begin to know how cold it really is—the wind cuts like a knife, and our frozen breath curls up into the air like smoke and covers our coat collars, caps and hair with a white frost.

Now we have crossed the valley of the St. Charles and passed through the village of Lorette. The road becomes much narrower and the fir trees growing thick and close on each side give a welcome shelter from the wind. Passing over a succession of steep hills we dive down into the primeval forest along a very narrow road on which the snow lies soft and deep. The bush on each side is very thick, and I notice the dotted track of the Alpine hare in every direction.

"*Arrive,*" shouts Antoine, and the mare trotting very fast for about half a mile stops suddenly at Madame Lachance's, which is our terminus for that day and our point of departure for the next.

The house or rather cabin is nothing more than a backwoods shanty formed of hewn logs—the roof is of bark and the smoke finds exit through the pipe of the stove which is carried out through the gable. Madame comes out to welcome us. She is a tall, bony, gray-haired woman with a suntanned face, and the bare arm she holds up to shade her eyes is as dark and muscular as a blacksmith's; but the good soul is very hospitable and keeps repeating her welcome, until we all crowd into the one room which is all her house; a huge double stove is burning fiercely almost in the middle of the room, and a large bed curtained with a very gay patterned print takes up a large portion of what small space remains—a deal table and a few home-made chairs with basswood seats comprise the rest of the furniture, while an open cupboard in one corner exhibits the family crockery of a splendid yellow, bright and clean, of which the old lady is not a little proud. Coming from *"la ville,"* of course, I am expected to tell Madame all the news, which she receives with oft uplifted hands and a running comment of never more than one word—thus I tell of the last large fire, *"misère"*; the new railway, *"bonté"*; the price of wood, *"tiens"*— while the frequent pinch of snuff she indulges in is constantly stayed midway to its destination, while she listens intently to a glowing description of the last fashionable marriage. The mare having been made comfortable for the night, Antoine comes in.

Madame's two sons, stout lads of 19 and 17 come home from chopping in the bush, and after supper we all draw round the stove and spend a couple of hours in talking. Antoine is now in his glory and tells his stories with a mimicry that convulses the two boys and even draws a grim smile from Michel who sits next to me smoking silently.

I had, during the evening, made arrangements that Madame's eldest son should come with us in the capacity of cook and woodcutter, as it is no joke to get home to camp after a hard day's work and find no fire and no dinner. So in the morning having breakfasted we at once commenced to pack our traps on the two toboggins, or Indian sleighs, which we brought with us from Quebec.

I have with me a double Westley-Richards shot gun and a double Purdy rifle.

We slip on our snow-shoes and start—each Indian drawing a toboggin by stout deer-skin thongs passed over the shoulder and under the arm-pits. The party now consists of four—the two Indians, Lachance and myself, and passing down a few yards from the cabin the road ends and we strike into the woods—the primeval forest, which is to be our home for the next two weeks. Michel has decided to make for Lac Rond, a favourite hunting ground of his; and, after a couple of hours' walk, we reach the river leading to the lake; now, of course, frozen, and covered with about six inches of snow. The walking is good and we calculate to reach the lake in a day and a half; the scenery is wild but rather monotonous; the mountains, not of any great height, are very much alike; and the white highway on which we are travelling winds about, offering to view snow scenes—the one you are looking at being the counterpart of the one you have just left behind. But the air is splendid—cold and bracing, and although I had taken an excellent breakfast at Madame Lachance's I am not sorry when Michel calls a halt for dinner. Cold pork, biscuit and a cup of tea—a pipe and an hour's rest and off we go again until four o'clock, when Michel turns off the river into the forest and selects a place to camp for the night. We have done a good twenty miles, and I am hungry again, so we all set to work to form a camp, and this is how we do it. The snow for about 10 feet by 6 is cleared away—all of us at work, using our snow-shoes as shovels—and thrown up on each side forms a trench about 1½ feet deep. One of the men then goes off for fuel, and soon a roaring fire is blazing up in the middle of the trench, over which a forked stick suspends the cooking pot, while a thick layer of spruce boughs, on each side of the fire, makes a very comfortable seat and bed for the night; stout stakes planted in the snow at each end of the trench, and sloping towards the fire, are covered with pine or spruce branches, affording a good shelter. We are soon very snug; the fire leaps and crackles, sending up showers of sparks into the frosty air, and tinging the forest trees near by with a red light; but the Indians have done a hard day's work and we are all ready for sleep as soon as supper is over, so rolling myself up in my blanket, with my feet to the blaze, I am soon sound asleep on one side of the fire and the three men on the other are snoring heavily. The men replenishing the fire during the night wake me up once or twice, but I sleep well, and in the morning rise fresh, and, I am almost ashamed to write it, hungry again; but this wolfish appetite is a leading feature in camp life, and one seems at all times ready to eat.

Breakfast over we are off at half-past seven, and by two o'clock, hurrah! Turning a sharp bend in the river we come suddenly on the famous Lac Rond. Following Michel we skirt the lake for about half a mile, then turn into the bush for a few yards, and halt before a small log-hut half buried in snow, which the men commence to clear away, and entering the cabin I find a good sized chamber, rather low in the roof, with a wide chimney, the lower part of which is built of round stones from the lake, while the upper portion is of thick bark. The small quantity of snow which has drifted in is swept out, and the dry spruce boughs which formed the beds of last year are bundled into the chimney—a match is applied, and instantly a ruddy flame leaps up and makes the old hut look quite cheerful. Leaving the men to get the cabin in order I light my pipe and stroll back to look at the lake, which I take to be about two miles in width, and apparently round in shape, from whence it takes its simple name. Frozen to a depth of six or eight inches, and covered with about the same quantity of snow, the even surface lies before me looking cold and dreary in the intense stillness of that calm winter evening. The round mountains, clothed with forest trees of small growth and snow-covered summits, surround it on all sides, and seem in some places to come sheer down to the water's edge; but if you were to make the circuit of the lake, you would find that all round it there lies, between the water-mark and mountains, a thick belt of dark spruce, varying in width from one hundred yards to half a mile, while large patches of cranberry bushes — the favourite resort of the grouse — rear their sturdy stems by the lake side under the shelter of the spruce. Nothing can exceed the sombre appearance or dreary solitude of a cariboo-swamp at about the evening hour — the dark formal trees, almost black in colour, throw a deep gloom around, which the near mountains serve to deepen, while long festoons of grey moss depending from their stems sway to and fro in the moaning wind, and give a weird and ghastly apearance to the scene. But it is this strange looking moss which I have seen hanging yards in length that forms the favourite food of the cariboo deer, and makes Michel consider this lake in particular one of his best hunting grounds. When I return to camp I find the men have put everything in order, the snow round the cabin is all cleared away, a goodly pile of dry wood is collected for the night, and through the open door I see a large cheerful fire burning brightly.

Next morning Pierre goes off at dawn, and, as soon as breakfast is over, Michel who is in high spirits, takes his departure, leaving me alone with Lachance, and explaining before he goes that I am to remain in camp for that on finding the fresh tracks of cariboo he will come at once for me, and we are then to stalk the deer together. Even at this remote period my ears will tingle when I think of the terrible error, as a sportsman, which I committed on that glorious winter day. Michel had been away about an hour, and seated on a log near the cabin, I was smoking my pipe, and trying not to feel impatient, when Lachance passed on his way to the lake for water. Very soon afterwards I hear the beat of his snow-shoes, and see him coming back at a trot without his bucket. I see at once that there is something up, so knocking the ashes out of my pipe, I advance to meet him. Turning his head, he points back at the lake, and whispers excitedly: *"Une belle bande de perdrix!"* "By Jove," thinks I, "the very thing: I can knock over a few brace; it will pass the time, and the birds will be a valuable addition to our larder." So I return to the cabin, throw off my blanket coat, and taking my Westley-Richards in hand I place a stout ash stick in Lachance's eager fingers, and we both make for the cranberries. The *perdrix de savane*, or swamp partridge, as the Canadians call this bird, is properly speaking a grouse — a splendid bird, very strong on the wing and delicious eating, but in these wilds extremely stupid — so much so, that I have seen a cock bird stand four shots from a very short-sighted man who was trying his hand with a pea-rifle. On reaching the bushes I see the fresh tracks of a large pack of grouse which have come out of the swamp to have a cranberry breakfast, and telling Lachance to move slowly on my right, I keep twenty yards behind him, knowing that the birds will lay like stones, and when flushed will fly across me to the cover, which is on my left. The boy understands his work well; moving slowly, and keeping his right distance from me he thrashes away at the cranberry bushes with the ash stick, and soon, almost at his feet, a grouse rises with a loud whirr, and flying across me on balanced pinions, makes for the spruce wood at a tremendous pace. I shoot well in front of him, and the bird pitching forward falls dead in the snow. Lachance waits quietly until he sees I have re-loaded, and on we go again. This time a brace of splendid cock birds rising together cross me about thirty yards; the opportunity for a right and left shot is not to be lost, and I take advantage of it, both birds are down, and the mountain echo roars back — bang! bang! The boy is delighted, and so on we go, until I bag five brace of splendid birds. Towards the end of this impromptu *battue* the grouse had got somewhat wild, and a few birds rising while I loaded got away without being shot at, and as we return I see one of them sitting on the dead branch of a spruce, and with outstretched neck intently watching us. I point the bird out to Lachance, and placing my gun in his hand tell him to shoot — he takes a good half-minute aim, and then knocks the grouse over — the boy bags his game, and coming towards me looks out at the lake and exclaims: "Here comes Michel."

The Indian hunter nears us rapidly, coming with a long, swinging stride, and handing me my gun, Lachance trots off to meet him, but there is something about Michel's look and gait that makes me think all is not well, and when the lad reaches him he stops a moment and I can hear the volley of abuse which he pours out on the head of that ingenuous youth. Poor Lachance with many shrugs of his shoulders seems to be trying to excuse himself, but apparently it won't do, and, calling him a *tête de veau*, Michel brushes past and goes straight to camp. Lachance then comes to me and in a few words makes me acquainted with the cause of the Indian's wrath. In order that you may fully appreciate the sad sporting blunder which I committed that morning, we will follow Michel in his search for fresh deer tracks. On leaving the camp that morning he turned along the margin of the lake and entering the spruce woods, which I have already described, he hunts it carefully backwards and forwards, beating his ground as close and careful as a well-trained pointer; but though he sees many tracks of deer, none are fresh, and he has nearly made half the circuit of the lake without success when he comes quite suddenly on the deep track of two deer. There is no need to stoop and examine the tracks; his practised eye tells him at once that not more than two hours have elapsed since the deer have passed. They had come over the mountain facing the cabin, and he knows well are now feeding in the spruce swamp by the lake and very likely not more than a mile off. Swift as a hound he runs along the track until fresh signs warn him that the dull beat of his snowshoes on the soft snow must cease. He stops and listens intently for some time and taking careful note of the wind again advances, but now only at a walk, with head slightly bent and ear turned in the direction to which the deer tracks lead he moves quietly and carefully without the slightest noise, well aware that a false step — the snapping of a dry bough or an unlucky fall may alarm the cariboo, which he knows are now close at hand; he has just paused to listen when a familiar sound reaches his ear — clack! clack! clack! a low indistinct rattle. If you or I heard it we would not pay much attention, but it is music to this keen, sagacious hunter and, faint as the sound is, he knows it to be the noise made by the antlers of a buck as he rubs his head against the branches of a forest tree. Michel now takes off his snowshoes, and laying his gun on them he creeps forward on hands and knees, frequently stopping to listen; then on again, stealthy and silent, as a cat. The bleating call of a buck rises on the frosty air, and gives Michel the exact position of the deer; rising on his knees he takes a rapid survey of the ground, and then gently steals forward to an excellent shelter formed by the trunks of two forest trees which have fallen across each other. For a minute or two the Indian lies buried deep in the snow, and then carefully raising his head he peers keenly over the barricade — and this is what he sees — a small, open space in the middle of which an old and blasted spruce, leaning over many feet from the perpendicular, spreads forth its withered branches, beneath which stands a magnificent buck cariboo, with upturned head, nibbling at the long festoon of moss which hangs from the tree, pausing now and again to rub his antlers against the dry boughs. Almost at the feet of the buck lies a splendid doe. Her ladyship has evidently breakfasted, and is lazily licking her nut-brown, glossy side. Michel gazes with all the admiration of a true-born hunter and, being satisfied that the deer will remain in the swamp for that day, at least, he is about to retrace his steps and return for me, when boom across the lake comes that unlucky shot of mine, and the mountains' echo answers hoarsely back. Suppressing an oath of surprise, Michel is swiftly down behind his ambush and buried in the snow, listens intently. "*Que diable*," he thinks, "what can it mean? Doubtless some accidental discharge of a rifle; 'tis well the cariboo are not off." Thus thinking, he raises his head again and peers over the logs in front of him, but he looks on another picture now. Both deer are on their feet, and slightly thrown back on their haunches with outspread legs and heads erect are gazing fixedly in the direction from which the sound has come. The Indian is just beginning to hope that the deer may possibly calm down, when again bang! bang! my unfortunate gun awakes that dreadful echo. Well, the deer can't stand *that* you know, and wheeling round with a velocity that sends a fountain of snow high into the air they vanish instantly into the forest; their flying forms glance for a moment from tree to tree and they are gone — gone, as the Indian said afterwards to me, "*au diable*." Michel listens for a moment to the rush of the two deer through the woods; then, jumping to his feet with a fierce oath, walks back to the place where he had left his gun and snow-shoes and with many a bitter imprecation walks savagely back to camp.

"Oh it was horrible, most horrible."

It takes the best part of my choice tobacco to soothe the outraged feelings of the keen old hunter; but he is firm in the belief that it will be of no use trying the Lac Rond ground for deer during the next two days.

Pierre returns to camp soon after dark, to my great joy, speaks well of the ground he has been examining, and after a consultation with Michel, it is decided that we shall try it. The marching orders are short and simple: each man beside his firearms and short-handled axe is to take two ship biscuits, a small piece of pork and a supply of matches; in addition to this simple fare I slip into the pocket of my blanket coat a small flask of brandy.

The early dawn sees us leave the camp, moving ghost-like over the soft snow, all of us clad in white blanket coats and leggings, our gun covers being of the same material. Michel leading, in Indian file, we move quickly across the lake and make for the big mountain opposite. No word is spoken by the men and yesterday's mishap makes me quiet enough. What a breather it was getting up that steep mountain side, but we *are* on the top at last and halt for a few minutes' rest.

As the summit is covered only by stunted hard-wood, I get a good view of the surrounding country and can make out nothing but lakes and round-shouldered mountains which roll away from the dark fir-clad hills close by into the far distance grey and indistinct; but Indians have not much love for scenery and we soon commence the descent. Down we go leaning well back on our snow-shoes and keeping our toes well up; we half-trot, half-slide and, in a very short time, are once more on level ground; a couple of hours' walk brings us to the edge of another large lake and, here happens to me one of the most exciting day's sport I have ever enjoyed. It was about eleven o'clock and the lovely calm of the early morning yet continued although the sky was overcast with grey clouds and it was evident that the two previous fine days were weather breeders, and that a severe storm was not far off. We had advanced about two hundred yards on the surface of the lake, when bringing up the rear, I suddenly saw Michel fall flat on his face; Pierre followed suit, and not knowing the reason why, I cast myself headlong in the snow at his heels, and there we all lay, not a word being spoken to explain the cause of this very sudden movement. I feel very much inclined to laugh, but knowing that something is up, I manage to keep quiet and presently Michel whispers "Look," and raising my head very slightly, I peer along the smooth white surface of the lake and a sight meets my eye that sets my heart beating high with intense excitement. At first I see only some dark forms about a mile off, but showing plainly on the snow. These dark forms on the lake are a herd of seven cariboo deer coming straight for us. Michel now gently calls me and I wriggle along through the snow and lie down beside him. The deer are coming rapidly toward us and are now plainly discernible — three splendid bucks and four does, quite unsuspicious of danger for they are trotting briskly, they gambol as they come. I am shaking with suppressed excitement, and the two men stolid as wooden images lie by me keenly watching the deer, when, to my great disgust, the whole herd suddenly halt about two hundred yards off, surely they have winded us; but no! see that noble buck leads off and then begins the prettiest game of romps I ever looked at — they charge each other with lowered antlers, but deftly the thrust is avoided, they leap into the frosty air with a grace and elegance that is charming to behold, and then race round and round, turning and leaping as gracefully as kittens. And now their romp is over, and bending his knees under him, a large buck quietly sinks down in the snow, and in a moment the rest of the herd follow his example; so there we are left on our faces in the snow watching the cariboo who are about two hundred yards off. The deer have unconsciously checkmated us for a time, for the Indians armed only with very wretched smooth-bores could not pretend to shoot at that distance, and though I carried an excellent Purdy rifle I felt so much excited that I was glad the men did not ask me to fire, in fact, they would have prevented me had I wished to shoot, as these men do not know the power and accuracy of a first-rate English rifle, and will always stalk their deer within fifty or sixty yards before they attempt a shot. Then Michel whispers his instructions in my ear. A belt of spruce wood ran out into the lake for a short distance and was about one hundred yards behind us and a little to our right, I was to make my way to this cover on my stomach and when he saw I was in position, he and Pierre would try and get within shot of the herd, approaching the deer in such a way that if alarmed, some, if not the whole herd, would pass near enough to give me a shot. After listening very carefully to some hurried instructions as to what I should do if forced to camp out alone, I slip my feet out of my snow-shoes and turning, slowly commence to creep through the snow towards the cover. The process is decidedly cooling and the snow gets up my sleeves and down my throat, but I am determined to do my best to-day, and at last I reach the spruce wood and am soon under cover and watching the further advance of the two Indians — slowly, slowly, they seem to glide through the snow like snakes, and I mentally contrast their really scientific approach to my own unwieldy waddle. They have got about half the distance to the herd when the large buck which is nearest to them quickly turns his head in their direction and then I hear that whistling snort which proclaims that the cariboo is sensible of danger, and turning his head he butts the doe lying next to him, when both deer spring to their feet, the other five immediately follow their example and gaze anxiously about. They know there is danger but cannot tell where to look for it for the wind is favourable for the hunters and they cannot scent their foe, and as the two men lie quiet in the snow they cannot see them; but the big buck has taken a slight alarm, and as luck will have it, comes quietly trotting in my direction, the doe accompanying him, the other deer remain standing and gazing about. Now is the time for me to wipe out yesterday's disgrace—the two deer are coming at a slow trot with rather a loose and shambling gait, I can distinctly hear the clatter of their large, broad hoofs, and make pretty sure of the doe who will pass at about 75 yards, the buck will be a more difficult shot for he is further off, and the first shot will send him away like the wind; but now the doe is just opposite me, and dropping on my knee I bring the sight of my double Purdy to bear on her, low behind the shoulder, and at the report of the rifle she springs up into the air and comes down dead with a ball through her heart: to my great surprise the buck immediately trots up and stands sniffing the dead carcass.

This sudden and to me, very strange movement, rather upsets me, and before I can recover he is off, but he offers a fine side shot, and when I fire he stumbles forward and comes down heavily on his knees, but it is only for a second—he is up again and away at a tremendous pace. I load as quickly as possible, and as I run back for my snow-shoes I see a dark form on the snow, which shows the Indians have killed another of the deer, and are now in full chase of the others, but going in the opposite direction to that taken by the deer I had just shot at. Confident that I had hit the buck very hard, I go forward and examine the spot where he came down, but to my surprise I find no blood, and I make up my mind for a long chase and the prospect of a camp out alone. So tightening the belt which supports my axe, I start off at a sharp trot on the track of the cariboo, which leads straight through the bush to the foot of a mountain—the steep sides of which rise before me. I thought so! the buck has gone straight up, but there is no help for it; up I go after him, soon I come to where the deer has laid down to rest, and a small patch of blood on the snow shows that my shot has told. Quickening my pace, I am soon on the summit: the cariboo is still going strong, and as I half slide down on the other side I am amazed at the tremendous strides with which he has descended. Again on level ground the track leads me out by a small river, down which the deer has taken, apparently going as strong as ever; down this river I follow for at least an hour, and am beginning to feel very much fagged, for it is now late in the day and I have worked very hard since dawn. I should be much relieved if I could throw off my coat, but I dare not do so yet, as beyond doubt I must sleep in the bush alone that night. But now the track of the wounded deer turns off the river, and I feel rather disheartened when I see another mountain before me, far up that hill the buck will go, and I doubt if I have the

94

strength left to follow. But see! he has lain down again, and this time a large, deep-red patch on the snow shows that the wound is severe. Now is the time to push him and, throwing off my coat, I start off at a rapid pace, and, running hard for about ten minutes, suddenly come on the gallant buck lying with outstretched neck on the snow stone dead. Fairly done up I place my rifle against the antlers of the buck and, seated on the carcase, take note of the sitaution. Michel and Pierre are probably thirty miles away, for I calculate that I have come fifteen, and they no doubt have gone quite as far in an opposite direction—it is now, by my watch, four o'clock, and, if I felt equal to walking home to camp, there would not be light to follow my tracks back, so as it is quite clear that I must camp out alone, the sooner I commence making preparations the better. The first thing to be done is to go back for my coat. This is soon recovered, and I return to the deer, and selecting a good spot, take off my snowshoes, and using one as a shovel clear a space large enough to build my fire and make my bed. It takes some time to collect sufficient fuel for the night, and, by the time all is ready, darkness has fallen on the forest, and the red glare from the fire throws flitting shadows on the trees near by, while the solemn stillness is only broken by the crackling of the dry logs and branches with which I keep feeding the flames. It is an awfully cold night, and I soon find out that sleep is impossible, so I take a little brandy, and cutting a steak from the deer, impale portions of the meat on hardwood skewers and roast them before the fire, the meat tastes delicious to me, and the cooking serves to pass the time. Again I try to sleep, but it is too horribly cold, and I jump up and once more build the fire—and thus I spend that long winter night wishing for morning. Squatted on a log before the fire, I think I must have dozed occasionally, for I know that on looking at my watch for about the hundredth time I am surprised to find that the long, long night has passed, and the hands are pointing to seven o'clock.

The cold pale green of the eastern sky is beginning to change to yellow, and it is already light enough to commence preparations for my return to camp, and I am thinking what portion of the buck I shall take beside his head and antlers, when to my great joy I hear a welcome shout, and Michel soon after dashes in, and, giving a ringing whoop at the sight of the dead deer, shakes me vigorously by the hand. The good fellow had wounded one of the cariboo, and followed for many miles; then, thinking he had better look after me, had left Pierre to continue the chase, and returning on my track had camped

95

within five miles of me. We take the skin and antlered head of the cariboo, and after eating some more steak and biscuit we tramp homewards, and arrive at the cabin at about four o'clock—the last two hours of our walk being made through a driving storm of snow, for the threatening weather of yesterday has broken, and a fierce gale of wind is roaring through the forest.

Lachance has been very lonely, he says, and is *bien content* to see us. The good lad is soon preparing supper, the fire is blazing brightly, and we are just sitting down to a good hot meal, when the wind lulls for a moment, and we hear a faint shout coming from the lake, and Michel, throwing open the door to allow the light to be seen, answers back—the long quavering whoop rises high over the storm, and the mocking demon-like shout is a fit accompaniment to the howling wind—but the signal is answered again, and soon Pierre comes in with the heads of two cariboo, making four killed out of the herd of seven. His arrival is all we require to make us perfectly comfortable, and we fall to on our supper, winding up with a glass or rather tin of hot brandy and water all round; after which, rolled up in my blanket and thoroughly tired out, I am sound asleep.

I spend another week at the famous lake, and stalk five different deer, three of which I kill, and then we pack up for return home, and on the second day of our departure from the lake we reach Madame Lachance's. The good old soul is delighted to see us, and Pierre, who is bent on getting home that night, promises to send Antoine over for me in the morning. Early the next day, while taking a smoke at the door, I hear the sound of sleigh-bells and a clear voice, chanting one of the simple hymns of the Church, rises on the frosty air, and Antoine comes driving quietly up the narrow road—the good fellow is as light hearted as ever, and profuse in his congratulations at the successful termination of my *chasse*. Carefully he stows away the antlered heads of the five cariboo, and, taking leave of Madame and Michel, I return to Quebec, and once more enjoy the undeniable comforts of civilized life.

Caribou Migration.

THE STUDENT EXAMINED

Allan A'Dale

"The Proctors. A Sketch of Canadian University Life"*

OH! NOX AMBROSIANA, on which Dobson and I first met under the roof-tree of St. Innocents'! With what a grand sense of independence did we lounge in the battered easy-chairs of the absent senior-man, whose castle had been assigned to me as a temporary refuge. Banqueting on the dainties and the ginger wine which a careful parent had provided to support me through matriculation, we recounted to each other such traditions of the college as we had heard, and agreed that we were both uncommonly good fellows, and that, come sorrow or come joy, we should stand by each other. We did stand by each other on many trying occasions, and the friendship which originated on that night continued without interruption till Dobson, having twice failed to conquer his "little-go," gave up his design of entering the Church, and exiled himself to the far west, with a view to cattle-dealing.

We may have been carousing, in the innocent manner I have described for an hour or more, when a knock at the door introduced a young gentleman, unknown to us, of mild and benevolent aspect.

"The Senior Proctor," said the mild and benevolent young gentleman, in hurried tones, "asked me if I'd be so kind as to look up all the new gentlemen in residence, and beg them to come to his room to see about their preliminaries." The Senior Proctor! Who, in the name of terror, was he? The preliminaries! What fateful thing were they?

*The Canadian Monthly and National Review, Oct. 1872, pp. 362-66.

"Didn't know about the proctors?" the mild young gentleman inquired, "why the proctors put you through the preliminary examination, to see if you're fit to go before the Professors to-morrow. Come on, and I'll take you to them. Exam. hard? Well, a leetle, though fellows often get through. Particular about Euclid? Oh no, not in the least; oh perhaps not; by no means. Here's the door. You come in first." And before Dobson could bid me one farewell, the benevolent young gentleman had him inside the mysterious chamber, and the heavy door closed with a bang upon them both.

A high sense of honour forbade my listening at the key-hole, as curiosity prompted, so I paced the floor in nervous expectation, and vainly endeavoured to fix in my mind some faint conception of the thirteenth proposition of the Second Book.

In about fifteen minutes Dobson re-appeared. His face was deadly pale; his eyes fixed on vacancy.

"Dobson!" I murmured. He smiled sadly.

"Dobson!" I said again. "Tell me the worst. Speak, I adjure you."

Again that sad smile. Still that long look into the future.

At length he spoke, and with unnatural calmness. "I wouldn't like to swear to it; but I rather think — indeed I may positively say — that I'm plucked — and you're to go in at once."

I stood aghast. An icy terror chilled my heart.

"Oh Dobson," I asked tremulously, "do you think I'll pass?"

"No," said Dobson, with a faint gleam of cheerfulness.

"One word more, Dobson. Did they give you the thirteenth of the Second?" But he was again exploring the future, and, with trembling hand, I opened the door.

I stood in a large room, lined from floor to ceiling with books. Before me, and behind a green table, sat three preternaturally solemn gentlemen in academic costume. The centre person of the three first caught my gaze. He was robed in a gown gorgeous with purple and gold. (The next time I saw it was on the Chancellor, at Convocation.) A college cap, with velvet top and gold tassel, adorned his striking head. He had bushy whiskers of uncompromising redness, corresponding nicely with his complexion, which was florid. His cheeks probably blushed for his nose, which was most fiery red of all, and moreover larger, and less decided in shape, than that of the Apollo Belvidere. The nose supported a pair of heavy spectacles, or rather spectacle rims, for I could see that no glasses dimmed the lustre of his keen eyes. Wearing spectacles, with the glasses knocked out, I put down as merely a learned eccentricity. He appeared to have a contempt for the barber's art, for his hair was unshorn and his chin unshaven, and as he was, on the whole, extremely ugly and rather slovenly, I felt myself to be in the presence of a man of singular genius. The gentlemen on each side were much younger, and cleaner. They wrote a good deal in ponderous books which lay open before them, and seemed inclined to laugh at times at the learned gentleman's peculiarities, which I thought very irreverent. Besides these, three other individuals, in gowns and tremendous white bands, sat in three great arm-chairs. They assisted occasionally in the examination which ensued, and evinced a kindly interest in my domestic affairs.

"I shall not conceal from you the fact," said the learned gentleman, with much affability and a Celtic accent, "that I am the Senior Proctor, and Emeritus Professor of Things in General. These gentlemen who support me are the junior proctors, and the three gentlemen on your right are members of the Senatus, who have kindly consented to assist with their valuable suggestions in the preliminaries of the matriculants."

The junior proctors here bent over their books, and took notes diligently, which struck me as a little superfluous, as they ought to have known all this before.

"You will oblige us, in the first place," continued the courteous Senior Proctor, "by candidly stating your name in full, your post-office address, your age next birthday, and whether you have ever been vaccinated."

Though exceedingly surprised at the peculiar nature of the opening questions, I answered them without reservation, and the junior proctors made a frantic note.

At this point a member of the Senatus anxiously inquired if I had any uncles in the lumbering business. I set his mind at rest, when another member of the Senatus asked me if my mother's family name was Hobbs. I was catechized at some length after this fashion, and when I had made a clean breast of all my domestic secrets, though with some unwillingness and resentment, we came to sterner matters.

"Would you prefer to translate a passage from a Latin, Greek, or Sanscrit author?" said the Senior Proctor. "Latin," I answered, without a moment's hesitation.

"The Latin," soliloquized the Senior Proctor, in a sort of learned reverie, "is undeniably a fine language, a very fine language. At the same time, it lacks the peculiar joyousness, the vivacity, the sparkling humour of the Sanscrit. In no Latin writer do we find the delightful pleasantry, the irrepressible love of fun, which makes the Rigvedas the pastime of the student's leisure hour. Nor is there, in the Latin, that solemn grandeur and unfathomable mystery which establishes the Greek verb deep in the affection of the scholar. But, in spite of these disadvantages, I consider the Latin a fine, a highly respectable language, and you will be so good as to mention any favourite passage of yours from any Latin author."

The junior proctors appeared struck with the comparative merits of the three tongues, so lucidly expounded, and took a note.

I did not hesitate to mention the opening lines of the Second Book of the Æneid, as possessing peculiar attractions for me. I must confess that my choice was not grounded on any particular excellence of style, or loftiness of imagination, which distinguishes this passage, so much as on the circumstance that I had been familiar with it from my earliest years, and considered myself equal to its translation. That pleasing delusion was soon dispelled. I was requested to pause at every full stop, and my construing was most unsparingly criticized by the Senior Proctor, whose comments were echoed by the other learned dignitaries. Thus, having rendered the first two lines in a time-honoured fashion—

"All became silent, and kept their looks intently fixed upon him;

"Thereupon father Æneas thus began, from his lofty couch"— the Senior Proctor interrupts me.

"Pardon me, but you entirely fail to transfer the poetic fire, which flashes through the original lines, to your translation."

Chorus of senators and junior proctors—"Not a spark of poetic fire!"

S.P. "Where, in your construction, is the breathless, eager multitude, hushed into awe and reverence? Where the benign countenance of the pious Æneas, beaming with benevolence, fascinating the gaze of the love-sick queen?"

Chorus—"Where, indeed?"

I might have suggested, "Nowhere, that I can discover," but I didn't.

Then followed questions, critical and explanatory:

By the Senior Proctor—"Can you quote from Homer to prove that the habit of whistling and imitating the cries of domestic animals, at public meetings, was held in contempt?"

Answer—"No."

By a member of the Senatus—"What was the name of the step-mother of pious Æneas?"

Answer—"I'm afraid I've forgotten."

By a junior proctor—"What was the exact height, in cubits, of the 'lofty couch' from which 'father Æneas thus began?'"

"I knew that once, but it has escaped my memory."

In this style did the examination proceed till I was completely bewildered, and had resigned all hope of passing these appalling pre-liminaries. Yet, at times, in such unseemly levity did the junior proc-tors indulge, and so utterly unintelligible did their questions become, the idea flashed across my mind that the learned examiners were not all they pretended to be. In the midst of a rather noisy argument between a junior proctor and a senator, as to whether the police of Troy wore helmets (during which I learned a good many facts hitherto unknown to me), the door opened quietly behind me. Glancing over my shoulder I observed a gentleman in clerical clothes, and a trencher. The discussion went on, for the scholars, heated with their argument, did not notice the new arrival.

"I tell you sir," shouted the junior proctor, "I have heard the Dean himself say that the helmets of our modern police are constructed on the model of one brought by faithful Achates, for he was a policeman, to Italy, and preserved in the Roman Capitol."

"Are you sure the Dean said that, Mr. Thompson?" said the clerical gentleman at the door, stepping into full view. Then my suspicions were proved true. In an instant a complete transformation came over the scene. The junior proctors looked foolish, and turned as red as their senior. They closed their note-books with celerity, and attempted the impossible feat of dragging them, unnoticed, out of sight. The members of the Senatus abandoned their chairs of state, consulted the nearest book-shelves with close attention, and, in an abstracted way, tried to transfer their long bands to their pockets.

The Senior Proctor alone preserved his equanimity. Without the least embarrassment he rose from his chair, elegantly doffed his trencher, removed his spectacles from his nose, and with the suavity he had all along exhibited, expressed the hope that he saw the clerical gentleman in good health, and that the long vacation had restored his shattered faculties to their usual vigour.

"It is a very strange circumstance, Mr. O'Rourke," said the clerical gentleman, in frigid tones, and taking no notice of these considerate inquiries, "that this is the third time I have found you in this very position, tricked out in the Chancellor's robes."

The Senior Proctor appeared to assent to this, and muttered that it *was* strange when you came to think about it.

"I don't think the Master would feel gratified if he knew his senior men were in the habit of desecrating his lecture-room, and usurping his authority. He would probably tell you that your own knowledge is not so extensive that you can afford to waste time, which should be devoted to reading, in undignified practical joking of this sort. We can get through the examinations without any assistance from officious undergraduates. Get off to your rooms, gentlemen, every one of you, and Mr. O'Rourke must expect that the next time he is found here, the Master will hear of his vagaries."

The Senior Proctor smiled with unruffled sweetness of temper, divested himself of his borrowed plumes with much deliberation, gave the clerical gentleman "good night" with charming affability, and left the room humming a psalm tune. Then followed the senators, conscious of their bands, and his junior disciples, who only waited to get through the door to indulge the laughter with which they had been struggling all evening.

"You're one of the freshmen, I suppose?" said the clerical gentleman, addressing me, "and these amiable young fellows have been trying to frighten you a little. You'll soon learn to know professors from undergraduates. Come with me and have a glass of wine."

And this was my introduction to the Dean.

ICEBERGS, NORTH ATLANTIC. (AUGUST, 1883.)

Rev. M. Harvey

"The Castaways of Gull Island"*

TO A STRANGER the sea-coast of Newfoundland presents, for the most part, a dreary and repulsive appearance. Dark, frowning cliffs, lofty headlands, miles on miles of rocky walls, from two to three hundred feet in height, with little verdure, even in summer, crowning their summits; bold promontories sculptured into grim, fantastic shapes by the blows of Atlantic billows—these are what greet the eyes of the voyager as he sails along the eastern coast. The iron-bound shores present no pebbly beaches on which the summer waves break, in softened music; but rugged, precipitous cliffs frown defiance on the stormy Atlantic, and not unfrequently shape themselves into forms of stern, majestic beauty. At intervals the coast-scenery is varied by the occurrence of those majestic estuaries for which the Island is so celebrated, some of them fifty or sixty miles in width at their entrance, and stretching away inland from forty to nearly one hundred miles. These noble bays, reaching out their countless arms on all sides far into the interior, and shaping their indented sides into some of the finest harbours of the world, serve to entice the finny tribes, with which the surrounding seas are swarming, into the deep recesses and shallower waters where their food abounds, and thus bring them within the grasp of man. Around the shores of these great bays the fishermen

*The Maritime Monthly, May 1873, pp. 435-47.

cluster, every little harbour, creek and cove having its fishing hamlet. In almost every spot where a fishing boat can find shelter, the rough stage and "fish-flake," for the landing and drying of cod, may be seen; and, in the summer season, the fishing banks, all around the shores, are dotted with the little boats dancing over the waves. It is wonderful to think how prolific are these fishing grounds, and how inexhaustible their resources. It is calculated that an acre of good land carefully tilled, will produce, once a year, a ton of corn, or two or three hundred weight of meat or cheese; while the same area, at the bottom of the sea, will yield an equal weight of food to the fisherman, each week of the year, provided he can carry on his operations, — and this without any ploughing, manuring, or sowing.

Between Cape Race, the most southern point of the Island, and Cape Freels, three of these great estuaries open, — Conception Bay, Trinity Bay and Bonavista Bay. After passing Cape Freels and running through Hamilton Sound, the great bay of Notre Dame is entered, being more than fifty miles wide at its entrance, and perfectly studded with islands. From this great bay, numerous smaller bays run many miles inland, the most considerable being Green Bay and Hall's Bay, each about twenty miles in length. Both these bays are famous hunting-grounds, from whence the trappers not unfrequently cross the Island to the Bay of Islands, on the western coast.

The most northern point of Notre Dame Bay is named Cape John. Seven miles south of it lies Tilt Cove, now famous as the location of a rich copper and nickel mine. In the year 1857, Mr. Smith McKay, an intelligent and enterprising explorer, arrived at this little Cove, then containing about a dozen poor huts of fishermen. His visit was not quite a casual one. The magic wand of science had pointed to this region as a spot where, among the serpentine rocks, a search for copper ore would, in all probability, be attended with success. To Dr. Dawson, of McGill College, Montreal, belongs the honour of this scientific vaticination. A hint from him induced Mr. McKay to visit this part of the coast. When at Tilt Cove, his eye lighted on a piece of bright yellow stone which stood on the mantel shelf in a fisherman's hut. The poor fisherman had no idea that the piece of yellow rock, which he had picked up at the bottom of a neighbouring cliff, was anything more than a curiosity. "Knowledge is power." The experienced eye of the explorer saw in it the treasure of which he was in search. For a small reward, the fisherman conducted him to the cliff where the fragment had been found. There, amid the clefts of the rock, he saw the outcropping of the precious lode. The mine was discovered; the fortune of the explorer was made. In a few years the little fishing hamlet had undergone a complete transformation. Its population had increased to more than a thousand, among whom might be seen scores of stout Cornish miners, with their wives and children. Neat, comfortable cottages had displaced the old dilapidated huts; and several handsome frame houses, for the superintendents of the works, had been erected. Ships, with all the necessaries and luxuries of life, were opened. A handsome Church and a Roman Catholic Chapel added much to the appearance of the village. Signs of comfort and prosperity were abundant on all hands. Great heaps of ore might be seen near the openings of the "levels" that were driven into the lofty cliffs; and far within the bowels of the hill the blows of the miners resounded, and, at times, the rumbling noise of their explosions, like peals of distant thunder, were heard, as they blasted the mineralized rock. An excellent jetty and wharf adorned the little harbour, alongside of which large vessels lay in safety, moored by great chains which were fastened to bolts driven into the rocks. The cove was often crowded with shipping, the larger vessels being engaged in loading the ore for Swansea. A coastal steamer, carrying mails, visited the locality fortnightly during summer, and connected it with the Capital. Altogether, Tilt Cove was a pleasant sight; and its prosperity has gone on increasing to the present hour.

On the 5th December, 1867, a vessel named the *Queen*, of Swansea, John Owens master, left St. John's with supplies of various kinds for the miners at Tilt Cove, and with the view of taking on board there a cargo of ore for England. There were fifteen souls on board, including the Captain and crew, two of them being females. The vessel was an excellent one; and as she had only to make a run of some two hundred miles along the coast, and had on board a pilot, the thought of danger entered the mind of no one. One of the passengers was Mr. Dowsley, of St. John's, who was about to open a drug store at Tilt Cove. On the evening of the 5th a fearful gale arose; the vessel being light in ballast, was driven out to sea about 160 miles. The storm lasted nearly three days, those on board expecting, every instant, that their vessel would be capsized or swamped, as she was tossed about like a cork on the surface of the water. A far worse doom, however, was in store for the ill-fated voyagers. When the gale abated, they ran in for the land, and on the evening of the 11th December made Gull Island, a small rocky islet off Cape John, and about three miles from the shore. As the night was closing in, they did not venture to run for Tilt Cove, and accordingly stood out to sea till daylight should appear. On what trifles, as we call them, the most important events appear to turn! About twelve o'clock that night, the pilot felt so sure in regard to his course, that he took the fatal resolution of running for the harbour, without waiting for daylight. The ship was put about, and held on her course safely till six o'clock on the morning of the 12th December, when, in the midst of a blinding snow-storm, the sea running mountains high, she struck with fearful violence on Gull Island. The shock was awful; and soon the gurgling inrush of the water told them that the ship was fatally injured. As the frightened passengers, startled from their slumbers, rushed on deck, they could dimly discern, through the snow-drift, a low cliff only a few yards distant. No time was to be lost. A sailor managed to scramble ashore, and a rope was passed from the ship to the rock. By means of this rope, those on board were dragged up the cliff. Eleven out of the fifteen on board were thus drawn, as speedily as possible, to the summit of the cliff, when the cable parted, the vessel slid off the shelving rock and drifted out of sight, a sinking wreck, with the pilot and three others on board. No doubt the latter found a watery grave; but a death of lingering agony, such as it makes the heart ache to think of, awaited the poor unfortunates on the Island.

Only ten or fifteen minutes elapsed from the time the vessel struck till the cable gave way, and she then glided off into the darkness, drifted across the bay, and was broken to pieces on the opposite shore. Those who escaped were unable to save anything: and in the rush and scramble to get ashore, thought of nothing but how to preserve their lives. When the morning came, they found themselves in a most forlorn position — partially clad, drenched to the skin with spray and the falling snow, shivering under the December blasts, and among the eleven castaways there was not a single particle of food of any description. The only thing obtained from the ship was a portion of an old sail which by some means had drifted ashore. The spot on which they had been cast is a low, rocky islet, about a quarter of a mile in length and the same in breadth, utterly barren, uninhabited, and with no vegetation except a few patches of low scrub-bushes. Worst of all — it does not contain a single spring or brook; and not a drop of water could be had. No materials for kindling a fire were available. Without tools or resources of any kind, the poor sufferers could only crouch together under the scrap of canvas, in a small "gulch" or hollow, hoping that some boat or vessel might pass within hail and rescue them.

At first, no doubt, their hopes of deliverance must have been strong. They were but three miles from the nearest main land, on which were some scattered dwellers; and but five or six miles from a village called Shoe Cove. The first day after they landed was bright and clear. They could see the smoke from the cottages ascending into the morning air, and cheerful signs of life ashore. Boats too were moving about in the bay, for a number of fishermen were out shooting sea-fowl. With what eager eyes these poor shipwrecked men and women must have watched throughout that day the movements of the boats, hoping that they might come near enough to see their signals of distress; and how their hearts must have sunk as they saw them return to the harbour, and the short winter day closing in gathering gloom, as the sun went down beneath the waves! How appalling the prospect of their first long night on the cold rock, hunger already gnawing fiercely at their vitals, and a burning thirst beginning to fever their blood. As they sent up their heart-wrung prayers to heaven for deliverance, they watched, one after another, the lights ashore disappearing, till only the pitying stars looked down upon them, and then, clinging close to one another, they sank into an uneasy, fevered slumber, to dream of home, with its love and warmth, where were the dear ones, all unconscious as yet of their sad fate. The weary hours of that long first night on the rock — a night that seemed to them as if it would never close — slowly passed away, and at length the dull, gray light of the winter morning began to creep over the moaning sea, awaking them to a full sense of their misery, and of the awful present that now seemed more and more threatening. Still, the thought that they must die there slowly, of cold and hunger and thirst, was too terrible, especially when help was so near — when only that little breadth of the hungry sea severed them from those who would welcome them with open arms, and even risk their lives to save them. Strength returned and hope revived as the sun arose; and they comforted one another with the thought that they were so near human succour, that surely this day would witness their deliverance. They would be missed and sought for, and no doubt Gull Island would be searched. It was not possible, the sanguine spirits among them thought, that they should be left to die unaided within two or three miles of human habitations. There were still many chances in their favour, and many ways in which help might come. The coasting craft, running for Tilt Cove, or some of the fishing boats, would be sure to pass near the Island. Alas! had they but known it, on that bright, clear day alone had they any chance of rescue; and unhappily they were either stupefied by the suddenness of the calamity, or so benumbed with cold and suffering that they failed to light a signal-fire, the smoke of which could have been seen along the shore, and would have brought them help. As events proved, some of them had matches in their pockets, and some combustible materials might have been gathered, which a portion of the sail might have been spared to ignite; but if the attempt was made, it would seem to have been soon abandoned as hopeless. They seem to have been trusting solely to the chance of a passing vessel, which, at that period of the year, was most uncertain, on that lonely, storm-beaten coast. It does not even appear that they managed to hoist a signal, owing probably to the want of anything to serve as a flag-staff. Their utter inability to do anything to help themselves, and their being compelled to wait impotently, under the gnawings of hunger and the more terrible pangs of thirst for the approach of death, looking out on the pitiless sea breaking on its cold gray stones, must have been the most bitter portion of their sufferings. So long as brave men feel they can do something they do not lose heart; it is when they find themselves powerless they sink into despair.

When the morning of their second day on the desolate islet dawned, dark heavy masses of cloud to windward indicated that another snow-storm was approaching. We can fancy the poor, pale, shivering castaways dragging their stiffened limbs from beneath the frozen canvas, and eagerly scanning the bay for the sight of some friendly sail, seeing only the angry scowl of ocean, hearing the mutterings of the approaching storm, and then searching one another's countenances for some gleam of hope, and meeting only looks of blank despair. And then, as the fierce nor'-easter rushed across the bay, hurling the snow-drifts on its wings of gloom, freezing the blood in their veins, we can see them, in imagination, cowering beneath their wretched shelter, huddling together for warmth, and perhaps trying to cheer one another with the expression of a hope which they but feebly realized. All day the snow continued to fall, shutting out the sight of sea and sky, and all hope of present deliverance. A terrible thirst now consumed them, far harder to bear than the dull gnawings of hunger. Another dreary night dragged through its slow hours, which were broken by death-like slumbers, from which maddening dreams aroused them at intervals. The storm had abated, and their rocky prison was now covered with snow. Hunger and thirst were doing their deadly work: and some were so weak they could scarcely stand upright. Hope began to die out, and dull, leaden despair crept closer to each heart. Rapidly failing strength told them that the end could not be distant. Some who thought themselves sinking, and who expected they would be the first to die, left messages of love and farewell for the dear ones they should see no more, with those who were likely to survive, and had a further chance of rescue. We can fancy the two poor women, reading their fate in each other's eyes, quietly clasping hands, leaning their cheeks close together, offering a prayer for mercy, and silently awaiting the approach of death.

One secret, unuttered dread, lay heavy on each heart in that sad group—more awful than even the fear of death—"should I be the first to die, ravenous hunger will at length drive the others to the last extremity—my body will never lie in a quiet grave, it will be devoured by my famishing companions." Alas! the poor sufferers were not to be released by death so soon as they expected. They had yet to lie many days and nights on that snow-covered rock, in the last extremity of human woe, looking into the stony eyes of death, as, like a hungry lion, he slowly crept nearer.

How the hapless group spent the dreary hours, what words were spoken, what prayers were uttered, which of them bore their sufferings most calmly; what arrangements they made for keeping an outlook, or what efforts for lessening their sufferings—of all these nothing can ever be known: Let us hope that some, if not all, felt the sustaining, comforting power of religion in those trying hours, and even from such a terrible death-bed, could look heavenward with humble hope. On the fifth day, one of the sufferers, Mr. F. Dowsley, feeling that there was no longer any hope, wrote a farewell letter to his wife, with a pencil, in his pocket-book. I have been permitted to copy this letter, and to make use of any portions of it which are suited for publication. It is pathetic and mournful in the last degree. After describing the circumstances under which they had been cast on the island, he wrote:

"This is our fifth day, and we have not had a bit or sup, not even a drink of water, there being no such thing on the island. It is void of everything which would give us any comfort. It is so barren and bleak that we cannot get wood to make a fire to warm us; our bed is on the cold rocks, with a piece of canvas, full of gutter, to cover us. You may fancy what my sufferings have been and are. You know I was never very strong or robust. My feet are all swollen, and I am getting very weak. I

113

expect that if Providence don't send a boat or vessel along this way to-day, or to-morrow at the farthest, that some of us will be no more; and I very much fear I will be the first victim. If so, you will not even have the gratification of getting my body, as they will make use of it for food. I am famishing with the thirst. I would give all I ever possessed for one drink of water. If I had plenty of water, I know I should live much longer. I feel a dreadful feverish thirst and no means of relieving it. Is it not a hard case that I cannot even get a drink of water? Oh! did I ever think my life would end in this way — to be cast away on a barren rock, in the middle of the ocean, and there to perish with cold and hunger and thirst, and our bodies to be bleached by the winter's frost and the summer's sun, and to be food for the wild fowl! Oh! is it not sad to think of this, and such a little thing would save us! We are only six miles from Shoe Cove where we would be received with open arms. Now, my darling, as I plainly see that in a few hours I must appear before our God, I wish to say a few words about your future prospects." (Here follow directions about family affairs.) "Whilst I am writing this, under our little bit of canvas, I am shivering with weakness and cold, from head to foot. I don't know how I have written what I have, but this I can say — the facts are worse than I have named. Give my love to my darling children, and tell them to think often of my sad fate. Tell them I leave it as my dying request to be kind and obedient to you, and to be advised by you in everything. Oh, my darling Margaret, you will feel, you will pity me, when you know of my unbounded sufferings and sad fate. Oh do, and pray for me, with the children, incessantly. I must now conclude, my darling, as I am unable to write more. Embrace my darling children, and tell them to be obliging and kind to each other, for, without this, they cannot expect to prosper. Tell them their unfortunate father leaves them his blessing. Should our fate be known before the Spring, if George would think it worth his while to come round, he would be able to get my body or bones, which I would like to have laid in Belvidere cemetery. If I were with you and my dear children, and had the priest, I don't think I should fear death quarter so much.

"I must now, my darling, take my last farewell of you in this world. May we meet and enjoy one another where there is no sorrow, no trouble, no affliction. I leave you, my love, my blessing. Your loving but unfortunate husband,

F. DOWSLEY."

We can fancy with what bursting hearts and streaming eyes the poor wife and children read these touching utterances of a love that beat strongly for them in death, when many months afterwards the poor remains were brought home, and how they will treasure these last solemn words of tender farewell! This letter is dated "December 16th, 1867," but it was not destined to be the last. Days and nights of fearful sufferings still awaited them before death came to their release. The following letter is dated December 18th:

"My darling Margaret —

"I have been out to see if there might be any chance of a rescue, but no such thing. I am almost mad with the thirst. I would give all I ever saw for one drink of water, but I shall never get it. We are all as wet as a sink. My clothes are all wet and frozen. I am going under the canvas to lie down and die. May God pity me and have mercy on my soul.

"Your loving and unfortunate husband,

F. DOWSLEY."

The foregoing letter was written on the seventh day of their sufferings; and we would naturally conclude, considering their circumstances, that, without food, drink or shelter, life could not be prolonged for many more hours. It is, however, startling to find that, six days later, all of them were still living. A third letter, written by poor Dowsley, is dated "December 24th, 1867":

"My darling Margaret —

"We are all still alive, only that we have had no relief ever since, nor any sign of it. We have not tasted a bit of food, up to this time, of any kind, with the exception of the dirty snow-water that melts around and under our feet, which we are glad to devour. The place we are sheltered in, if I can call it a shelter, is up to our ankles in water. Oh, what a sad Christmas Eve and Christmas Day it is for me! I think I can see you making the sweet-bread and preparing everything comfortable for to-morrow. My feet were very painful last night. I was in complete agony with them. My clothes are completely saturated. Oh, I never knew how to appreciate the comforts of a home, or a bed, until now. We shall never see one another again in this world. I had no idea we should have lasted so long. Our case is now hopeless. There is no hope of deliverance. My sufferings have been beyond description since I landed on this barren rock. Don't forget to give my love to George and Eliza. Oh, how I dread" — (words illegible — probably "another night.") "I would write more but feel unable. Oh, my darling, if I could but once see you and the children, I think I would be satisfied to die. Embrace them all for me. Give my love to Mary —— and Mrs. G——, and all her family! Tell them all to pray for me.

"Your loving husband,

F. DOWSLEY."

This is the last sad record which was discovered; and probably the hand that wrote it was, soon after, cold in death. A more touching memorial of affection amid awful sufferings, it would be difficult to imagine. From it we learn, on the most unquestionable evidence, what would otherwise have been incredible, that eleven human beings lived, under the circumstances I have described, for thirteen days without food or drink. In all probability, their lives were prolonged for such a length of time by their swallowing the half-melted snow around them, as described in the last letter I have quoted; though this seems to have still left them consumed by a raging thirst. Moisture too must have been absorbed by the skin, from their saturated clothing, and would help slightly to meet the cravings of nature. I believe instances are on record of persons having subsisted without food for more than a fortnight when access to water was obtained. In the case of the sufferers on Gull Island, we know, for certain, that they were all alive on the thirteenth day; after that we know nothing, except by inference, of what took place, and can only conjecture how many more days elapsed before kind death released the last sufferer. It is too painful to dwell on the possible horrors of the closing scene, or to imagine one after another dying, till the last man, looking around with glazing eyes, saw the ghastly faces of ten frozen corpses, and was glad to crouch among them, under the same wretched canvas covering, praying for death to release him from the terrors of their stony gaze. This much is certain, that the fierce cravings of hunger at length drove some of the unhappy sufferers to that extremity from which nature revolts most strongly. Two skeleton forms, lying apart from the other dead bodies when discovered, and almost denuded of flesh, told a sad tale. May heaven preserve us all from such an awful death!

At length, on that lonely spot, the last groan of the sufferers was hushed in the sleep which was never to be broken. All was still. Through the cloud-rack the pale moon looked down upon the two ghastly skeleton forms—upon the dead women, their hands clasped, the head of the one reclining on the shoulder of the other,—upon the wan, worn faces of the dead men, some so calm and peaceful, others with traces of anguish and woe, which once seen would haunt the dreams of the beholder till the close of life. But the snow-drifts, shaken from the wings of the storm, fell softly on the sorrowful scene, wrapping the sleepers in a spotless winding-sheet, hiding all traces of suffering, effacing all records of the dreadful past, even as the divine mercy and love wrap our poor world around, hiding in their beneficent folds the scars of our sinning and suffering humanity, and quieting its convulsive sobs. The storms of January came and raved around the sleepers, but they heeded them not. The foam-crested billows dashed themselves far up the cliffs, with angry roar, but did not disturb "the sleep that knows no waking." The vast ice-fields floated down from the frozen north, encirling the lonely sleepers on the rock, and converting the face of the ocean into a white, solid table-land far as the eye could reach. The glittering icebergs glided past in silent grandeur, as if they feared to disturb their slumbers. But, at length, the April sun came with its warmth, dissolving the frozen masses, bringing the soft breezes off the land which drove away the chilling ice-fields, and thus gently uncovering the faces of the dead, that sorrowing friends might see them once more, lay them, with loud weeping, in the soft bosom of earth.

On the 21st of April, a small schooner was cruising near Gull Island, in search of seals. A boat was despatched from it to shoot some birds that were hovering near the shore. One of these was fired at and fell wounded on the Island. A fisherman landed to recover it, and had gone but a few yards when he was struck with horror and consternation at the sight of the two skeletons lying almost close together. He called to his companions, who were speedily beside him. On further search, they found, underneath the frozen canvas, the dead bodies of seven men and two women. Horror-stricken, they hurried back to their vessel with the doleful intelligence. The truth at once flashed upon them—that these were a portion of the crew and passengers of the ill-fated *Queen*, all of whom were believed to have gone down on the wreck, but had really perished of hunger and cold close to their very doors! It was a harrowing thought to the poor fellows, that had they known of their mishap on the fatal 12th December, they could have rescued all in a couple of hours; had they even within a fortnight after, observed any signal of distress on the uninhabited island, it would not have been too late to save them. Dark and mysterious providence! All things seemed to have conspired to cut off help and hope. Had the *Queen* been wrecked where she struck, an immediate search for survivors would have resulted in the rescue of all. With sad hearts they headed their vessel for Tilt Cove, in order to make known the sorrowful news, and get aid for the removal of the bodies. The little village was convulsed with grief. Coffins were hastily got ready, and a schooner was despatched to convey the bodies from Gull Island to Tilt Cove for internment. The horror of the scene was completed when it was found that the bodies were frozen so firmly together that it was necessary to separate them with crowbars and force. In the cemetery at Tilt Cove all found a quiet resting-place, except the body of Mr. Dowsley, which was transmitted to his family in St. John's, and, in accordance with his dying wish, was interred in Belvidere cemetery.

As everything connected with the sad fate of these castaways is of interest, I subjoin copies of two other documents found on the persons of the sufferers. The first is one which was found written in the memorandum book of the Captain, and ran as follows:

"No. I.

"We left St. John's N.F., on the 5th December 1867, with 80 tons stone ballast, about 10 or 12 tons general cargo and lumber and a mail bag full of letters for the Union Mine, Tilt Cove. When running for Gull Island, Cape John, in a snow-squall, struck on it, when not able to see anything even when on top of it, at 6 o'clock A.M. on December 12th, 1867. Did not save anything only this book and the ship's papers, which are in a tin case now here, — and Lord have mercy on our souls. We will all perish here, without food or clothes or fire.

"JOHN OWENS,
"Master of the Queen, of Swansea"

"No. II.

"The *Queen*, of Swansea, got on the rocks on Gull Island on December 12th. The captain, mate, and seven men landed on Gull Island on December 12th by means of a rope, just as we stood, neither bread, nor eatables, nor clothes. Boatswain, pilot, and one of the ship's crew went away with the ship, and a married man, a passenger, and all these four perished with the ship. This is written on the Island, after landing, by me.

"JOHN OWENS,
"Master of the Queen"

The following letter was found on the person of William Hoskins:

"Whatever person or persons pick this up I hope they will send this small box, with its contents, and a revolver which is in my coat pocket, to Captain Hoskins, Tilt Cove Union Mine.
"Dear Father, Mother, Sisters and Brothers, — I expect this is the last you will hear or see of us. We have been here 108 hours. We could not get any thing on shore to eat. There were fifteen on board. We lost four men that were driven off in the vessel. We got on shore by means of a rope on the morning of 12th December. Dear friends, do not grieve for us, we are giving our time to prayer. There is no one dead yet, but all are getting very weak. We shall have to wish you a long farewell. If we do not meet on earth, may we meet in heaven. The revolver belongs to Willy Parsons — give it to him for me. We must bid you good bye. We remain your affectionate children,

"WILLIAM AND GRINELDA HOSKINS."

The tale of the poor castaways of Gull Island will continue to be told, for many a year to come, around the winter hearths of the

Newfoundland fishermen, while the storm is raging without; awakening gentle pity in many a heart, and helpful compassion towards the suffering and sorrowful, of whom the world is so full.

REVEREND MOSES HARVEY was born in Armagh, Ireland, in 1820 and died at St. John's, Newfoundland, in 1901, where he had been the minister of St. Andrew's Free Church from 1852 until 1878. A dedicated Newfoundlander, Harvey contributed a large number of articles and sketches on the history, capabilities, and natural resources of Newfoundland to the newspapers and periodical press of Britain, the United States, and Canada. As well as writing descriptive and statistical articles in the *Encyclopaedia Britannica* and *Johnston's Univ(ersal) Cyclopedia*, Harvey was the author of various texts including, *Across Newfoundland with the Governor. A Visit to our Mining Region; and This Newfoundland of Ours. Being a Series of Papers on the Natural Resources and Future Prospects of the Colony* (1879), *A Short History of Newfoundland. England's Oldest Colony* (1883), *Where Are We and Whither Tending? Three Lectures on the Reality and Worth of Human Progress* (1886), *Guide* (1894), *Newfoundland in 1897. Being Queen Victoria's Diamond Jubilee* (1897), *Newfoundland in 1900* (1900), *Newfoundland at the Beginning of the 20th Century* (1902) and, in conjunction with Joseph Hatton, *Newfoundland, Its History, Its Present Condition and Its Prospects* (1883).

It was said of Harvey, "What Mr. H. does not know about Newfoundland is not worth knowing."

On the Road to Baddeck.

W. D. Dimock

"A Visit to the Mineral Spring, East Bay, Cape Breton"*

HOW EAGERLY AND HOW NATURALLY mankind grasp at every possible means that will beget health! The most visionary objects we essay in our attempts to gain a sound body, and prolong, if possible, our span of life. The *mens sana in corpore sano* is an Eldorado that with unwearied strength we are ever striving to attain. Disease is a sleepless monster of hideous mien that no Medea can overcome, and that too often vanquishes the skill of the modern Æsculapius, whose staff, knotted and thorny though it be, can never half symbolize the aches, pains and sorrows that weak, frail man is heir to.

A "*parva rura* and the old fashioned family salt-cellar on a frugal board," Horace may exclaim; but what are these, even with a "contented mind," when the blood boils with fever and the parched tongue lies burning in the mouth? We must have health and we seek for it everywhere. Time and money are mere ciphers that we may multiply and divide at pleasure, with no great gain, in our search for health. At one time we may madly rush to a Ponce De Leon's *Fountain of Life*, or again, bathe in the chalybeate waters of Spa or Saratoga, and fondly imagine we will emerge invulnerable from these Stygian waves.

A few years ago I visited a tiny spring, the waters of which were highly impregnated with carbonate of iron, and whose reputed medi-

The Maritime Monthly, July 1873, pp. 63-70.

123

cinal properties were so wonderful that hundreds were crowding to it. From far and near invalids were flocking to drink of the health-restoring water, which, it was said, lost much of its efficacy to cure unless drunk on the margin of the spring. Summer after summer it was the "rage." Every season brought a new crowd of visitors and health seekers. At last I decided to join a party that had planned a trouting excursion up the waters of the Bras d'Or; and on our way, by a slight deviation, we could stop and see the mineral spring, then in full blast, and satisfy ourselves of the wonders its waters possessed.

As the Spring was distant some forty miles or so from North Sydney, the chief coaling port on the Island of Cape Breton, we found we must make an early start. One of those lovely mornings in June, the air so balmy and invigorating that even the sad heart must rejoice as the youth, found us at day-dawn rapidly whirling off to our destination. What new vigor the fresh morning breeze instils! How lovely all nature appeared! In what beautiful robes she was decked! The green fields on our right sloping seaward, with their thousands of dewy crystals reflecting the face of the rosy-fingered Aurora, now gently emerging with golden light from the eastern ocean, and to the left, the ever-heaving sea, silently breaking on the pebbly beach into tiny waves of the most brilliant coruscations, added new charms to the scene around, and made us all feel that

"Sweet is the breath of morn; her rising sweet,
With charm of earliest birds."

What resolutions were formed that beautiful morning! How much did we lament the hours of the never-to-be-recalled past, that we had lost in idle slumber. What pledges we gave one another, for the future, to be up with the lark, and enjoy the most divine part of the day, I well remember. The novelty and beauty to most of us of a "sun-rise," was so entrancing, that we made good promises of reform in our late rising, which Punic faith, alas! was so soon broken.

For miles our course was through a lovely country, with rich and fertile arable lands on every side. The early ploughman was at his work. The herd-boy was watching his cattle. The birds were singing in the neighboring groves. Everything seemed to be at work, and realized that soft, balmy spring would soon give place to summer, and then would come winter, against which preparation must be made at once. Soon all these fine fields are left behind, the habitations of men disappear, and we enter the "forest primeval."

Across jolting, bouncing, rattling bridges; through soft and clayey roads, over-shadowed by tall beech trees that above us seem to join in fond embrace; past little brooks that run seaward, and moss-clad springs that, oozing from the hill-side, run trickling over our path, we wind our way. A ray of sunlight now and again flashes through the thick wood, and the shadow that the dark, damp forests, wet with the night-dews, threw over our spirits, is chased away.

Once more we burst into the wide and open country. The flashing surface in the distance tells us that we have arrived at that favorite resort of Walton's disciples, Gillies' Lake. We agree to wait till our return, before we tempt the silvery trout from the great, dark depths of the waters before us. In the distance stands a large, white chapel, so, Aristippus-like, we argue we are yet in the confines of civilization. Dense forests once more. Tall hardwood trees, hoary with age, every-where. The timid, panting hare sits crouching on the roadside, or goes leaping away before the dust cloud of our wagon. The owl hoots overhead, and the morning song of a thousand birds fills the air.

The public way is now left behind, and we turn off into the lone road, frequented only by the weak and weary invalids that have come to recuperate on the banks of this spring. What jolting, and tossing, pitching and rolling, bumping and thumping we experience as our heavy van sways along on this uneven road. The twisted roots of mighty trees, as old almost as the rocks they grow on, stretch serpen-tine over our way, as if to trip us. Deep ruts that some lumbering cart, perhaps bearing a family and their Penates to the spring-side have gouged out, we sink into,—this gives us all a forward motion, till we bring up in a pile against the driver, who is firmly braced against the foot-board.

The forest is thicker and the road rougher. We have had nothing like this before. We are told that we must leave our wagon and take to our horses, or walk. I immediately seize upon the quietest looking beast and endeavor to mount him, with the assistance of a tumble-down old stump. The stump sinks beneath my weight, I sink hurriedly beneath the horse. With the friendly hand of a companion I manage to mount, and spanning the beast with my legs, I hold on in spite of his prancing and rearing. My friend, almost worn out by the rough tossing we had received, can walk no further. He will risk a seat behind me. I feel perfectly safe too. But, oh, how fleeting are worldly projects! No sooner had my companion touched the horse, then high up in the air went his legs, forming a straight line with his back, his head dropped downwards, a kind of centrifugal motion seized me, and in a second I

125

was coiled up in a rude heap amid the thick furzy underbrush and the thorny prickles of the raspberry. I concluded to walk to the spring. I was not the least tired. Always preferred walking to riding on horseback.

As we tugged and scrambled along the mere footpath, we met numbers of men, women and children returning from the celebrated waters. Every one had a flagon, jug, or bottle filled with the healing liquid. They are a happy group on their homeward march. The trip through the rough forests has put new life into them, which they attribute to the healing power of the precious waters they are bearing with them. Our curiosity is greatly increased, and jostling about from side to side, we hurry on.

Here we are at last, sure enough. Little canvas tents, camps of the evergreen spruce and temporary huts rudely constructed, dot the little mounds, and everywhere peer through the trees. Only one permanent habitation appears, a little removed from the general encampment, with a roughly finished barn attached, and a sloping plot of land surrounded by a rustic fence. Two cows cooling themselves in the shade of the barn, a rickety looking horse grazing near by, a pig grunting at the doorstep, and numberless flocks of domestic fowls indicated that their owner did not belong to the nomadic crowd housed in the white tents, but was a resident of the valley, and probably, by profession, would call himself a farmer. The valley before us was the spot that, for the last eight or ten years, had been visited by so many. As you approach the Mineral Spring, at the top of a densely wooded hill, you are met by a host of little ragamuffins all offering their services to point out the great wonder of the place. These ragged little urchins belong to the settlements some five miles away, and are ever on the lookout for the few coins travellers may throw to them. They are a hardy set of boys, living on the most homely fare, sleeping on the dewy grass, and seeking shelter from storms beneath the protecting arms of some mountain tree. Under the leadership of one of these we make our way to the spring. Here and there we pass groups of worn-out travellers resting beneath the shady forest trees. Some are pitching their tents, similar to those that already glisten in the mid-day sun, and others are preparing their scanty meal.

It is almost impossible to follow our bare-footed guide as he nimbly pushes through the trees, and rapidly hurries over the under-brush. He has the agility of a squirrel, and we are left far behind. As we come up, he looks first at his own dirty bare feet and slimly formed limbs, then a look of contempt passes over his equally dirty face, as he gazes on our legs carefully ensconced in heavy knee-boots, and our hands protected by thick gloves.

He would not exchange places with us. He rather pities us. No feeling of jealousy enters his untutored mind as he gazes on us equipped cap-a-pie to protect our bodies from the merciless twigs and broken wood that are ever assailing us. Rather the reverse. He feels sorry for us, and smiling, chuckling to himself, he starts on again.

"This here's the spring," came from a clump of small bushes a little beyond us. We hurry up, and, as our guide parted the thick brambles with his hands, a mud hole about as large as a bucket is disclosed to view. Shades of the departed! is this the celebrated mineral spring? An insignificant hollow with a red clay bottom, the ground for some distance round a little moist, is what we have pointed out as the natural curiosity that we have encountered a nine hours' journey to visit. We look aghast. Speechless we gaze on the filthy, empty bog-hole before us. We scan one another's countenances in mute surprise. Were we fools enough to travel all this long distance to see what was visible a stone's throw from our homes?

"They've been dippin' out o' it all day," ventured the little fellow, who was holding the bushes apart and vainly peering into it for water. "It'll soon fill up," he said, as he saw our disappointd looks. Perhaps he imagined we would think him an impostor. Perhaps, also, he thought of the few coins he expected. He was alarmed, from our conversation, that we did not appreciate the beauties and wonders of East Bay mineral spring.

We waited almost breathless for an hour on the bank of the spring. The waters were indeed rising. The little cavity was fast filling. However small it might be, there was a spring, certainly. The cup was soon taken from a pocket-flask by Jake, the boldest of our party, and the bubbling, boiling water was tasted. We watched his countenances carefully to see what effect the healing balm would have. Jake was a little round-shouldered; we imagined he would straighten up immediately. He was somewhat deaf,—had been so from childhood. Of course, his hearing would be as keen as our own. He was cross-eyed, too. Surely these great waters would make him a perfect man again. Imagine our surprise when, with "Ugh, what trash! it's as brackish as bilge water," he dashed the cup to the ground. No apparent change came over his physical constitution, except the awfully distorted and woe-begone countenance before us. What can be the matter? Do the

Naiads no longer brood over the waters? We all decided that, however potent to cure, the water was by no means palatable, and that it was the meanest looking spring we had ever seen. We went to the brook that flowed near by. A general call brought Jake's flask out again. Mineral water was at a discount after that. It might do to pour over rheumatic limbs and shower around invalids, but the healthy, sane man would certainly choose *eau de vie*.

We slept pretty well that night on the floor of the farmer's house. He had as many in his house as could possibly be crowded in, he said; but we made a rush, and a jolly field-bed was given us, where, before morning dawned, we got a few hours sleep. We rushed at daybreak to the spring. It was filled to overflowing, and around it were scores of people ready to get their share of the limpid waters. There was the old grey-headed man and the mere child making their way through the thickets, knocked rudely aside by the more energetic and persevering. Some poor creatures could barely drag themselves along; others were carried by their friends. One little boy was in tears because he had got no mineral water for two days, and his mother had threatened him with summary punishment, if he again returned empty-handed. He sobbed as if his little heart would break, when he found his chances were no better than on previous visits. Kind-hearted Jake seized his tin dipper, disappeared in the crowd, and from the brook near by, dipped a full dish of the running water, which, with a fifty cent piece, he put into the boy's hand, who soon scampered off with a joyous heart to his friends. It likely had the same effect as if drawn from the medicinal spring.

The smoke curling up from before each tent and camp gave the place a wild and romantic appearance. The morning meal was being prepared, and as we passed along we observed that the culinary operations were of the most rustic description. Two forked sticks with a cross-pole supported the kettle, or pot; a broken-nosed tea-pot sang away among the embers; here and there a potato showed its scorched head from beneath the ashes, while the smell of broiled herring floated thick on the morning breeze. As a general thing, the visitors were of the poorer classes, — those who were too reduced in circumstances to employ medical attendance, — so they came to try the free waters of this Bethesda; or those who were so illiterate that the superstition of the great power to cure all manner of diseases that this spring possessed, had firmly seized their minds, and nothing would satisfy them but to bundle up and make the wearisome journey. There were others, too, from strange countries, all seeking the great Elixir, health. The jeweled invalid, carefully waited on by a long line of attendants, and the poor, emaciated, wretchedly clad pauper, with yearning eyes, day by day watched for health.

When we were seated around the farmer's humble board, with its yet more homely fare, we heard many strange and wonderful stories of the mineral spring. Ten years before, the farmer was accustomed to drive his cows every morning to the little brook to drink. He noticed that after a time, they always sought the spring near by. It surprised him. It was difficult to get at; the open brook with pure water was before them, yet the spring was their drinking place. He noticed the strange taste in the waters, and at last carried them to the neighboring village. It was pronounced a mineral spring. Hundreds had since been to it. Scores once weak and crippled with physical infirmity, were now hearty and well,—living monuments of what these chalybeate waters had achieved. Sight had been restored, hearing improved, rheumatism had fled in dismay at the touch of the water. Every one we met had something new to tell of this wonderful spring. Its praises were in every one's mouth; and so, year after year, it had been frequented by crowds of sickly human beings.

We stayed for a number of days around this little reservoir that was attracting so many. We listened to the marvellous stories about the place, till, surfeited, we decided to continue our trip. Our hearts ached as we left, to think of so many of our fellow creatures, racked with disease and pain, still lingering behind, cherishing the delusive hope that beneath the health-inspiring influence of this little fountain, they might yet regain their wonted strength.

The spring yet oozes from the earth, but its banks are almost deserted. The thick brambles are growing up again with a new vegetation. The morning and evening air is broken only by the natural melody of the birds. Occasionally the curiosity-seeker may tramp over the rough road and taste its waters, but no more do weary pilgrims, with disease-stricken bodies and sore-distressed souls, congregate on its mossy banks. Its silent and undisturbed bubblings have outlived the wild frenzy that brought so many to drink of its waters, and gently tell that men may come and go but it moves on the same, for ever.

WILBERT DAVID DIMOCK was born in Onslow, Nova Scotia, November 27, 1846. After receiving his B.A. from Acadia University in 1867, he worked as a teacher, becoming principal of the North

Sydney Academy, then of the Model Schools at Truro. In 1883 he filled the office of Secretary Treasurer of the Canadian Department at the International Fisheries Exhibition in London; his success at this position earned him a special diploma of honour and many similar assignments, including Secretary of the Canadian section at the Chicago World's Fair in 1893. From 1894 to 1897 he tried his hand at active politics, sitting first in the Nova Scotia House of Assembly, then in the House of Commons. In 1894 he became editor of the Truro *News*, a position he held for many years.

ICE CUTTING ON THE ST. LAWRENCE.

Morgan Coldwell

"Ice-Cutting on Lake Huron"*

THE ICE CROP of 1874 having failed in the United States, a number of Americans in the business turned their attention to Canada, and at the invitation of one of them—a particular friend of mine—I went to see the operation of cutting and stacking ice. It was in the afternoon of a Monday in the beginning of April that we started—Mr. Le Stair and I. The place we were bound for was a distant point on Lake Huron. The place we started from was near Saugeen, on the shores of that Lake. Our conveyance was—a cutter, you say: no, it was a buggy, drawn by two grey horses. Mud was on the earth beneath; sunshine in the heavens above.

It was the worst ride I had had for an age.

"We'll soon be over this bit," says Le Stair, as we bounded over a corduroy road, he driving and smoking, and the other passenger smoking and abusing the roads, the buggy making mad attempts to get off its springs, and the horses doing incipient somersaults front and back without intermission. We did get over that "bit," but not soon. Then we got into the mud, and had a comparatively peaceful time of it for a long spell. We got over this "bit" very well. Sometimes one wheel went up suddenly into the air, and I dashed sideways against Le Stair; and sometimes the other wheel went up, and Le Stair precipi-

*The Canadian Monthly and National Review, Feb. 1875, pp. 135-41.

tated his left shoulder upon me. We did not converse much on this "bit." Several times my fellow-traveller began to say something, evidently about the damage the buggy was sustaining, but he never got beyond the first syllable of the first word of the sentence, and then he sunk into wrathful silence and played with the whip.

"It's a lucky thing we brought the buggy," he remarked, as a new idea struck him, when we were three hours and a half on the road, and fifteen miles on our way. "A cutter," he continued, "would not have done at all."

I was speechless with conviction.

"We must get a cutter at Stewart's Mills," he went on, "and then we'll make for the Lake and get along splendidly."

We made Stewart's in five hours, and on looking at the horses and his watch, he said, "We have not done so badly after all."

It was not so good, however; for here we got nothing to eat ourselves, and only a wisp of hay for the horses.

"Now," says Le Stair, as we left Stewart's an hour later, packed into the cutter, "we'll get along nicely, once we get to the Lake." He did not say how we should get on before we reached the Lake; but I soon found out.

The road we had to travel was simply no road. Now we were wending our way over a ploughed field, and again we were doing the same thing in the bush. We jolted against a log on the right, and turned sharp round and brought up against a stump on the left; we fled headlong into ravines and toiled up hills. We—that is Le Stair—performed innumerable skilful feats in driving; but success elated him. He tried to "cushion" off the side of a steep hill, and we went over. As an upset it was successful, especially as it was done on the off side, and I fell upon Le Stair.

"First adventure," said he, as we righted the cutter and replaced the robes.

"Yes," I replied; "and it was thoughtful to let it come off in daylight. It will be dark in less than an hour."

"Don't mind," said he. "We'll be on the Lake in five minutes." It was twenty-five, however.

Once in view of the Lake, Le Stair grew reckless. He encouraged the greys with voice and whip, and we bowled on to its frozen waters just in time to admire the setting sun. It was a glorious sight. Along the shore ran a belt of ice-hills, dazzling white, formed into a thousand fantastic shapes by the furious Nor-westers of Huron. A huge bank of

black clouds was piled up at the horizon, making a striking back-
ground for the sparkling ice-hills. Behind the black clouds the sun had
just gone down—a magnificent halo of brightest gold marking the
spot, while every cloud in the western heavens glowed with a fiery
fringe.

"This is what I call enjoying life," says Le Stair, in a burst of admiration. "Look at these matchless colours!—what beauty, brilliancy, delicacy, harmony! Talk to me of the painter's art! What in art can compare with nature?"

"A cigar, old fellow," I replied, producing one, and not knowing at
the moment anything better to suggest.

He took; he lit; he smoked it.

We both gave way to the enthusiasm of the moment. The horses
were left to find their way by sight or instinct. We lay back and gazed
in delight, whiffing the light blue clouds of the fragrant weed, and
indicating each charming change in the scene by a nod, a sign, or a
monosyllable, until the heavenly fires grew dim, and darkness
descended upon the face of the deep.

On we went, and down came the night, black and blacker, and cold
and colder. We moralized that it would have been better if we had
started earlier; that it was a pity there was no half-way house, or any
house, or any living thing to meet with on the Lake between us and
our destination, and then we remained silent for miles.

"Can you see the track at your side?" said Le Stair.

I gazed through the darkness on my side, and not seeing any track,
reported my disappointment.

"We've lost it," he remarked.

"Best let the horses find it," I suggested and with slackened rein and
drooping heads the greys were left to their own devices. After wandering half an hour whither they listed, they did find the road. Again
we made a little spurt, and after a couple of hours driving found
ourselves among what are called the "Fishing Islands," a group of
many uninhabited islands, large and small, that stud Lake Huron west
of the Bruce peninsula. Here we again lost our way, and this time
completely. In the darkness we had gone west instead of east of one of
the islands, and, as if apprehensive of danger, the horses attempted to
turn back. To turn back, however, was infinitely worse than to go on,
for it was now pitch dark, and late, and it was much farther to return
than to go ahead. Le Stair persisted that he could find a way out of our
difficulties by proceeding, and on we went, slowly and painfully. As a

135

preventive against melancholy we discussed the thickness of the ice. It was giving forth some of those collapsing, sobbing sounds, startling in daylight, frightful at night. We had got upon new ice, weakened by currents flowing between the islands. "Just think of it," says Le Stair, "Two thousand pounds is no joke on rotten ice; and twenty feet to the bottom!"

I did think of it, and, rashly perhaps, advised speed. Again the greys were put to it. They broke into a trot, and one of them broke through the ice almost simultaneously. A crash, a short mad struggle, the off horse tearing himself almost out of the harness, the nigh horse making frantic efforts to get on the strong ice. A series of yells and vociferations, a lash of the whip, a bound forward, and we came out of the peril, pale and panting, and with an indescribable feeling of relief.

"I'll walk ahead and see if there are any more holes in the ice," said Le Stair, hastily disengaging himself from the cutter and handing me the lines, and off he started into the darkness at a brisk pace, whilst I followed with the team, and reflected on the coldness of the night and the coolness of some people.

After a long walk, Le Stair waited for me and got into the cutter again, preferring the risk of being drowned to the certainty of being fatigued. He confessed to some misgivings that troubled him. He did not know where he was—he did not know exactly where he was going to. It was an island in the Lake, but it was so dark that unless we ran over it we could not see it, or distinguish it from the surrounding group. "It is not this, however, that bothers me most," he said: "it is that confounded bridge."

"What confounded bridge?" I asked, with aroused curiosity. "Bridges in the middle of Lake Huron are the last things I should expect to bother any one."

"The fact is," he said, "there is an opening in the ice formed by the currents flowing between the islands. It lies between us and our destination. It is many miles in length and some twenty feet in width. It has been bridged over by our men with planks on the track leading to Main Station Island—the island we are bound for, and if we miss the bridge we shall drive into the water, and be drowned. Now," he exclaimed, with returning animation, "you know the worst of it. So keep a sharp lookout for that track, for the track leads to the bridge."

We strained our eyes peering into the darkness, until they ached again, but there was nothing to see. We drove in this way for an hour, when a black streak suddenly loomed up, dimly discernible across our

136

path, a hundred feet ahead of us. "What is that?" "Who-a-h! By George that is the water."

We pulled up like a flash, and once more Le Stair got out and left me with the horses, while he went coasting along the chasm on foot to find the bridge. As luck would have it, he found it after a long walk, and we paused to hold a consultation, he near the brink of the water, alone; I a couple of hundred yards in the rear with the greys.

"Now," said he, "can you see me?"

"No."

"Drive on a little. There now, look sharp. I'm at the bridge. Follow in my tracks, and be sure you keep straight, or else you'll get into the Lake."

"Had you not better come back and drive over?"

"No! Follow me quick."

Le Stair started on at a run. There was a splash, a skip, and a jump, and an "all right, I'm over! come ahead." With a kind of desperation I prepared to follow with the horses.

"Keep straight for me," he sung out of the darkness. Throwing back the robes so that I could spring out in an instant, and tightly grasping whip and reins, I put the greys to it in the direction of the voice. "Get along." Crack went the whip, and on they went. "Gee-gee! to the right. For me, for heaven's sake!" yelled Le Stair, as the brutes, scared at the water and the yielding of the ice, began to haw, and crowd, and shy to certain destruction. A few vigorous lashes—a spring as if they were clearing a double ditch—a splash and dash across the loose planks, and over we went, safe and sound.

Now that we were over the bridge and on the track, we trotted along, if not merrily, at least with a load off our minds. In and out, in the darkness, among the islands. Rounding a large one, a gleam of light in the distance—scarcely time to say "look!" and utter darkness again! Another turn. "There it is again!" All right this time. It shines out with a bright, friendly blaze. It comes from the window of one of the shanties on Main Station Island, where our men are. I call them "our" men, having come so far and gone through so much to see them stacking ice. Fifteen minutes more, and we pulled up under the window, and made the island ring with "Hollo! will some of you come and take these horses!" "Frank! Louis! Bob!" Half a dozen came, and we stumbled out of the cutter, shouldering each a buffalo robe—our blankets that were to be—and, tired and hungry as tired and hungry could be, we handed over the cattle, went into the shanty, and after

137

doing ample justice to a welcome meal, turned into bed and slept the sleep of the weary.

It seemed no time when I was awakened by the uproar attendant upon the natives turning out. I peeped through the planks of my shanty and saw a streak of daylight. The crows began to caw vociferously all over the island. It seemed to me that at least fifty of them were performing a matinée on the roof, just a foot over my head. As I had not travelled so far merely to enjoy the pleasure of sleeping in a shanty, I was soon on the floor, performing an elaborate toilet. We sallied out. It was a glorious morning. A few fleecy clouds flecked the firmament. As he rose above the tree tops the sun poured down his rich, ruddy, gladsome rays, enlivening man, and beast, and bird. The lake sparkled as if sown with diamonds. But the gentle reader does not care about these things, or the breakfast we had, or anything, in fact, but the cutting of ice and the piling of it into huge stacks as high as a house, and as long and broad as a good size block of buildings.

The force employed in cutting and stacking ice numbered over forty men and six horses. The operation is as follows: — First a spot is chosen on the lake, where the deepest water is nearest the shore. The locality is selected for two reasons: the ice is thicker and purer the deeper the water, and the deeper the water the easier for a vessel to come alongside the Island, and load from the ice stack. A space of say a square acre or two of ice is then scraped as bare as possible of the surface snow. This is done by means of common wooden scrapers. Two ice ploughs, each drawn by one horse, are then set to work to cut the ice into blocks about two feet square. An ice plough is not like an earth or a snow plough. It is more like a saw. Its action, however, is not up and down like a carpenter's engine, but along the plane of the ice field like an ordinary plough working on a meadow — hence it is called an ice plough. It is composed of a blade of steel a quarter of an inch thick, six feet in length, and from nine inches to one foot in depth — according to the thickness of the ice to be cut. It has only six or seven teeth, but they are very large and strong, and in shape each one is like the stem of one of those ironclads called rams — the six or seven immense teeth looking like a fleet of those rams sailing close behind one another. The blade is fixed into an iron bracket, which gives it all the solidity and fixity it requires when in use. At the front of the plough is an iron ring, to which is attached the chain by which it is drawn by the horse. At the back are a pair of handles — the same size and shape as those used in an ordinary plough — by which it is guided;

one man guides the plough, and a boy leads the horse so as to insure his walking in a straight line on the level surface of the ice field.

The manner in which so thin a machine is made to work in parallel lines running along the surface of the ice, is simple. From the centre of the plough, where the blade is fixed in the bracket, an iron bar two feet long springs out at right angles; from this depends a small blade two feet in length, the same height as the blade of the plough, and running parallel with it. This small blade has no teeth and is called the marker, and its use is twofold. It enables the plough to be driven with the requisite steadiness along the ice field, an operation like pushing a saw along the plane of a board, instead of cutting through it; and it secures a uniformity of size for all the blocks cut, for after the first line is cut from end to end across the ice field, the plough is shifted to cut another line, and then the marker is placed in the first line already cut, in the groove of which it runs, keeping the plough cutting exactly parallel to it all the way across the field.

Two ploughs will cut up a square acre of ice eighteen inches thick in a short time. They work as follows: Supposing the sides of this acre to lie north-south-east-west, by way of easy illustration. One plough will be set to work from north to south to cut the ice into parallel lines two feet apart, and the whole length of the acre. The other plough will at the same time be set to work from east to west to cut the ice into parallel lengths, two feet wide, also the whole length of the field. In a short time the acre of ice begins to look like a chequer board — all marked off into squares. It is necessary to state that the ice in no instance is cut through all the way to the water. There is no necessity for that: besides it would be dangerous, if not impossible of execution. The depth to which, say eighteen inch ice is cut would not be more than twelve inches. It is then firm enough to walk over and work upon without showing the least sign of weakness, while at the same time, it is so sufficiently cut through that it can be easily divided into separate lengths and blocks by a few strokes of the ice bar. The ice bar is an iron bar the end of which is broad and sharp. This is struck into the grooves cut by the plough, and a few strong leverage pulls will detach a line of ice twenty feet long by two feet broad. It is also necessary to state that in no case can the ice be cut to the required depth by the first cutting of the plough, which constitutes another difference between ploughing land and ploughing frozen water. When first driven across the ice field the groove made would not be more than an inch deep. Back the plough comes again on the same groove and cuts another inch deeper, and so on across and recross until the required depth is reached, when the next length is attacked. The time occupied in the operation is short, as the horses go through their work at a smart walk.

Stacking ice is a more exciting operation, and it too, is done in quite an easy way. The ice to be cut and stacked is selected, as before stated, at a place where the deepest water is nearest the shore. A level place on the shore opposite the ice that is cut is cleared and levelled off to a space of say one hundred by two hundred feet. The place chosen is as near the water's edge as is compatible with the safety and preservation of the ice when stacked. A skid is then erected, one end of which touches the spot where the ice is to be lifted out of the lake, while the other end reaches to the cleared and levelled place where it is to be stacked upon shore. A skid is composed of two inclined planes: one, about say a hundred yards in length, reaching up from the lake towards the shore to a certain height, say twenty feet, and the other perhaps the same length, reaching down from this height to the stacking ground. The length of the skid depends upon the distance of the ice field from the shore: that used on the present occasion was some six hundred feet. It is constructed as follows: A tressel work of poles somewhat in the shape of a bridge is erected from the stack to some point as near the ice field as possible: the centre is, say twenty feet high, and the breadth six feet. In the middle is a flooring of plank hard and smooth, and two feet and a half wide, with a three inch raised scantling running its entire length on each side. Up this flooring or skid the ice is drawn, the scantling keeping it on the track. Beside the flooring are narrow run-ways with pieces of wood nailed across them to form stairs, up and down which the men guiding the ice travel when it is being drawn up. The end of the skid touching the ice field is, I must add, carried under the water to a depth of three feet and a length of nine feet, so that the ice blocks are easily floated up to it and on to the skid.

Having now described how the ice is cut, and how the skid is made, I will describe how the ice is lifted and stacked. We will suppose it all cut up into blocks two feet square. The first thing to be done is to cut out a long canal leading from the ice field to the end of the skid where its point is submerged. This canal is as long as is required, and is only three feet in width. Up this narrow passage the blocks are floated until they touch the skid. They are separated by the ice bar as they come up the canal, so that when they reach the skid they are ready to be stacked. The stacking is accomplished by ropes and pullies. At the centre of the skid are two tall poles and two sets of tackle. The rope passing through the top pulley is attached to a large iron hook or clasp which catches with a sure grasp the block of ice intended to be lifted.

A large handle is fixed to the hook by which the blocks are guided when being drawn up. The rope passing through the bottom pulley is yoked to a span of horses. When the hook is fixed on the ice, the word is given, off go the horses, and up comes the ice until it is drawn to the top of the incline reaching from the canal; the hook is then whipped off by the guide who goes up with each load, and down flies the block by its own momentum on the incline leading to the stacking ground. It is there seized by another man who drags it to its place in the stack. To make the description clear, I have spoken as though only one block of ice was lifted at a time. Five blocks were lifted every time while I was present, the hook being placed at the back of the fifth block in the canal, and the whole five coming up the narrow channel, and so on to the skid, and up the skid and down again to the stack — just as easily as one block could be handled. As every block weighed over two hundred pounds, it will be seen that each lift brought up half a ton of ice. And as there were two teams of horses busily at work, one at each side of the skid, hauling up half a ton at a time, it can easily be imagined that ice went up one incline of the skid very rapidly, and came down the other incline very lively, and required a large number of men, and smart men too, to handle it and arrange it in the stack. Four skids, each worked by two teams of horses, are sometimes used in putting up a stack — and then there must be an awful rush; but this is done mostly when an emergency, such as threatened bad ice weather, occurs.

The ice stack that I saw was two hundred feet in length, a hundred feet in depth, and twenty feet in height, composed of solid ice, and contained I was told above five thousand tons. It is easily built. The blocks are placed side by side, in rows, close together, until the space intended for the foundation is covered. Then a second tier is laid upon the first; a third upon the second; and so on until the top is reached. As each tier is laid, the incline of the skid leading to it is raised by means of pulleys, until finally, as the stack grows in height, the incline which at first led to the foundation, becomes part of a long incline leading all the way from the canal to the top of the stack.

The celerity with which the ice is stacked as I have described it, is astonishing. Le Stair and I timed them for a spell of their ordinary mode of working, and saw no less than eight tons lifted out of the water and placed on the stack in five minutes. A ton a minute is slow work. No wonder then that the cutting and stacking of ice as I witnessed it, is an exhilarating sight. Some forty men and six horses were hard at it. Some were driving the ploughs, cutting the ice up into convenient lengths. Others were separating the lengths into squares by blows from the ice bar. A dozen of men with long poles, tipped with iron spikes, were pushing the floating blocks from the place where they were cut to the canal, and up the canal to the skid. Another dozen men and four horses were unceasingly at work at the skid, hauling the floating ice out of the water on to the skid and up the incline, from the top of which the blocks rushed down with a crash upon the stack, where another dozen men were as busy as bees grasping them with iron ice hooks, and dragging them to their places. It was nothing but strings of ice blocks running up one incline and thundering down the other without intermission, at the rate of over sixty tons an hour.

It is hard work; sometimes it is dangerous. The men that guide the blocks up the incline have been known to be thrown from the top of the skid, which is over twenty feet high, down upon the ice below, by reason of the hook slipping; and, said Louis to me—when in the course of full blast operations, suddenly there were a series of cries and shouts, and a man was seen staggering to his knees while the horses were thrown back on their haunches by the frightened drivers, and there was a crashing of ice in the canal—said he: "We lost a couple of men a few years ago, just in that manner. Hook slipped; man holding it suddenly yanked over the skid, fell on his head, killed. Ice blocks went smashing back amongst the workers—man in the way—broke his leg." Not the least discomfort to be endured in cutting ice, is snow-blindness. This affects all the workmen. In the morning when I saw them there was scarcely a man whose eyes were not greatly inflamed, and one of them had to give up work. To save their eyes the men wear green veils, and amongst the novel sights I saw at Main Station were these great, rough, bearded fellows flitting about with their delicate green silk veils. For myself, however, I soon had reason to admit that such things are useful; for I had not been four or five hours on the ice when the glittering reflection of the sun on the ice and my always looking down watching the work, inflamed my face and eyes so that I could not have stood such a glaring scene unprotected for twelve hours. The shipping of ice from the stack is conducted by means of the skid. Upon the opening of navigation three or four vessels are sent to remove the ice to the nearest railways or markets in the States. The skid is continued out into the lake until water is reached deep enough to enable the ships to come alongside of it. The ice is then conveyed along the skid from the stack to the vessel, where it is packed in sawdust and taken away. Loading ice from the stack is no trouble and requires but few hands. During the interval that elapses between the stacking of the ice and the opening of navigation, the stack is protected from the wasting effects of the weather by being covered either by lumber or by green boughs; the former, I understand, is the dearest mode at first, but in the end it is said to be the cheapest and best.

We returned home very tired, very sun-burnt, and very well pleased with our trip to see how our enterprising American friends cut and stack ice, making, I am glad to say, tens of thousands of dollars out of a raw material of which Canada has an unlimited supply—sometimes an unwelcome monopoly—and upon which as a staple we have hitherto placed little or no value, but which if rightly handled would yield a handsome revenue in return for private enterprise.

144

Canniff Haight

"Canadian Life in the Country Fifty Years Ago"*

'I talk of dreams.

*   *   *   *   *

For you and I are past our dancing days.'

I WAS BORN in the County of———, on the 4th day of June in the beginning of this century. I have no recollection of my entry into the world, though present when the great event occurred; but I have every reason to believe the date given is correct, for I have it from my mother and father who were there at the time also, and I think my mother had pretty good reason to know all about it. I was the first of the family, though my parents had been married for more than five years before I presented myself as their hopeful heir, and to demand from them more attention than they anticipated. The Psalmist said in his day, that 'children are an heritage,' and he who had 'his quiver full of them shall not be ashamed; they shall speak with the enemies in the gate.' I do not know what effect this had on my father's enemies, if he had any; but later experience has proved to me that the couple that rear a numerous progeny go through a vast deal of trouble and anxiety. At any rate I made my appearance on the stage, and began my performance behind the footlights of domestic bliss. I must have been

*Rose-Belford's Canadian Monthly, 1880, pp. 2-12.

a success, for I called forth a great deal of applause from my parents, and received their undivided attention. But other actors came upon the boards in more rapid succession, so that in a few years the quiver of my father was well filled, and he might have met 'his enemies in the gate.'

My father, when he married, bought a farm, — all woods, of course; — these were the only farms available for young folk to commence life with in those days. There was a good deal of romance in it, doubtless. Love in a cot; the smoke gracefully curling; the wood-pecker tapping, and all that; very pretty; but alas, in this work-a-day-world, particularly the new one upon which my parents then entered, these silver linings were not observed; they had too much of the prose of life.

A house was built, a log one, of the Canadian rustic style then much in vogue, containing one room, and that not very large either, and to this my father brought his young bride. Their outfit consisted, on his part, of a colt, a yoke of steers, a couple of sheep, some pigs, a gun, an an axe. My mother's *dot* comprised a heifer, bed and bedding, a table and chairs, a chest of linen, some dishes, and a few other necessary items with which to begin housekeeping. This will not seem a very lavish set-out for a young couple on the part of parents who were at that time more than usually well-off. But there was a large family on both sides, and the old people then thought it the better way to let the young folk try their hand in making a living before they gave them much. If they succeeded they wouldn't want much, and if they did not, it would come better after a while.

My father was one of a class of young men, not uncommon in those days, who possessed energy and activity. He was bound to win. What the old people gave was cheerfully accepted, and he went to work to acquire the necessaries and comforts of life with his own hands. He chopped his way into the stubborn wood, and added field to field. The battle had now been waged for seven or eight years; an addition had been made to the house; other small comforts had been added, and the nucleus of future competence fairly established.

One of my first recollections is in connection with the small log barn he had built, and which up to that date had not been enlarged. He carried me out one day in his arms and put me in a barrel in the middle of the floor; this was covered with loosened sheaves of wheat, which he kept turning over with a wooden fork, while the oxen and horse were driven round and round me. I did not know what it all meant then, but I afterwards learned that he was threshing. This was one of the first rude scenes in the drama of the early settlers' life to which I was introduced, and in which I had to take a more practical part in after years. I took part, also, very early in life, in sugar making. The sap-bush was not very far away from the house, and the sap-boiling was under the direction of my mother, who mustered all the pots and kettles she could command, and when they were properly suspended over the fire on wooden hooks, she watched them and rocked me in a sap-trough. Father's work consisted in bringing in the sap with two pails which were carried by a wooden collar about three feet long, and made to fit the shoulder, from each end of which were fastened two cords with hooks to receive the bail of the pails, leaving the arms free except to steady them. He had also to cut wood for the fire. I afterwards came to take a more active part in these duties and used to wish I could go back to my primitive cradle. But time pushed me on whether I would or not, until I scaled the mountain top of life's activities; and now, when quietly descending into the valley, my gaze is turned affectionately towards those early days. I do not think they were always bright and joyous, and I am sure I often chafed under the burdens imposed upon me; but now how inviting they seem.

My next recollection is the raising of a frame barn behind the house, and of a niece of my father's holding me in her arms to see the men pushing up the heavy bents[1] with long poles. The noise of the men shouting and driving in the wooden pins, with great wooden beetles, away up in the beams and stringers, alarmed me a great deal, but it all went up, and then one of the men mounted the plate (the timber on which the foot of the rafter rests) with a bottle in his hand, and swinging it round his head three times, threw it off in the field. This was the usual ceremony in naming the building. If the bottle was unbroken, it was an omen of good luck. The bottle, I remember, was picked up whole, and shouts of congratulation followed; hence, I suppose, the prosperity that attended my father.

The only other recollection I have of this place was of my father, who was a very ingenious man, and could turn his hand to almost everything, making a cradle for my sister, for this addition to our number had occurred; but I have no remembrance of any such fanciful crib being made for my slumbers. Perhaps the sap-trough did duty for me in the house as well as in the bush. The next thing was our

---

[1]The term bent, whether correct or not, is used by carpenters for a part of a frame put together, and then raised as indicated.

147

removal, which occurred in the winter, and all that I can recall of it is that my uncle took my mother, sister, and myself away in a sleigh, and we never returned to the little log house. My father had sold his farm, bought half of his old home, and came to live with his parents. They were Quakers. My grandfather was a short, robust old man, and very particular about his personal appearance. Half a century has elapsed since then, but the picture of the old man, taking his walks about the place, in his closely-fitting snuff brown cut-away coat, knee breeches, broad-brimmed hat, and silver-headed cane is distinctly fixed in my memory. He died soon after we took up our residence with him, and the number who came from all parts of the country to the funeral was a great surprise to me. I could not imagine where so many people came from. The custom prevailed then, and no doubt does still, when a death occurred to send a messenger who called at every house for many miles around to give notice of the death and when and where the interment would take place.

My grandmother was a tall, neat, motherly old woman, beloved by everybody. She lived a number of years after her husband's death, and I seem to see her now sitting at one side of the old fire-place knitting; she was always knitting, and turning out scores of thick warm socks and mittens for her grandchildren.

At this time a great change had taken place, both in the appearance of the country, and in the condition of the people. It is true that many of the first settlers had ceased from their labours, but there were a good many left—old people now who were quietly enjoying, in their declining years, the fruit of their early industry. Commodious dwellings had taken the place of the first rude houses. Large frame barns and out-houses had grown out of the small log ones. The forest in the immediate neighbourhood had been cleared away, and well-tilled fields occupied its place. Coarse and scanty fare had been supplanted by a rich abundance of all the requisites that go to make home a scene of pleasure and contentment. Altogether a substantial prosperity was apparent. A genuine content, and a hearty good will, one towards another, in all the older townships existed. The settled part as yet, however, formed only a very narrow belt extending along the bay and lake shores. The great forest lay close at hand in the rear, and the second generation, as in the case of my father, had only to go a few miles to find it, and commence for itself the laborious struggle of clearing it away.

The old home, as it was called, was always a place of attraction, and especially so to the young people, who were always sure of finding good cheer at grandfather's. What fun, after the small place called home, to have the run of a dozen of rooms, to hunt the big cellar, with its great heaps of potatoes and vegetables, huge casks of cider, and well-filled bins of apples, or to sit at table loaded with the good things which grandmother only could supply. How delicious the large piece of pumpkin pie tasted, and how toothsome the rich crullers that melted in the mouth, that came between meals! Dear old body, I can see her now going to the great cupboard to get me something, saying as she goes, 'I'm sure the child is hungry.' And it was true, he was always hungry; and how he managed to stow away so much is a mystery I cannot now explain. There was no place in the world more to be desired than this, and no spot in all the past the recollection of which is more bright and joyous.

My father now assumed the management of affairs. The old people reserved one room to themselves, but it was free to all, particularly to us children. It was hard to tell sometimes which to choose, whether the kitchen, where the family were gathered round the cheerful logs blazing brightly in the big fire-place, or a stretch on the soft rag-carpet beside the box stove in grandmother's room. This room was also a sanctuary to which we often fled to escape punishment after doing some mischief. We were sure of an advocate there, if we could reach it in time.

The house was a frame one, as nearly all the houses were in those days, and was painted a dark yellow. There were two kitchens, one was used for washing and doing the heavier household work in; the other, considerably larger, was used by the family. In the latter was the large fire-place, around which gathered in the wintertime bright and happy faces, where the old men smoked their pipes in peaceful reverie, or delighted us with stories of other days, and the old lady plied her knitting,—where mother darned our socks, and father mended our boots, where the girls were sewing, and uncles were scraping axe handles with bits of glass to make them smooth. There were no drones in farm-houses then; there was something for every one to do. At one side of the fire-place was the large brick oven with its gaping mouth, closed with a small door, easily removed, where the bread and pies were baked, and in the fire-place an iron crane securely fastened in the jam and made to swing in and out with its row of iron pot-hooks, of different lengths, on which to hang the pots used in cooking. Cook-stoves had not yet appeared to cheer the housewife and revolutionize the kitchen. Joints of meat and poultry were roasted on turning spits, or were suspended before the fire by a cord and wire attached to the ceiling. Cooking was attended with more difficulties then. Meat was fried in long-handled pans, and the short-cake that so often graced the supper table, and played such havoc with the butter and honey, with the pancakes that came piping hot on the breakfast table, owed their finishing touch to the frying pan. The latter, however, were more frequently baked on a large griddle with a bow handle made to hook on the crane; this, on account of its larger surface, enabled the cook to turn out these much-prized cakes, when properly made, with greater speed; and in a large family an expert hand was required to keep up the supply. Some years later an ingenious Yankee invented what was called a 'Reflector,' made of bright tin for baking with. It was a small tin oven with a slanting top, open at one side, and when required for use was set before the fire on the hearth. This simple contrivance was a great convenience and came into general use. Modern inventions in the appliances for cooking have very much lessened the labour and increased the possibilities of supplying a variety of dishes, but it has not improved the quality of them. There were no better caterers to hungry stomachs than our mothers, whose practical education had been received in grandmother's kitchen. The other rooms of the house comprised a sitting-room, — used only when there was company — a parlour, four bed-rooms, and the room reserved for the old people. Up stairs were the sleeping and store-rooms. In the hall stood the tall old fashioned house clock, with its long pendulum swinging to and fro with slow and measured beat. Its old face had looked upon the venerable sire before his locks were touched with the frost of age. When his children were born it indicated the hour, and had gone on telling off the days and years until they were grown. And when a wedding day had come, it rung a joyful peal through the house, and through the years the old hands travelled on, the hammer struck off the hours, and another generation came to look upon it and grow familiar with its constant tick.

The furniture was plain and substantial, more attention being given to durability than to style or ornament. Easy chairs — save the spacious rocking-chair for old women — and lounges were not seen. There was no time for lolling on well-stuffed cushions. The rooms were heated with large double box-stoves, very thick and heavy, made at Three Rivers, and by their side was always seen a large wood-box well filled with sound maple or beech-wood. But few pictures adorned the walls, and these were usually rude prints far inferior to those we get every day now from the illustrated papers. Books, so plentiful and cheap now-a-days, were then very scarce, and where a few could be found, they were mostly heavy doctrinal tomes piled away on some shelf where they were allowed to remain.

The home we now inhabited was altogether a different one from that we had left in the back concession, but it was like many another to be found along the bay shore. Besides our own family, there were two younger brothers of my father, and two grown up nieces, so that, when we all mustered round the table, there was a goodly number of hearty people always ready to do justice to the abundant provision made. This reminds me of an incident or two illustrative of the lavish manner with which a well-to-do farmer's table was supplied in those days. A Montreal merchant and his wife were spending an evening at a very highly-esteemed farmer's house. At the proper time supper was announced, and the visitors with the family gathered round the table which groaned, metaphorically speaking, under the load it bore. There was turkey, beef, and ham, bread and the favourite short-cake, sweet cakes in endless variety, pies, preserves, sauces, tea, coffee, cider, &c, &c. The visitors were amazed, as they might well be, at the lavish display of cooking, and they were pressed, with well meant kindness, to partake heartily of everything. They yielded good-naturedly to the intreaties to try this and that as long as they could and paused only when it was impossible to take any more. When they were leaving the merchant asked his friend when they were coming to Montreal, and insisted that they should come soon, promising if they would only let him know a little before when they were coming he would buy up everything there was to be had in the market for supper. On another occasion, an English gentleman was spending an evening at a neighbour's, and as usual the supper table was crowded with everything the kind-hearted hostess could think of. The guest was plied with dish after dish, and thinking it would be disrespectful if he did not take something from each, he continued to eat and take from the dishes as they were passed, until he found his plate and all the available space around him heaped up with cakes and pie. To dispose of all he had carefully deposited in his plate and around it, seemed utterly impossible, and yet he thought he would be considered rude if he did not finish what he had taken, and he struggled on, with the perspiration visible on his face, until in despair he asked to be excused, as he could not eat any more if it were to save his life.

151

It was the custom in those days for the hired help (the term servant was not used) to sit at the table with the family. On one occasion, a Montreal merchant prince was on a visit at a wealthy Quaker's, who owned a large farm and employed a number of men in the summer. It was customary in this house for the family to seat themselves first at the head of the table, the hired hands then all came in and took the lower end. This was the only distinction. They were served just as the rest of the family. On this occasion, the guest came out with the family and they were seated, then the hired men and girls came in and did the same. Whereupon the merchant left the table and the room. The old lady, thinking that there was something the matter with the man, soon after followed him into the sitting room and asked him if he was ill. He said no. 'Then why did thee leave the table?' said the old lady. 'Because,' said he, 'I am not accustomed to eat with servants.' 'Very well,' replied the old lady, 'if thee cannot eat with us thee will have to go without thy dinner.' His honour concluded to pocket his dignity and submit to the rules of the house.

I was sent to school quite early, more, I fancy, to get me out of the way for a good part of the day, than from any expectation that I would learn much. It took a long time to hammer the alphabet into my head, but if I was dull at school, I was noisy and mischievous enough at home, and very fond of tormenting my sisters. Hence, my parents — and no child ever had better ones — could not be blamed very much if they did send me to school for no other reason than to be rid of me. The school house was close at hand, and is deeply graven in my memory. My first schoolmaster was an Englishman who had seen better days. He was a good scholar, I believe, but a poor teacher. The school house was a small square structure, with low ceiling. In the centre of the room was a box stove, around which the long wooden benches without backs were ranged. Next the walls were the desks, raised a little from the floor. In the summer time the pupils were all of tender years, the large ones being kept at home to help with the work. At the commencement of my educational course I was one of a little lot of urchins, who were ranged daily on hard wooden seats, with our feet dangling in the air, for seven or eight hours a day. In such a plight we were expected to be very good children, to make no noise, and to learn our lessons. It is a marvel that so many years had to elapse before parents and teachers could be brought to see that keeping children in such a position for so many hours was an act of great cruelty. The terror of the rod was the only thing that could keep us still, and that often failed. Sometimes, tired and weary, we fell asleep and tumbled off the bench, to be roused by the fall and the rod. In the winter time the small school room was filled to overflowing with the larger boys and girls. This did not improve our condition, for we were more closely packed together, and were either shivering with the cold or being cooked with the red hot stove. In a short time after, the old school house, where my father, I believe, had got his schooling, was hoisted on runners, and with the aid of several yoke of oxen, was taken up the road about a mile and enlarged a little. This event brought my course of study to an end for a while. I next sat under the rod of an Irish pedagogue, an old man who evidently believed that the only way to get anything into a boy's head was to pound it in with a stick through his back. There was no discipline, and the noise we made seemed to rival a Bedlam. We used to play all sorts of tricks on the old man, and I was not behind either in contriving or carrying them into execution. One day, however, I was caught and severely thrashed. This so mortified me, that I jumped out of the window and went home. An investigation followed, and I was whipped by my father and sent back. Poor old Dominie, he has long since put by his stick, and passed beyond the reach of unruly boys. Thus I passed on from teacher to teacher, staying at home in the summer and resuming my books again in the winter. Sometimes I went to the old school house up the road, or to the one in an opposite direction, which was larger, and where there was generally a better teacher. But it was much farther, and I had to set off early in the cold frosty mornings with my books and dinnerbasket, often through deep snow and drifts. At night I had to get home in time to help to feed the cattle and get in the wood for the fires. The school houses then were generally small and uncomfortable, and the teachers were often of a very inferior order. The school system of Canada, which has since been moulded by the skilful hand of Dr. Ryerson into one of the best in the world, and will give to his industry and genius a more enduring name than stone or brass, was in my day very imperfect indeed. It was, perhaps, up with the times. But when the advantages which the youth of this country possess now, are compared with the small facilities we had of picking up a little learning, it seems almost a marvel that we learned anything. Spelling matches came at this time into vogue, and were continued for several years. They occasioned a friendly rivalry between schools and were productive of good. The meetings took place during the long winter nights, either weekly or fortnightly.

Every school had one or more prize spellers, and these were selected to lead the match, or, if the school was large, a contest between the girls and boys came off first. Sometimes two of the best spellers were selected by the scholars as leaders, and these would proceed to 'choose sides,' that is, one would choose a fellow pupil who would rise and take his or her place, and then the other, continuing until the list was exhausted. The preliminaries being completed, the contest began. At first the lower end of the class was disposed of, and as time wore on one after another would make a slip and retire, until two or three only were left on either side. Then the struggle became exciting, and scores of eager eyes were fixed on the contestants. With the old hands there was a good deal of fencing, though the teacher usually had a reserve of difficult words to end the fight, which often lasted two or three hours. He failed sometimes, and then it was a drawn battle to be fought out on another occasion.

Debating classes also met and discussed grave questions, upon such old-fashioned subjects as these: 'Which is the most useful to man, wood or iron?' 'which affords the greatest enjoyment, anticipation or participation?' 'which was the greatest general, Wellington or Napoleon?' Those who were to take part in the discussion were always selected at a previous meeting, so that all that had to be done was to select a chairman, and commence the debate. We can give from memory a sample or two of these first attempts. 'Mr. President, ladies and gentlemen, unaccustomed as I am to public speaking, I rise to make a few remarks on this all-important question—Ahem—Mr. President, this is the first time I ever tried to speak in public, and unaccustomed as I am to—to—ahem. Ladies and gentlemen, I think our opponents are altogether wrong in arguing that Napoleon was a greater general than Wellington, ahem—I ask you, Mr. President, did Napoleon ever thrash Wellington? Didn't Wellington always thrash him, Mr. President? Didn't he whip him at Waterloo and take him prisoner? and then to say that he is a greater general than Wellington, why Mr. President, he couldn't hold a candle to him. Ladies and gentlemen, I say that Napoleon wasn't a match for him at all. Wellington licked him every time,—and—yes, licked him every time. I can't think of any more, Mr. President, and I will take my seat, sir, by saying that I'm sure you will decide in our favour from the strong arguments our side has produced.'

After listening to such powerful reasoning, some one of the older spectators would ask Mr. President to be allowed to say a few words on some other important question to be debated, and would proceed to air his eloquence and instruct the youth on such a topic, say, as this: 'Which is the greatest evil, a scolding wife or a smoky chimney?' After this wise the harangue would proceed: — 'Mr. President, I've been almost mad a-listening to the debates of these 'ere youngsters — they don't know nothing at all about the subject. What do they know about the evil of a scolding wife? Wait till they have had one for twenty years and been hammered, and jammed, and slammed, all the while. Wait till they've been scolded, because the baby cried, because the fire wouldn't burn, because the room was too hot, because the cow kicked over the milk, because it rained, because the sun shined, because the hens didn't lay, because the butter wouldn't come, because the old cat had kittens, because they came too soon for dinner, because they were a minute late — before they talk about the worry of a scolding wife. Why, Mr. President, I'd rather hear the clatter of hammers and stones and twenty tin pans, and nine brass kettles, than the din, din, din, of the tongue of a scolding woman; yes, sir, I would. To my mind, Mr. President, a smoky chimney is no more to be compared to a scolding wife than a little nigger is to a dark night.' These meetings were generally well attended and conducted with considerable spirit. If the discussions were not brilliant, and the young debater often lost the thread of his argument, in other words, got things 'mixed,' he gained confidence and learned to talk in public, and to take higher flights. Many of our leading public men learned their first lessons in the art of public speaking in the country debating school.

Apple trees were planted early by the bay settlers, and there were now numerous large orchards of excellent fruit. Pears, plums, cherries, currants, and gooseberries were also common. The apple crop was gathered in October, the best fruit being sent to the cellar for family use during winter, and the balance to the cider mill. These mills were somewhat rude contrivances, but answered the purpose for which they were designed. It was a universal custom to set a dish of apples and a pitcher of cider before every one who came to the house: any departure from this would have been thought disrespectful. The sweet cider was generally boiled down into a syrup, and with apples quartered and cooked in it, was equal to a preserve, and made splendid pies. It was called apple sauce, and found its way to the table thrice a day. There is no better cure for biliousness than a dish of apple sauce.

Then came the potatoes and roots, which had to be dug and brought to the cellar. It was not very nice work, particularly if the ground was damp and cold, to pick them out and throw them in the basket, but it had to be done, and I was compelled to do my share. One good thing about it was that it was never a long job. There was much more fun in gathering the pumpkins and corn into the barn, where it was husked, generally at night, the bright golden ears finding their way into the old crib, from whence it was to come again to fatten the turkeys, the geese, and the ducks for Christmas. It was a very common thing to have husking bees. A few neighbours would be invited, the barn lit with candles, and amid jokes and laughter the husks and ears would fly, until the work was done, when all hands would repair to the house, and after partaking of a hearty supper, leave for home in high spirits.

Then came hog-killing time, a heavy and disagreeable task, but the farmer has many of these, and learns to take them pleasantly. My father, with two or three expert hands, dressed for the occasion, would slaughter and dress ten or a dozen large hogs through the day. There were other actors besides in the play. It would be curious, indeed, if all hands were not employed when work was going on. My part in the performance was to attend the fire under the great kettle, in which the hogs were scalded, and to keep the water boiling, varied at intervals by blowing up bladders with a quill for my own amusement. In the house the fat had to be looked to, and after being washed and tried (the term used for melting), was poured into dishes and set aside to cool and become lard, afterwards finding its way into cakes and pie-crust. The out-door task does not end with the first day either, for the hogs have to be carried in and cut up; the large meat tubs, in which the family supplies are kept, have to be filled; the hams and shoulders to be nicely cut and cured, and the balance packed into barrels for sale.

Close on the heels of this, came sausage-making, when meat had to be chopped, and flavoured, and stuffed into cotton bags or prepared gut. Then the heads and feet had to be soaked and scraped over and over again, and when ready were boiled, the one being converted into headcheese, the other into souse. All these matters, when conducted under the eye of a good house-wife, contributed largely to the comfort and good living of the family. Who is there, with such an experience as mine, that receives these things at the hand of his city butcher and meets them on his table, that does not wish for the moment that he was a boy, and seated at his mother's board, that he might shake off the phantom cat and dog that rise on his plate, and call in one of mother's sausages.

As the fall crept on, the preparations for winter increased. The large roll of full cloth, which had been lately brought from the mill, was carried down, and father and I set out for a tailor, who took our measure and cut out our clothes, which we brought home, and some woman, or perhaps a wandering tailor, was employed to make them up. There was no discussion as to style, and if the fit did not happen to be perfect, there was no one to criticise either the material or the make, nor any arbitrary rules of fashion to be respected. We had new clothes, they were warm and comfortable. What more did we want? A cobbler, too, was brought in to make our boots. My father was quite an expert at shoe-making, but he had so many irons in the fire now that he could not do more than mend or make a light pair of shoes for mother at odd spells. The work then turned out by the sons of St. Crispin was not highly finished. It was coarse and strong, but what was of greater consequence, it wore well. While all this was going on, for the benefit of the male portion of the house, mother and the girls were busy turning the white flannel into shirts and drawers, and the plaid roll that came with it into dresses for themselves. As in the case of our clothes, there was no consulting of fashion-books, for a very good reason, perhaps—there were none to consult. No talk about Miss Brown or Miss Smith, having her dress made this way or that, and I am sure they were far happier and contented than the girls of to day, with all their show and glitter.

The roads at that time, in the fall particularly, were almost impassable until frozen up. In the spring until the frost was out of the ground, and they had settled and dried, they were no better. The bridges were rough wooden affairs, covered with logs, usually flattened on one side with an axe, and the swamps and marshes were made passable by laying logs as nearly of a size as possible close together through them. These were known as corduroy roads, and were no pleasant paths, as all who have tried them know, to ride over for any distance. But in the winter the frost and snow made good travelling everywhere, and hence the winter was the time for the farmer to do his teaming.

One of the first things that claimed attention when the sleighing began, and before the snow got deep in the woods, was to get out the year's supply of fuel. The men set out for the bush before it was fairly light, and commenced chopping. The trees were cut in lengths of about ten feet, and the brush piled in heaps. Then my father, or myself, when I got old enough, followed with the sleigh, and began drawing it, and continued until the wood yard was filled with sound beech and maple, with a few loads of dry pine for kindling. These huge wood-piles always bore a thrifty appearance and spoke of comfort and good cheer within.

Just before Christmas there was always one or two beef cattle to kill. Sheep had also to be slaughtered, with the turkeys, geese and ducks, which had been getting ready for decapitation. After home wants were provided for, the rest went to market.

The winter's work now began in earnest, for whatever may be said about the enjoyment of Canadian winter life, and it is an enjoyable time to the Canadian, there are few who really enjoy it so much as the farmer. He cannot, however, do like bruin, roll himself up in the fall and suck his paw until spring in a state of semi-unconsciousness, for his cares are numerous and imperious, his work varied and laborious. His large stock demands regular attention, and must be fed morning and night. The great barn filled with grain had to be threshed, for his cattle wanted the straw, and the grain must be got out for the market. So day after day he and his men hammer away with the flail, or spread it on the barn floor to be trampled out with horses. Threshing machines were unknown then, as were all the labor-saving machines now so extensively used by farmers. His muscular arm was the only machine he had to rely upon, and if it did not accomplish much, it succeeded in doing its work well, and provided him with all his modest wants. Then the fanning mill came into play to clean the grain, after which it was carried to the granary, from whence again it was taken either to the mill or to the market. Winter was also the time to get out the logs from the woods and to haul them to the mill to be sawed in the spring—we always had a use for boards. These saw mills, built on sap-streams, which ran dry as soon as the spring freshets were over, were, like the cider mills, small rough structures. They had but one upright saw, which, owing to its primitive construction, did not move as now with lightning rapidity, nor did it turn out a very large quantity of stuff. It answered the purpose of the day, however, and that was all that was required or expected of it. Rails, also, had to be split and drawn to where new fences were wanted, or where old ones needed repairs. There was flour, beef, mutton, butter, apples and a score more of things to be taken to market and disposed of. But, notwithstanding all this, the winter was a good, joyful time for the farmer,—a time in which the social requisites of his nature, too, received the most attention. Often the horses would be put to the sleigh and we would set off, well bundled up, to visit some friends a few miles distant, or, as frequently happened, to an uncle or an aunt quite a long distance away in the new settlements. The roads often wound along for miles through the forest, and it was great fun for us youngsters to be dashing along behind a spirited team, now around the trunks of great trees, or under the low-hanging boughs of the spruce or cedar, laden with snow, which sometimes shed their heavy load upon our heads.

But after a while the cold would seize upon us, and then we would wish our journey at an end. The horses, white with frost, would then be pressed on faster, and would bring us at length to the door. In a few moments we would all be seated round the glowing fire, which would soon quiet our chattering teeth, thaw us out, and prepare us to take our place at the table which had been getting ready in the meantime. We were sure to do justice to the good things which the table provided.

'Oh! happy years! once more who would not be a boy.'

Many of these early days start up vividly and brightly before me, particularly since I have grown to be a man and to live amid other surroundings. None of these recollections, however, are more pleasing than some of my drives of a moonlight night, when the sleighing was good, and when the sleigh, with its robes and rugs, was packed with a merry lot of girls and boys. We had no ladies and gentlemen then. Off we would set, spanking along over the crisp snow, which creaked and cracked under the runners, making a low murmuring sound in harmony with the sleigh-bells. When could a more fitting time be found for a pleasure-ride than on one of those clear calm nights, when the earth, wrapt in her mantle of snow, glistened and sparkled in the moonbeams, and the blue vault of heaven glittered with countless stars, whose brilliancy seemed intensified by the cold. When the aurora borealis waved and danced across the northern sky, and the snow noiselessly fell like flakes of silver upon a scene at once inspiriting, exhilarating and joyous. How the merry laugh floats away in the evening air, as we dash along the road! How sweetly the merry song and chorus echoes through the silent wood, while our hearts were a-glow with excitement, and all nature seemed to respond to the happy scene!

We were always on the *qui vive* when the frosty nights set in, for a skating revel on some pond near by, and our eagerness to enjoy the sport frequently led to a ducking. But very soon the large ponds, and then the bay, were frozen over, when we could indulge in the fun to our heart's content. My first attempts were made under considerable difficulties, but perseverance bridges the way over many obstacles, and so with my father's skates, which were more than a foot long, and which required no little ingenuity to fasten to my feet, I made my first attempt on the ice. Soon, however, in the growth of my feet, this trouble was overcome, and I could whirl over the ice with anyone. The girls did not share in this exhilarating exercise then, indeed it would have been thought quite improper. As our time was usually taken up with school through the day, and with such chores as feeding cattle and bringing wood in for the fire when we returned at night, we would sally out after supper, on moonlight nights, and full of life and hilarity fly over the ice, singing and shouting, and making the night ring with our merriment. There was plenty of room on the bay, and early in the season there were miles of ice, smooth as glass and clear as crystal, reflecting the stars which sparkled and glittered beneath our feet, as though we were gliding over a sea of silver set with brilliants.

> Away, away, on the smooth ice we glide,
>   Fair Cynthia shines bright above us;
> We heed not the old, while gaily we glide
>   O'er the water that slumbers beneath us.
> Our hearts are light as the falling frost,
>   That sparkles on the snow-banks' brow;
> The north wind's blast we feel it not,
>   For we're warmed by excitement now.
> Hurrah! boys, hurrah! skates on and away,
> You may lag at your work, but never at play;
> Give wing to your feet, and make the ice ring,
> Give voice to your mirth, and merrily sing.

CANNIFF HAIGHT, who was born in 1825 at Adolphustown, Ontario, and died in 1901 in Toronto, is described in Henry Morgan's *Canadian Men and Women of the Time* (1898) as a "Canadian through and through...proud of his country, its progress and institutions." A druggist and bookseller by trade, Haight also participated in the educational life of his community and in 1842 was instrumental in establishing the first country library in Upper Canada. A frequent contributor on historical and other subjects to magazines and newspapers, he is also the author of *Country Life in Canada Fifty Years Ago* (1885) — a compilation in book form of sketches which first appeared in *Rose-Belford's Canadian Monthly* and *The Canadian Methodist Magazine* — *Here and There in the Home Land. England, Scotland and Ireland, as Seen by a Canadian* (1895), *Before the Coming of the Loyalists* (1897), *Coming of the Loyalists* (1899), and *A Genealogical Narrative of the Daniel Haight Family* (1899).

BLACKFEET INDIANS CROSSING A RIVER.
(From a Sketch by Sydney Hall.)

Captain E. D. Clark

"In the North-West with 'Sitting Bull'"*

TO ATTEMPT TO WRITE ANYTHING for public perusal about this vast territory, or one's experiences in it, is only to follow in the footsteps of many others, and perhaps to fail signally. However, at the urgent request of one very dear to me, for whom I would do almost anything, I nervously make my virgin effort—namely, to write, in as concise a manner as possible, about what I have seen and done during my four years' sojourn in the wilds.

To faithfully describe the great North-West is not an easy task. To call it a huge, endless prairie, sometimes rolling, sometimes level, intermixed with vast, swift-running rivers, gives but a poor idea of what it really is. As one travels from the east towards the setting sun, one passes through a variety of climates and of countries. In 1875, I was in a country where one received but a faint idea of what the prairie really is. During a day's ride, I met with beautiful lakes, fine belts of tamarac, red pine, and birch, and places where nature had formed the most picturesque of parks—really laid out farms. Though one sees but little game there beyond the feathered tribes, yet carcasses of the mighty buffalo point out that they too were there one day. Such is the country from the Province of Manitoba to what is called The Fertile Belt, by which I presume is meant the Valley of the

*Rose-Belford's Canadian Monthly, 5 July 1880, pp. 66-73.

Saskatchewan. Along this valley, which has been described by the author of the 'Lone Land,' it has been my lot to travel many hundreds of miles; and truly may it be called 'the fertile belt.' The soil is of the richest kind, the timber good and in large quantities, and farming could easily be carried on. The summer, while it lasts, is most glorious, and vegetation is very rapid. But winter, in all its intensity, comes to this part of the North-West early in November, or sooner, and holds it in an iron grip for six long, weary months. Everything is hushed into solemn and oppressive silence. The mighty Saskatchewan rolls on, but under massive blocks of ice. Terrible storms sweep over the country, and the settler has naught to do but tend his few cattle, trap a little, and try to sleep away the rest of the day. The red man seeks the timber, where blue smoke rolling up from his lodge indicates his whereabouts. The cold is severe. I remember that, in February, the thermometer for over one week averaged forty degrees below zero; and generally there was a good breeze. Between that country and the one I now write from, two vast barren plains lie, to cross which it takes many a long, weary march. It is on these two plains where one meets the huge bands of buffalo and antelope, of which I will subsequently write. On these stretches the eye rests on naught, for day after day, but one long, everlasting line of horizon. Here it is where the traveller has often to make 'a dry camp' — a camp without water — and if he carries no grain his weary steed makes but a sorry supper. In crossing these plains, the vastness and the endless space oppresses one; there is nothing but sky and land, and an indescribable stillness reigns over all — a stillness such as one often notices before the burst of a storm. On these prairies fire is most alarming. The parched grass is like tinder. I have seen a spark from a pipe occasion a fire which, in a very short space of time, rolling its smoke sky-ward, travelled at a tremendous pace before the wind, and could be seen for many days afterwards, both by day and night. The only way to stop these prairie fires, if one is coming directly on your road, is to set fire to the prairie behind you. This stops the advancing fire, but the new one goes on, till it either meets some burnt place or the wind turns round. It rains so seldom that to trust to rain to check a fire is somewhat of a forlorn hope. Once these plains are crossed, one meets with a different country and a different climate. I refer now to the country lying at the foot of that magnificent range the Rocky Mountains. Here we have large undulating plains, with rivers of the most transparent water; and along these rivers are fine valleys — or bottoms, as they are called here—in which is found excellent pasturage. In many places the rivers flow through 'cut banks,' frequently more than one hundred feet in height. Cattle and horses feed out the whole winter long, and in the spring look well. There is a species of grass of which the buffalo are very fond called 'bunch grass,' and from this great nourishment is afforded. The climate during the summer is very fine, and here also vegetation is rapid. The weather during the winter is greatly influenced by the Pacific breezes, which come to us across the mountains. The thermometer occasionally falls low, but on the whole the weather is very temperate. For instance, on the 3rd of February last, I see by my diary, that I played cricket, and well I remember the day—genial and warm, not a trace of winter to be seen, with the exception of the leafless trees. The principal tree-growth on these river bottoms is cotton-wood, but fir and pine can be got at the foot of the mountains, and also in the Porcupine Hills, a range some sixty miles in length which lies close under the Rockys. The Pacific breezes which float to us over the mountains are called 'chanoukes,' and last many days at a time. They come very suddenly. In an incredibly short space of time, the thermometer has been known to run up to thirty-five degrees. When these chanoukes blow, all the windows and doors are thrown open. This in mid-winter is not what one may see in the Valley of the Saskatchewan.

Here is the country of that great and warlike tribe the Blackfoot Indians, a race always held in great awe by other tribes. The Blackfeet are a fine people, but, from all I can learn, greatly degenerated. Small-pox, some years ago, made havoc among them, taking off many hundreds. But what helped to impoverish them, and kill them morally, was the illicit traffic in whiskey, carried on for many years by gangs of desperadoes from the neighbouring territory of Montana. These men, many of whom had a halter awaiting them in their own country, were of the most desperate character, whose business was to traffic alcohol to the wretched Indians for their horses and robes. Many a good horse has been purchased for a quart of this poison. As long as this traffic was permitted, the Indian sank lower and lower. He lost all he had, his children and women were starved, and murder and rapine swept the country. As you know, the Government of Canada organized, some years ago, a mounted constabulary of 300 strong, for the sole purpose of maintaining order and discipline in these vast territories, and truly the small force has worked wonders. The Indians now are tractable and amenable to the law, and have, also, a pretty good idea of what that law is. Here, in the very heart of the great Blackfoot country, where formerly a man never ventured abroad without his Henry rifle, and that man, for the most part, one of the Montana desperadoes before mentioned, all is now as quiet and orderly as in any civilized country, and the farmer and stock-raiser carry on their vocations without fear of molestation. And all this change has been wrought by a handful of red-coated constabulary! But their mere presence has not done all this. It has taken downright hard work, the utmost of vigilance and perseverance, to extinguish the liquor traffic. The advent of the police naturally caused many settlers to swarm round their different posts, and to these, and even to the police themselves, did the whiskey dealer transfer his trade from the Indians.

Few people out of these territories have any conception of the hardships and privations that have been undergone by the police in their endeavours to break up this whiskey traffic. Day after day on horseback; night after night sleeping out with but one blanket; your provisions generally a buffalo tongue and a hard biscuit, stuffed into your wallet; and these expeditions, as a rule, during the winter. Canada has good reason to be proud of the stuff of which her hardy sons are made, and England has no reason to feel ashamed of their pluck and endurance.

Comparison has often been made between our own and our neighbours' treatment of the Indians. There large military forces have to be kept on the frontier; the Indian steals and pilfers; he fears and distrusts a white man, and is in perpetual warfare with the 'Long Knives,' as he terms the Americans. If one Indian kills another the authorities simply compel him to pay the deceased's family so many horses. The Indian policy of the United States is rotten to the core. The United States Indian agent holds his office for a term, and gain is his sole object. If the wretched Indian steals, surely he is stolen from in return. To exterminate the Indian is the practical effect of the policy on the other side. How different it is with us! An Indian is made to understand that he is treated the same as a white man — if either does wrong he is punished. The Government makes a treaty with the Indian for his land, and that treaty is strictly observed.

Last year wild and conflicting were the rumours that spread over this country regarding the Sioux Indians, who were then at war with the United States. After the signal victory gained by these Indians over General Custer's command, the half-breed settlers felt that the climax was reached, and that no longer was there safety for them in the country, so they drew their stakes and 'cleared'—where to, apparently, no one cared. The police posts in this section were strengthened by four guns and one hundred men. But there was no occasion for alarm—everything remained as usual. The Blackfeet tribe offered their services to the Police in case the dreaded Sioux came, and for this they have been most graciously thanked by Her Majesty the Queen.

The war with the Sioux commenced in this way. Learning that gold was to be found in the Black Hills, the land of the Sioux—ceded to them, I understand, by treaty—the white men poured in by thousands. This the Sioux, naturally enough, resented, and of course skirmishes between the would-be miners and the Lords of the Soil took place. Troops were sent to protect the whites, and the whole summer a continual strife was kept up between the troops and the Indians, the latter fighting for what they considered their rights. The Sioux refused to go into the Indian Agencies and were consequently followed up by large forces of infantry and cavalry. At the 'Big Horn,' on the Yellow stone, 'Sitting Bull,' the head 'Soldier of the Sioux,' made a stand and for twelve days watched by his scouts the approach of General Custer's command. The result of the meeting is well known. The Americans call it a massacre, but I, an Englishman, fail to see it in that light. Since then 'Sitting Bull' and his people wandered about, until at last he found himself on British soil; and again the fright of last year came upon our timorous friends, the half-breeds. Hearing of the arrival of this much-talked of Indian warrior, the officer commanding the police in this district, Lieutenant-Colonel A. G. Irvine, determined upon at once visiting him, and ascertaining his intentions. I was lucky enough to be of the party; which consisted of three officers besides myself, two or three men who were on their way to another post, and two waggon drivers. These, with the interpreter, formed the whole of the party to meet the man whose name is held in terror throughout the Northern Territories of the United States. It was felt, and with no ordinary pride, that our scarlet coats were far greater protection than any armed escort. Here is a man who has caused regiment after regiment of American soldiers to be under arms, and many general officers to lay their heads together in consultation against him; a man whose strategy and generalship outwitted one of the best of rising general officers; a man held up as the most blood-thirsty of Indians, being quietly interviewed by a small party wearing Her Majesty's scarlet. Such an instance is, surely, a worthy tribute, if only from a savage, to the glorious colour which is the pride of every Englishman, and which has won respect in all quarters of the globe.

A ride of some hundred and forty miles brought our party within sight of 'Sitting Bull's' camp, and an hour after first seeing the camp through our glasses, we were smartly cantering up an incline, at the top of which hundreds of savages stood, with extended hands to greet us. So eager were they to shake us by the hand that it was utterly impossible to move on. Loud and prolonged were the grunts of approval as each Sioux grasped the hand of one of us. Poor wretches! What a red-letter day in their lives, grasping the hand of a white man as a friend! At length we were enabled to push through to the end of the camp, and turn our horses loose. Oh, would I had the pen that could describe the scene faithfully that ensued when dismounted. We were at once surrounded by men, women, and thousands of children, all eager to shake the hand of the red-coat chief. At first the women and children were very shy, almost afraid. Colonel Irvine chucked a small child under the chin, and they gained confidence. We apparently were to them objects of great curiosity, judging from the talk that they carried on among themselves. I was particularly struck with the looks of some of the women, many of whom were very pretty and graceful. The manner of throwing one blanket over two heads, gipsy style, added to the picturesqueness of the scene — many of the children as well as the squaws were handsomely dressed, which rather surprised me, knowing of their long and weary pilgrimage. Quantities of elk teeth were to be seen on their dresses. Elk teeth are very valuable, there being only two teeth in the animal that the Indian takes; so when you see a squaw with several hundreds of these teeth on her dress, it is sufficient proof that her 'lord' is well-to-do.

While standing in the midst of a large crowd of women and children, I observed one Indian of huge stature pushing his way towards us through the throng, and gesticulating towards some one on the outside of the crowd. We followed him to a group of Indians, in the midst of whom stood a man of middle size, with a face of great intelligence. He remained motionless until we were within a few feet of him, when his face lightened up, and with a bright smile he stepped forward and gave the white mother's chief a hearty grip of the hand. Then he shook hands with our whole party, followed by his huge companions. We stood before 'Sitting Bull' and his head men. The grip of those men spoke volumes to me. It spoke trust and confidence in the white mother's soldiers, and a complete throwing off of suspicion and dread. It appeared to say: 'You do not blame us unheard; we have been sinned against more than sinning. Now, at last, we have met you, and we know to-day what we never knew before—that we are safe. You don't want our lives—we can live in peace.' I may be thought sentimental in all this; but I maintain that none could have seen that proud warrior, with his head soldiers around him, as I did that day, and not have had some such thoughts.

We were then told that the council lodge was being erected, and we promised to go there as soon as we had dined. After dinner we went to the council lodge, a large erection of skins, capable of holding many hundred people. A buffalo robe was spread for us to sit down upon, close in front of 'Sitting Bull,' his head soldiers and chiefs. Here I must describe the difference between the soldier and the chief. The chiefs are the head men in the camp in the time of peace; they do not fight, but appear to look after the internal economy of the camp. In time of war they fall back, and the soldiers take command of the camp; in fact, martial law prevails. A 'chief,' named 'Pretty Bear,' opened the proceedings with a prayer. He sat on the left of 'Sitting Bull,' and taking his seat he let go his buffalo robe and displayed his huge muscular body, painted a bright orange. Next to 'Pretty Bear' sat 'Bear's Head,' an old Indian with a complete bear's head on his own. The skull had been hollowed out, and he wore this strange head-gear as a cap. When he looked down, and his face was hid, his appearance was most ludicrous. One saw before him what appeared to be a bear with an Indian's body. All the men had 'coup sticks' on their persons. A 'coup stick' is a flexible stick covered with buffalo hide, at the end of which is a heavy round or egg-shaped stone. These sticks are most formidable weapons, and are used for giving a wounded opponent his *quietus*. I understand they did terrible execution in the 'Custer Massacre.' All the men, women and children swarmed into the council lodge, and stood four or five deep inside, and many hundreds were unable to get in. Great was the interest and anxiety displayed by the women. The result of the council was to them a life of peace, or a return to what they had just left, with a pretty certain promise of speedy annihilation. No wonder that these poor people took a terrible interest in the proceedings of that day. The opening ceremony was very impressive. 'Pretty Bear,' holding the large peace pipe in his hands, called on God Almighty and the spirit of their grandfather (who this gentleman was, when in the flesh, I never ascertained) to look upon them that day and have pity on them. The warriors all held

169

their right hands aloft. 'Pretty Bear' reminded the Almighty that he had been raised to eat buffalo meat in order to be strong, but that to-day he was nothing. He pointed the pipe to the south, saying: 'Thunder is my relation there;' to the west and north, saying that there they would be friends; to the east, saying, if he had friends there, he would be strong. He then referred to the Queen, saying: 'My mother, take the pipe; understand, we will all smoke for the country to be full of plenty, and the land good.' 'I am going to light the pipe straight,' he continued. By the word 'straight' he meant with 'truth.' He then handed the pipe to 'Sitting Bull,' who lit it with a bit of buffalo dung, refusing a match that was offered him. (The Indian considers a lucifer match to be deception.) The pipe was a huge article, the bowl made out of some red stone, the stem very long and studded with brass nails. When it was lighted, it was in a very solemn manner pointed to the four quarters of the compass, and then held to the white mother's great chief, Lieutenant-Colonel Irvine, who smoked, great silence being observed. Sitting Bull, holding the bowl while everyone of us smoked, said in a solemn voice: 'My grandfather, have pity on me; we are going to be raised with a new people.' After all the party had smoked, 'Sitting Bull' smoking with each in turn, the pipe was handed back to 'Pretty Bear,' who dug a hole in the earth, deposited the ashes therein, covered the hole up, and, taking the pipe to pieces, placed it on the ground over the ashes. This they regard as a most solemn oath. Then the pow-wow was commenced by 'Sitting Bull,' followed by several of the warriors. The purport of their speeches was that they claimed to be of British descent; that all the rivers ran down to the sea, and so far was their land. The white men came from the other side of the sea. They all complained bitterly of the way they had been treated by the 'Long Knives,' and said they had been fighting on the defensive. They had been raised in a blanket, and to live on buffalo meat, and that was all they wanted, and to be allowed to trade their robes. They had come to see the white mother's country, where their grandfather's spirit told them they would have peace, and they wanted to know if the white mother would protect them, and prevent the 'Long Knives' from following them.

An incident which I have not mentioned caused them great uneasiness, namely, the advent of three Americans in their camp. They spoke with bitterness at being followed by these Americans, and had not allowed them to leave the camp until we arrived. These three people consisted of a Roman Catholic priest, a scout of the American army, who acted as guide, and an interpreter. The priest's mission, he informed us, was to tell the Sioux the terms on which they could return to their agencies, namely, the giving up of all their horses and arms. He also stated he had expected to find them on American soil, but had followed their trail up to the present camp. None but a priest would have dared to enter the Sioux camp on American soil, and the other two men trusted to his protection. Had not 'Sitting Bull' been told by one of the police officers, previous to the arrival of these people, that if any stranger came into their camp he was to send and notify the police of the fact, there is but little doubt that the scout's and interpreter's hair would have been dangling to some lodge pole shortly after their foolhardy act of entering the camp. 'Sitting Bull' as good as told us so.

After a short interview with the priest, he went with us, and we explained to 'Sitting Bull' the purport of this unlooked-for visit. After smoking a pipe with the priest, 'Sitting Bull' called the Almighty to witness that he was smoking with the Father; he never smoked with the whites: and adding if, in what they were going to say, there should be any lie between them, that all people might know it. The priest explained to him that if he returned, he must give up his horses and arms, when his life would be safe, and the lives of his people. The reply given to this was somewhat of a poser: 'You tell me you are a messenger of God. I hardly believe you, for God raised me on a horse, and you want me to give my horses to the Americans.' He also said to the priest: 'You know, as the messenger of God, that the Americans tried to kill me. Why did you wait till half my people were killed before you came? I don't believe the Americans ever saw God, and that is why they would never listen to me.' Another warrior asked: 'Did God or the Queen tell the American people to take our horses and arms away?' On the priest asking for an answer as to whether they were going to return or remain where they were, 'Sitting Bull' turned to the white mother's chief (Lieutenant-Colonel Irvine), and asked: 'The white mother, will she protect us if we remain?' On being again assured of this, he turned to the priest: 'Why should I return,' he said, 'to give up my arms and horses? The Americans have nothing to give me. I am going to remain with the white mother's children.'

The following is said to have happened in 1868, in 'Sitting Bull's' camp, and, if true, of which I have little doubt, it is no mystery why the Sioux doubt even the Church. A priest of the Roman Church visited the Sioux camp, baptized several children, spoke to the sol-

171

diers and chiefs about living at peace with the Americans, and very shortly after his departure a troop of cavalry rode into the camp, killing men, women and children right and left. It is said that 'Sitting Bull' then declared that he would never again believe an American, no matter in what garb he came. But the visit and intentions of the man of God—Rev. Father Abbot Martin—there is no doubt of. He considered it a part of his duty, and is deserving of great credit for his nerve and pluck in endeavouring to recall the lost sheep to the spiritual fold. But the conduct of the scout is open to serious criticism. That he came as a guide to the priest is, of course, a fact; but whether that was merely a cloak is another question. It is a patent fact that a good deal of jealousy existed among certain American officers at the amount of 'Kudos' gained by General Custer; and to make an Indian name such as Custer's is the ambition of not a few officers. This guide told us he was General Miles' head scout. Supposing 'Sitting Bull' and his people had moved across the line to go into the agency, the question is, would this guide have become again his real self, the head scout? Would he have given information to his chief of the exact strength and the feelings of the Sioux, and would this information have been to the detriment of 'Sitting Bull' and his band? Would they have been attacked? I don't say any of this would have happened, but I do say that finding a man in the camp who was employed all last year as a scout, naturally gave rise to these thoughts.

An Indian pow-wow is usually a long tedious affair, there being so much repetition, and this one was no exception. We all felt relieved when all was over. The priest came to our tent and had supper with us. We found him a very nice fellow, well-read and gentlemanly, a Swiss by birth. After supper I took a stroll through the camp, which was composed of some 200 lodges, and close by there were about 150 lodges of Yankton Indians, a branch of the Sioux. I never saw such a happy people as were those in the camp that night. Sounds of rejoicing were echoed far and wide. They felt *that* night, for the first time for many a long, weary month, that they might henceforth sleep in peace, with no fear of being suddenly awakened by the sharp, ringing report of the Springfield carbine, or by the clatter of horses galloping through their camp, with sound of trumpet. They had journeyed on and on, till at last they had found a haven of rest. Small nude savages were riding colts, two on the one animal, at miniature stone forts, defended by other little savages, who, as the mounted assaulting parties dashed up to their forts, rushed out, brandishing buffalo robes at the colts' heads. This had the effect of making the small animals buck and rear, much to the children's merriment. Although but children's play, it was in reality schooling both ponies and children for real warfare. A horse fears nothing so much as a buffalo-robe, and it is by no means an uncommon practice for the Indian to use a robe for the purpose of frightening an opponent's horse. In the lodges the tom-tom (a rude drum) was in full swing, and to this, coupled with the squaws' chants, which are not unmusical, was the dance going merrily on. I saw many horses with the brand of the late General Custer's regiment, 7th Cavalry, on the hip, and also numerous carbines and ammunition pouches taken from the same regiment.

In the midst of this rejoicing but one man seemed unable to shake off a feeling of sadness, and this was 'Sitting Bull.' He wandered about apparently musing over all that he had gone through. I went up to him and offered him my pipe, which he took and smoked with me. I fancy what was weighing on his mind was the idea of giving up what he calls his country, as well as thought for the rest of his people who are still on the other side. All days have an end, and at eleven o'clock I was by no means sorry to turn in under my blankets—which I did thinking what a singular event it was for three or four white men to be calmly sleeping in dreaded 'Sitting Bull's' camp. I was in the tent of Colonel Irvine, who had also retired for the night. I had just finished reading a little of 'Bleak House,' with my last pipe, when I heard some one moving near the tent, and the next minute 'Sitting Bull' and one of his head warriors pushed aside the curtain of the tent, and quietly sat down at the foot of our beds. This was a most unexpected visit, and in order to find out what he wanted the interpreter had to be awakened. On the interpreter coming in, it was found that 'Sitting Bull' wanted to see the white mother's chief about a man from whom some of his young men had, years ago, stolen some horses on the Missouri. He was anxious to know what he was to do. He was too poor to pay at present. To show that he was willing to do all in his power to repay the debt, he told Colonel Irvine he had given up some horses, and also some gold-dust. After this was settled, he, in quiet and subdued tones, answered all our questions about the battle at the 'Big Horn.' Many things he said about the Americans amused me greatly. The following shows his respective estimates of the Americans and himself. He stated that, shortly after the fight with Custer, some American soldiers came to him and asked him to go down to Washington with eight or ten of his head men to see the President, and so settle matters. His reply to them was, 'The President is as big a fool as you soldiers are; if he wants to see me he can come up here!' When telling us this and other things, he appeared much amused, for occasionally a broad smile broke over his face.

I was particularly anxious to get General Custer's watch and ring, which we heard was in the possession of one of the warriors, to forward them to the poor widow; but I was much disappointed to find that both had been lost when crossing the Missouri. The crossing of this river was one of 'Sitting Bull's' narrow escapes from the American troops. The day after he had crossed the river, and when camped on its banks, a sudden rising of the water carried everything before it. His people lost everything they had, even to their very lodges. Had they been one day later in arriving at the river, their fate would have been doubtful: crossing the river would have been impossible, and troops shortly after were marching up on the south side in search of them. 'Sitting Bull' says the great Manitou was with him.

E. DALRYMPLE CLARK was the son of a British major general and a nephew of Sir John A. Macdonald by his first marriage. He joined the Northwest Mounted Police upon its founding, in 1873, as one of nine officers. Clark began as paymaster and quartermaster, and quickly rose to the rank of Sub-Inspector, then to Adjutant. On October 2, 1880, just three months after the publication of "In the North-West with 'Sitting Bull,'" described by Clark as his "virgin effort," the young man became the first commissioned officer to die in service, succumbing to an attack of gastric fever while posted at Fort Walsh.

CANADIAN COW-BOY LIFE—DINNER IN THE TENT.

Drawn from life by A. H. Heming.

175

NIGHT FISHING IN THE CREEK.

ROLPH, SMITH & C.º

176

Archibald Lampman

"Fishing in Rice Lake"*

RICE LAKE, which is probably known to many of my readers, is a beautiful little sheet of water, embedded among hills gleaming in the autumn with yellow patches of matted rice, which lifts its thin stalks through five or six feet of water to a height of two feet perhaps above the surface. Sprinkled with small islands, steep-banked and covered with dark, thick wood, reflected in the sleepy stillness of its glassy surface, the lake seems on a calm summer's morning like a little patch of dreamland dropped into the midst of the woody hills that gird it round.

The sun had risen, and not a breath of wind stirred the magic stillness of the scene. Our boats, provided with the necessary tackle both for trolling and still fishing, shot out from the old wharves below the village of Gore's Landing, over the sleeping waters, as we watched the tangled weeds below us, tall and thick in the shallow bay — hiding place of many a staid, saturnine, black bass, who swept majestically away as we passed above him, scared by the whirl of the water from the glittering oar blades; or impudent sunfish, swaggering and indifferent, sunning his contented snub-face in the morning light; countless perch and minnows, skimming hither and thither, picking up occasional scraps of eatable matter, and often narrowly escaping the yawning jaws of their kingly tyrants, the bass.

*Forest and Stream, 10 Aug. 1882, pp. 28-29.

There were three of us in the boat—a fat old gentleman in the stern, myself, and a tough denizen of the neighborhood to pull the oars—a noted character, brown, hardened, muscles like wire, a miraculous fisherman, a miraculous duck shooter, thoroughly acquainted with all the best spots for fishing or shooting, and discreetly silent about the same. The old gentleman had command of the trolling line, which was accordingly let out as soon as we had got clear of the bay and into deep water, the brass spoon spinning merrily behind at a distance of perhaps a hundred feet. For some time we kept our course straight out into the lake, then turned and skirted the rice bed between two of the islands, in hopes of alluring from the tangled recesses of the rice shade one of those lounging fellows who are generally loafing lazily about the edges of the bed looking for something worth eating. The maskalonge is a swaggering, violent, greedy fellow, but not very cautious—like some of his avaricious counterparts among men he often snatches at anything that glitters, quite heedless of the uselessness and danger of it.

We had not gone far when we were startled by "Bless my soul," from the fat gentleman who was glaring, purple-faced, behind him and pulling hard at his line. I came to his assistance and as the oarsman pulled on we leisurely drew in the line. Our captive struggled bravely, flinging himself several times out of the water and whirling in wild circles as we got him nearer to our side. At length, tired and weakened, his long striped frame was transferred from his native element to the bottom of our boat, his desperate exertions to escape our grasp nearly terrifying our fat friend out of his wits. A blow on the back of the head from the "headache stick" which we had brought with us, soon, however, convinced the prisoner that a state of complete rest was most conducive to his happiness; though the old gentleman still looked with no very assured glance upon the long rows of sharp vindictive teeth that fortified the jaws of the fallen hero.

As we coasted along the side of one of the islands, a beautiful wooded hillock rising from the placid water, stony-shored with wild creepers and grape vines trailing to the water's edge, we captured another of the bright-eyed tyrants and one or two bass.

After this we resolved to row back again to the mainland, and try our chances at still fishing, for we had taken care to provide ourselves with the necessary tackle. The water was still glassy, smooth and too clear to afford us much hope of success. However, we dropped anchor a few yards from a stony point, between which and the mainland stretched a reedy swamp, lined with rushes. The great, white water-lilies, opened wide to the sunlight, gleaming here and there through the reeds, two or three dreamy cranes drifting off over the water, casting their long, dark shadows over its sleeping surface. Our anchor rested on a bed of stones and the water was clear, deep and almost free from weeds. It was a favorite place for the black bass, and our rods were quickly adjusted. The unsuspecting crawfish, gathered for us by some village urchin from his rocky habitation, was cautiously extracted from the swarming can, wherein but a moment before he had been lustily clawing his neighbors, and the sharp hook inserted under his tail—that lithe, graceful little tail that had so often aided him in dashing out of danger's reach at a magic speed—and drawn through his body, out at the throat. Now inert and almost lifeless, the tempting bait was cast into the still water and sank till the float rested upright on the surface.

Some time we waited under the hot sky and with the mirrored water between us, in that dreamy revery which makes the sedate amusement of fishing the philosopher's cherished enjoyment, and recalls to us the figures of genial Izaak Walton and many others whose footsteps will be traced beside these native brooks to the end of time. Presently my float descended to the depths, slowly, majestically, solemnly, evidently borne off by some proud old veteran, too philosophical to make a fuss over any bait however fat and tempting. I tightened my line, and instantly my captive was awakened to the danger of his position, made off for the open lake until he was brought to a halt by the cautious effort of my hand. I found him no compliant prisoner, and it was not without considerable trouble that I laid his black side upon the bottom of the boat. After this we caught several bass of from two to four pounds weight, and lost several, one of which saw fit to go off with the better part of the old gentleman's tackle, causing considerable trouble and a great deal of unnecessary blasphemy.

After this last event we weighed anchor at the intercession of our fat friend—who was convinced that the fish, having now learned the trick, would proceed to further violation of the principles of honor and run off with all the other rods and lines in the boat—and rowed over the rice-beds to the other side of the lake, a distance of about three miles and a half.

Here we found the mouth of the river Otonabee flowing through a vast marsh, overgrown with reeds, rushes and wild rice and fringed with stunted trees, the home of the frog and the mosquito. After pulling a few hundred yards up the stream, we cast anchor again in a bend of the river, and here, almost under the shade of the trees, we

179

dropped our lines into the deeps and found better luck than ever. Several magnificent fish were soon stretched stiff and stark on the inhospitable boards of our treacherous craft, and it was not till sunset that our hardy oarsman weighed his anchor and we took our contented way, sun-tanned and ravenously hungry, back to the quiet little village, nestling among its trees on the steep lakeside, where our stomachs were plentifully refreshed and our minds cheered by reflection upon the gratifying success of our day's work.

ARCHIBALD LAMPMAN was born in 1861 at Morpeth, Canada West, and died in 1899 at Ottawa, Ontario. When he was six his father, an Anglican clergyman, moved the family to Gore's Landing on Rice Lake. Here Lampman became acquainted with Susanna Moodie and Catharine Parr Traill. As a student at Trinity College in Toronto, Lampman began writing poetry which he contributed to the college magazine, *Rouge et Noir*. After graduating in 1882, he spent only four months as a teacher before deciding he would prefer the life of a civil servant. He worked in Ottawa as a clerk in the Post Office from 1883 until his death. Lampman's reputation rests on his poetry, above all on his nature lyrics which reveal the same faithfulness to detail so often expressed by the sketchers of the nineteenth century. From February 6, 1892, to July 1, 1893, he collaborated with William Wilfred Campbell and Duncan Campbell Scott on "At the Mermaid Inn," a weekly column in *The Globe* for the discussion of ideas. In 1895, he was invited into the Royal Society of Canada. The only volumes of poetry published during Lampman's lifetime were *Among the Millet, And Other Poems* (1888) and *Lyrics of Earth* (1895). Collections published posthumously include *Alcyone* (1899), *The Poems of Archibald Lampman* (1900), and *At the Long Sault and Other New Poems* (1943).

It may have been to this sketch that Lampman was referring when he wrote his friend, John Ritchie, on August 22, 1882 that: "I have been thinking lately that something might be done with short sketches, descriptions of character and the like in the manner somewhat of Dickens — subjects such as 'Village Life,' 'Musical Professors' ('School Boards'!), etc."[1]

---

[1] Carl Y. Connor, *Archibald Lampman: Canadian Poet of Nature* (1929; Ottawa: Borealis, 1977), p. 59.

'FROM THE OUTSIDE I DIDN'T THINK MUCH OF MRS. PORTHERIS'S HOUSE'

Sara Jeannette Duncan

[Buying Insurance], "Woman's World"*

I WOULD BE INSURED. Straightaway I betook myself to an English accident insurance company's office to ascertain the nature of the preliminaries. It was in an unfamiliar part of the city, dingy and populous and given over to the habitation of brokers. Not a petticoat was to be seen in all the length and breadth of the street. The elevator boy looked curiously at me as we ascended, the clerks stared. I felt like a book agent, but I persevered. Presently I was ushered into the inner sanctum of a tall and portly gentleman, who inquired, in a voice of patient condescension, what my business might be.

"I want to take out an accident insurance policy," I said. "May it please your gracious majesty," I wanted to add, but I didn't.

"Ah! You know, of course, the restrictions under which we issue policies to ladies!"

"No," I said, "I don't. I know of a good many restrictions under which my unfortunate sex is compelled to labor, but I haven't heard of any that apply specially to insurance policies."

"Well," responded Pooh Bah, "they unhappily exist. There is a strong prejudice against insuring women at all against accident. Our company, however, I am happy to say, has so far conquered this prejudice as to issue accident policies to such women as we consider good

*The Globe, 1 Sept. 1886, p. 6; 3 Sept. 1886, p. 6.

183

risks. Now you, I should think from your appearance, would be a very good risk."

"Indeed!" I said. "Thanks. I have been known as an excellent loss, but I think I would prefer being a good risk. And how much do you pay me if I get hurt?"

"That is a truly feminine interrogation," *dit* Pooh Bah, with a far away smile of superiority. "It wholly depends upon the amount of your policy what sum we pay you, and upon whether you are sufficiently hurt that we pay you anything at all."

"Really! And may I enquire how much is sufficient in your idea of accident that requires compensation!"

"Well, you see, our policies, when held by women, are only paid in the event of—of demise."

"Then I've got to die first?"

"That, unfortunately, is our rule."

"It makes a difference, doesn't it? Now, my idea of insurance included some sort of compensation to myself at so much per week for the long or short but more or less unpleasant time that should precede that event, in case the conspiracy of the Toronto contractors against my connection with the sidewalk should prove fatal."

He looked at me with some anxiety, but doubtless concluded that it was only temporary.

"Am I to understand that you grant policies to men payable in the event of death and partially payable in the event of accident, but to women payable only in the event of death? And why?"

"The prejudice is an old one and has its root in the absolute control that husbands formerly had over their wives. A man might insure his wife's life against accident and then take pains to bring the accident about, you see. He might—as an illustration—he might throw her into the well!"

Whereupon it occurred to me that we should be thankful for pumps as well as higher education.

"Further," said His Insuranceship, "it is much more difficult to define the precise extent of injury to a woman, or to know what constitutes accident in her case. A man might inflict a blow upon his wife with a domestic utensil—"

"Merely corroborative detail intended to give verisimilitude to an otherwise bald and uninteresting narrative." Said I absently—"He might hit her with a poker. Go on."

—"And she would doubtless consider it an accident, whereas we

184

might look upon it in the nature of legitimate warfare." "From a masculine point of view," I said, "it would doubtless be legitimate warfare. But proceed."

"Not—not precisely," he said, "not privately—personally—I mean —in my own opinion—it's very warm to-day?"

"Yes," I said, "it's very warm. I believe I will bid you good afternoon."

"And you think you will not take out one of our policies. I assure you you could not do a better thing for—for your future."

"Yes," I said, "no doubt—for the future. But as a present and ever-present defence against the possibilities of the King-street pavement your policy would be, in the language of 'Don Onofrio,' 'of no use at all.' "

If he had seen "Don Caesar" I suppose it would have been different, but as it was I heard him distinctly remark as I entered the elevator that they never issued policies to lunatics anyway.

* * *

—"Be not discouraged, O my soul!" I whispered to myself as I stood in the august presence of another insurance agent yesterday. "Though Pooh Bah and the British Association conspire against thee, yet will this Canadian company surely take thee up."

* * *

—And I addressed the head and front of a Canadian company's Toronto branch, a genial gentleman on a revolving chair, saying to him:—"Will you be good enough to tell me whether this company has progressed far enough along the lines of modern thought to grant accident policies to women, payable in the event of injury as well as death?"

* * *

"I am happy to say," responded the agent, urbanely providing me with a seat, "that our company has so far conquered the prejudice existing in our business against women as to have assumed the very most advanced position taken regarding them. You would like to take out a policy?"

"I would like to understand precisely the point which the most advanced position taken regarding them occupies, first, if it is quite the same to you."

"Ah! exactly. You would like to know the provisions under which we insure women. Well, we issue life and endowment policies to them upon the same basis as to men. We do not discriminate there. In insuring against accident we grant a woman compensation for the injury, but not for the disability following it."

"If I broke my arm, for instance, you would pay me what you consider compensation for the broken arm, but you would allow me no weekly indemnity for the time I should lose from my desk."

"Precisely. In the event of your demise, however, you would be treated with the same impartial justice which we bestow upon men."

"In the event of my demise," I returned, "I expect the unfortunate fact of my femininity to dwindle into comparative insignificance. But are you not aware," I said with severity, "that we have recently concluded not to wait for the event of our demise to obtain the same impartial justice which you bestow upon men?"

"We have been informed of your intention to that effect, and we consider our step in the matter, which has only been lately taken, a decided advance toward equality for women in this direction."

"So it is," said I, with sudden remorse, remembering Pooh Bah and the English company. "But why do you not take a further one, and pay women during disability as well as men?"

"It is difficult to fix the basis of payment, for one thing. A man is determined by his wages, etc., but his wife has usually no other occupation" —

"No," I interpolated, "she doesn't usually need any other."

— "And it is hard to determine the precise money value of her time. Then we think that the ladies might victimize us here as they do everywhere. They might impose in the matter of continued sickness as the result of an accident, and they would have no object, as men have, to get back to work. The nervous system of woman seems to be so much more intricate than that of man that it is really almost impossible to determine when she may be considered well. Another thing, we might not find women willing to submit to our examiners when cases arose where we would not be willing to take the verdict of the family physician."

"Your examiners are physicians?"

"Oh, yes."

"Then there should be no difficulty. Moreover, you might employ the services of a woman; there are plenty in the profession now. Indeed I think you should in any case."

"Yes," he said, "that objection is not particularly tenable, nor, indeed, are any. The prejudice is wearing away, and one by one the companies are coming to more philosophical conclusions regarding women. In time I have no doubt that the matter will be more equitably adjusted than at present."

* * *

—Before taking out a policy I concluded to inquire further, and betook myself to a gentleman of wide knowledge and experience in the matter.

"Women," he said, "have themselves to blame for the prejudicial attitude of the companies toward them. They are instinctively opposed to insurance. They regard it with horror, as blood money. Approach a woman on the subject of insuring her husband's life, and she will usually treat you as if you were conniving at his death. There appears to be among women a greater tendency to rely upon Providence than—than—

"Than the facts warrant!"

"Than in our business we think it wise to encourage. When it comes to paying premiums in life to insure her a comfortable provision upon the death of her husband, the Scotch Presbyterian female mind seems to be particularly given to trusting Providence."

I suggested a more obvious explanation.

"No," he said, "I don't attribute it to parsimony. Women have the notion that it is tempting fate to insure their husbands. They don't seem to consider that our standing toast is 'Long life to our policy holders!' But I really think that idea is disappearing among them, and of course as they become more reasonable toward insurance companies the insurance companies will become more reasonable towards them. But at present I do not know of any company that will grant you anything but a life policy, and very few that will grant you that."

—I made one more attempt to induce an association of capitalists to bind themselves to pay me an indemnity for the consequences of accident in consideration of a certain sum yearly. Behind a desk in the office which was my *dernier* resort I saw one encouraging sign, a woman. She wasn't the agent, but she was the agent's representative in

187

his absence, and appeared to be quite as well informed as any man I had seen upon the subject. "Surely," thought I, "a company that will employ women will insure them." Nor was I disappointed. The brown eyed young person on the high stool informed me that the company was willing to place women who earned money on the same footing as men with regard to the issuing of policies, the only stipulation being, that they should be wage-earners. "Of course," she said, "women being more delicately organized than men and more subject to risk of injury in their various occupations, the premiums are higher."

"Yes," I said, "that is to be expected—we are not good risks are we?"

"We are not so considered," she responded. "But the insurance companies have not had sufficient experience yet to judge. Although the insurance idea is growing among women, especially among widows who want to leave some provision for their children, it has not yet reached a point that would justify the company in expressing an opinion as to the expediency of the plan."

—This, I conclude, is the gist of the whole matter. There was a time when for many reasons it was deemed inadvisable to insure women. The time has gone by, and the reasons with it. A multitude of women are now in positions of responsibility and profit. Prudence and fore-thought and business sagacity are becoming characteristics of women as well as of men. As their dependence upon their wage earning power increases their desire for provision against emergencies will also increase. And any widespread demand by women for insurance on the same terms as are granted to men will surely be met. The sooner Canadian companies understand this matter fully the better it will be for them.

GARTH GRAFTON.

SARA JEANNETTE DUNCAN was born in 1861 in Brantford, Canada West, and died in England in 1922. She grew up in Ontario, where she began her literary career. A round-the-world trip in 1888 took her to India, where she met Everard Cotes, Curator of the Indian Museum at Calcutta at the time, and later managing director of the Indian News Agency. After their marriage she spent most of the next three decades in India with occasional visits to Canada and to England. A prolific and respected writer of fiction, in style Duncan was foremost a journalist.

After a short stint as a school teacher, she turned to writing for *The Week*, *The Globe*, *The Montreal Star*, and *The Washington Post*, sometimes under her own name, sometimes under the pseudonym "Garth Grafton," and sometimes anonymously. The style of the journalistic sketch, which gives the author opportunities to observe and comment, served her well in many of her novels which describe Britons and North Americans abroad. Among the novels based on her travels are *A Social Departure* (1890), *A Daughter of Today* (1894), *A Voyage of Consolation* (1898), *A Canadian Girl in London* (1908), and *Cousin Cinderella* (1908). Duncan's best known work, *The Imperialist* (1904), is her only novel to focus closely on Canada. Her realism reflects her training as a journalist, as she analyzes small-town life and reports the sentiments of Canadians faced with the question of Imperial Federation.

The first sketch presented here, from Duncan's "Woman's World" column in *The Globe*, commenced September 1, 1886, and concluded September 3, 1886. "A Visit to a Carmelite Convent" in *The Week*, appeared November 10, 1887.

THE MARKET-PLACE, QUEBEC

189

URSULINE CONVENT

Sara Jeannette Duncan

"A Visit to a Carmelite Convent"*

LET US WALK AWHILE FIRST. We shall find plenty along these narrow streets to repay us for exercise we are unaccustomed to in flat Ontario — pedestrianism at an angle of forty-five degrees. The first thing one looks for on arriving in Montreal is lodgings and a laundress; the next an alpenstock. By the time the first two are satisfactorily got we don't want the alpenstock. We are accustomed to the hills, and like them.

Dozens of loveable, habitable-looking, fine, old stone houses! That one especially, there on the corner of Bleury and another street that we must not mention, because we can easily see from the outside of it that the inhabitants do not love publicity. Is not that very good to look at with its suggestion of strength and endurance and comfort, and all the sentiment that gathers about a home! In architecture unpretentiously square, not at all grand in size but big enough to suggest comfortable capacity. Wide, hospitable eaves and old-fashioned projecting porch, tiny panes in the windows that make the people behind them feel as if they were indoors. Hard to keep clean? I suppose so; but few things that are worth having are got very easily. You think your broad sheets of plate-glass an improvement perhaps? Well, I don't. I like best the many broken pictures that the narrow panes make. Plate-glass is for invalids. If healthy people want all out-of-doors they can put on their hats and go out and get it. And of

*The Week, 10 Nov. 1887, pp. 800-01.

course there are trees about our old house, and places where flowers bloomed, I suppose, in June, and a barn that is as solidly built as the house itself. There is this advantage about the Quebec climate: it compels people to build houses that future generations may comfortably live in, and put their money into strength and solidity instead of ornamentally hideous exterior kickshaws, which lose even their tawdry worth in ten or fifteen years.

Judging from appearances the human boy is not the reviled member of society in Montreal that he is elsewhere. He is, in fact, conspicuously "wanted." Every other shop window bears the placard *"garçon demandé"* —which limited advertisement the boys disdain to notice apparently, for it remains there week after week. It appears to the sojourner that the Montreal *garçon* declines almost all his legitimate occupations. He does not cry the papers to any extent; he is no bootblack, nor crossing-sweeper, he! Nor does he drive grocers' carts nor run errands nearly so much as with us, which is perhaps owing to the fact that his father is content to do it. Altogether, unless the factories swallow him up, the small boy of Montreal may be believed to lead a life of enervating and luxurious leisure.

Next to the oft-quoted *Fameuse* —which by the way is neither more nor less than our own more modestly christened "snow-apple" —the fruit of the land appears to be the oyster. One does not require much capital to start in the bivalve business in Montreal. A pile of shells on either side of the door, to attest public appreciation and a flourishing trade; inside, half a barrel of stock, a broken knife and castor that has seen better days, and perhaps a wooden chair on which the proprietor sits and smokes his native tobacco at ten cents a pound and ponders, doubtless upon the advantages of unrestricted trade. The shells are the only indication the intelligent public requires, but some ostentatious firms scrawl the additional legend, *"huîtres,"* in chalk above the door. This is the humble beginning of the business; it ends somewhere in the magnificence of the Windsor, and all the way up one is struck with the diversity of its forms. Oysters not only at the fruiterer's and the fishmonger's, but in the market, at the grocer's, the confectioner's, the little woman's who sells odds and ends of buttons, lace, and the evening papers; oysters by the glass, quart, gallon, peck, small measure, basket, and barrel. I have not yet seen them in the millinery shops by the yard, but am willing to believe that they are sold covertly even there.

But we are a long way down St. Catharine Street, and our car is coming. Where are we going? To Hochelaga I think, to see the convent there. Our guide, who is a lively little French-Canadian lady, and luckily for us speaks English, says it is "the la-argest in Kennada—that convent;" and surely with the October sun shining on its pillared front, and the last yellow largesse of autumn scattered about its solid base, and the broad blue St. Lawrence flowing grandly past, it is the most beautiful in "Kennada." We are admitted to the reception room, which is really quite a large *salon*, adorned with oil paintings of His Holiness the Pope, the sister who founded the Order very humbly at Longueuil across the river there, and the usual religious subjects. This lady in the black habit and the plain white hood, which, with the veil, is the dress of the sisters of Jesus and Mary, who presents each cheek to be kissed by our French friend, and bows pleasantly to the rest of us, is the Mother Superior of the whole Order. The responsibility of her charge may be imagined when we hear that it has missions in Florida, California, British Columbia. She looks like an organiser and directress this nun, with her keen, intellectual face, ready speech, and nervous, energetic manner. She has been for eighteen years at the head of a mission in California, and it is a little odd to note the traces of Americanism in her voice and ways. One looks for national traits in secular flocks, but expects, somehow, nuns to be feminogeneous, if I may coin a word. The Superioress chats with us for a while, and hands us over to a smiling little English nun, who shows us the school-rooms, where one hundred and sixty-five young ladies, all the way from five to eighteen are receiving the usual convent instruction, and the chapel, a perfect copy of that of St. Marie Maguere of Rome, and very beautiful with carvings, and white statues of Saints, and dusky corners where single candles are burning.

"I will show you our Saint," says the little nun, as she leads the way to the place near the altar, where lies a wax figure, representing a beautiful young girl dead with a gash in her throat. "St. Aurelia," says the little nun in a whisper, "and the hair"—which is very long, shining, and curly—"was given by our sister St. Aurelia when she entered."

"Was it—was she—was the saint made here?" I enquire, in misery of uncertainty as to the proper pronoun.

"The head and hands and feet were sent from Paris," she responds, "but we made the body here and put it together, and all the embroidery of the dress was done here."

The embroidery is of gold on a robe of white satin, and a marvel of handiwork.

"Perhaps," says the little nun, "I can show you our other most precious relics." And she goes to see. Alas! she cannot show them to us — perhaps because we are heretics, and who knows what a heretic will do or say.

Just across the road from the Convent of Jesus and Mary stands a grim building with a very high thick stone wall. I have never seen so impassable a wall around a prison as this which confines inmates who have imposed a life sentence on themselves. The building is the worldly face of the cloistered cells of the Carmelites, and the wall is built about their garden. And this is the only Carmelite convent in America. In Spain, in France, in Italy there are others, but not on *this* continent. The Order has existed here since 1875 only. The money to establish it was given by a Madame Frémont of Quebec, and the French Carmelite *fondatrice* who came from Paris is dead now. So are all her sisters except three. The severity of their lives in our rigorous climate killed them. There are fifteen now cloistered here, but twelve are French-Canadian. You know, of course, what it means to take the vows of a Carmelite. It means the most literal renouncement of the world possible to a human being. The face of the Carmelite nun is never seen after her entrance except by her immediate relatives, and then only for half an hour once a month, through heavy gratings. Her hand is never touched save by her sisters. From behind the little door that is barred upon her on the day of parting with our pleasant world she never comes again. Her cell is of the barest; she sleeps on a mattress with one coverlet. Her diet is of the poorest, and meat never enters it. Her habit is of coarse brown cloth, with a veil of a similar colour and kind, and she wears sandals on her feet. Her occupation is prayer and penance, and the making of church decorations. She is a "favourite soul."

We ring, and the sound reverberates within, hollow and chill. A nun dressed like those of the convent opposite opens the door, and, after a whispered conference with our French friend, admits us. The hall we stand in is narrow, cold, and ill-ventilated, and we shiver as we pass along to a small, bare room with an opening in the wall about four feet square. From the iron bars which guard it project spikes half a foot long. On the other side of the opening is another barred network, and behind that hangs a black veil. The room is in semi-darkness, but we can read above the spikes and bars the words —

Au Carmel comme au jugement.
Dieu seul et moi.

They strike through the stillness upon one's consciousness like a text of half-comprehended truth. *Dieu seul et moi!* There is a ring of awful solemnity about that. This is where the Carmelite comes to get her pitiful sight of some one she loved in the days before she became a "favourite soul;" and these are the bars through which that loved one strains aching eyes for the tortured glimpse of the recluse. Through double bars—and then the tears! "Mark well and consider, all you who pass this way," runs a printed text upon the wall; "is there any sorrow like my sorrow?"

Yes, we may have speech with one of the nuns, the sister who let us in comes to tell us. This is by grace of the French lady, who is high in favour in her church. But not here. So we are conducted to another little room, where a circular shelf revolves in the wall for the admission of necessaries to the hospital. Behind this stands the nun. Madame addresses her. We cannot. We have a kind of fear as to what we might say, our conversation being in the world. We shrink from the possible profanation of the strange stillness that surrounds the life behind these thrice-mortared gray walls. But Madame does not shrink. She addresses the shelf with a sort of reverential gaiety, if there is such a thing, and enquires for the health of "*ma soeur.*" And in tremulous tones the nun responds that she is very well—oh, very well, indeed, and is Madame well? How her voice shakes as they talk in French, Madame turning occasionally to tell us that the Superioress is very ill; that if we desire the prayers of the nun we may have them; that the garden has not been very successful this year! It is a great license, this of conversing with strangers behind a heavy partition, and she must be very, very mindful not to forget for an instant that these are not "favourite souls." And she can speak in English? Yes, but can we?

"Are you happy, *ma soeur?*" I falter.

"I am most happy," comes the answer in a quiet cadence.

"And when you die, *ma soeur*, where are you buried?" I query.

"In the vault below," she responded, and I fancy I do detect a trace of hopefulness in the way she says this.

Do they sell the things they make? Oh yes, and if we wish to buy, some will be put on the shelf. And presently a box of wax flowers is pushed slowly around—pansies and camelias and roses, white and red, exquisitely wrought. How much? For the roses five or six cents apiece; for the pansies three. And, after getting change for the price of our souvenirs, she is distressed that we will not take the two or three coppers that are due us.

It is late in the afternoon when we go again through the narrow hall to the door, yet we must have a look at the chapel on the other side. So through another long passage we follow our guide, and into the rather empty, dreary, and bare edifice, where a candle or two burn dimly, and we can just make out the figures of a few bead-telling worshippers. As we stand silent a sound—a song (?)—a dirge sweeps through the gloom from somewhere behind the altar and beyond the knowable. It sinks and swells in its inexpressible mournfulness, as waves might beat on a desolate shore. It is the call—the cry—the chant of the Carmelite nuns.

Montreal.   GARTH GRAFTON.

CANADIAN FARM SNOWED-UP.

198

Archibald MacMechan

"The Last of the Hostelries"*

ONCE UPON A TIME, on my way through the world, I had occasion to stop over night at a little Canadian village called Krahwinkel. It owes its odd name, I may say in passing, to the first settlers, who were Germans, and whose heirs possess the land to this day. The journey was made by stage, and, unluckily for me, it was just about the turn of the year when our winter weather is at its wildest. The country through which I passed looked inexpressibly dreary. There had been a January thaw, which had taken off all the snow. As a matter of course, this was succeeded by a severe frost, which left the roads full of deep ruts. The sky was covered with clouds, and a little snow had fallen, but not enough to make sleighing possible or to cover the nakedness of the desolate fields. The cold wind blew the loose, dry wreaths of it about the brown stubble, now sowing it evenly and now driving it into little heaps. At such a time, the most uncomfortable way of travelling that can be imagined is by Canadian stage. I know of nothing worse; dromedary-back must be a joke to it. In the first place, the make of the vehicle renders keeping warm in it an impossibility. The cover, instead of shielding you, merely serves to keep in and concentrate the cold which leaks up from the floors and blows in from the front. The frost penetrates the most voluminous wraps, ulster, fur cap and

The Dominion Illustrated, 5 July 1890, p. 10.

gauntlets; overshoes are feeble defences against it. The discomfort is aggravated by the snail's pace at which the carriage crawls along. If it went fast you could bear it—for let not the word "stage" mislead the inexpert. The Canadian stage bears only the faintest family likeness to the stage coach of English fiction. It resembles the "flying mails" of Dickens and De Quincy only in having four wheels. The horses are always poor and old. The stage itself is never new; it rattles, it jolts, it pitches, it throws the passengers from side to side; in a word, it is only to be resorted to when all other methods of travelling fail. This particular stage was like all the rest. There was a sharp wind blowing in our faces, and the last ten miles of rough road left me numb with cold and utterly miserable.

The short winter afternoon was merging into night when the stage lumbered into the long main street of Krahwinkel. It drew up before the single hotel of the place, and out of the buffalo robes I crawled, perfectly stiff with cold. The driver's beard bristled with icicles, icy spikes hung from the horses' noses, and their flanks were white with their conjealed breath. The hostelry was a plain stone house, two storeys high, and not very promising in its appearance, for in America you cannot expect cleanliness or good food except in city hotels, a country tavern is never comfortable. A lean-to shed, open to the street, had been built at one side for waiting teams, and a pump with its ice-crusted watering-trough stood in front. The driver carried my portmanteau into the house and I followed him. The door opened directly into the bar-room, a low, dark-ceilinged room, the walls of which were ornamented with a few gaudy hand-bills. At one side three homespun farmers were gathered round the stove, talking politics. I caught the words "John A.," "Mail," "Blake" and "Globe" as I entered. Opposite the door was the bar. The dingy counter and shelves were graced with a few black bottles, decanters and cigar boxes. Here Jacob Schmidt, mine host, met us, and to him the driver handed over my portmanteau. The landlord was a short, thick set, brown-bearded German, arrayed in a brown cardigan jacket. He was a slow, deliberate man of few words; saying little because speech required him to take his pipe out of his mouth. The driver told me next day that he had the reputation of being the best hotel-keeper for three counties round, and the richest; a reputation, I am bound to say, he well deserved. Out of one of those black bottles Jacob poured some particular old schnapps which revived and partially thawed me. Then he picked up my portmanteau, led me out into a cold, dark passage and threw open a door, out of which there came a blaze of light. Half blinded, I stumbled in and Jacob withdrew.

It took me some time to realize where I was. The transition was too abrupt and unexpected. The first thing that I really saw was a huge coal-stove right in front of me, every one of its mica panes blazing red. Then I was aware, as the old ballads say, of one — two — three young women who were by no means bad looking. Then a piano, a sofa, arm chairs, tables, pictures gradually arranged themselves before my sight, and I perceived that I was standing in a snug, well-appointed parlour. The change from the bleak winter road, the jolting stage, the cheerless bar-room, to this torrid zone of comfort was almost too much. I began to think that I was the victim of some new Arabian Night, and recalled vaguely the one-eyed calender in the castle of the forty obliging beauties. Jacob had apparently thought introductions unnecessary; so I was quite at a loss to explain my presence there. The situation would have been awkward if one of the young ladies had not been equal to the occasion. This throwing a total stranger upon their hospitality seemed nothing unusual. She came forward with a smile and asked me if I wouldn't take off my coat and come up to the fire. This was enough to break the ice, and a conversation sprang up; but I did not care to come any nearer to the fiery furnace that glowed in the middle of the room. On the sofa at one side I was quite near enough to make the process of thawing out a pleasant one. At this safe distance I had a good opportunity to observe my fair entertainers and distinguish between them. They were all about a size, and bore an unmistakable family likeness to one another. They were dressed very much alike in plain, neat frocks of good material. Two had black eyes and hair, but one had rosy cheeks and the other was noticeably pale. These seemed to be the eldest and the youngest of the trio. The third girl was unlike her sisters in having brown hair and eyes. I never heard their names, so I christened them for convenience Black Eyes, Brown Hair and Pale Face. Their ages would probably range from sixteen to one or two and twenty. Evidently they were mine host's daughters. This was their living room, and Jacob, in the simplicity of his heart and contempt of modern notions, had made his transient guest a member of his family for the time.

I was just pleasantly warmed through again, feeling conscious once more of hands and feet, and we were deep in a four-cornered discussion of the weather when a bell rang, and the girls told me it was for supper. I plunged once more into the cold, dark passage, and found my way to another room on the same flat, well lighted and quite as comfortable as the one I had just quitted. It was not like a room in a tavern but in a well-to-do farm house, and conspicuous for neatness and order peculiarly German. Here I found about half a dozen men sociably seated around one large, well-set table, and chatting like old acquaintances. What a welcome sight that generous board presented to the gaze of the famished traveller. Besides preserves and hot cakes, cold meat and fried sausages, home made bread and country butter, there was a large earthenware dish containing some sort of pie. I cannot say what it was made of, beyond that it was brown and rich and savoury, and there was very little of it left when we rose from the table. It was like nothing I ever saw or tasted anywhere else. Probably the recipe was a family secret, and the pasty a dish as peculiar to this tavern as the "pudding" is to the "Cheshire Cheese." Brown Hair and Pale Face waited on us and handed us our steaming cups of tea and coffee without any abatement of their quiet self-possession. Black Eyes was invisible; in command at the base of supplies, the kitchen, by right of seniority, I imagined.

When the meal was over the other men went off—most of them were in business in the village—while a few adjourned to the bar-room to smoke a quiet pipe with the landlord. For my part, I returned to the parlour, which was empty, and amused myself turning over the books strewn on the piano, looking at the pictures and so on. I felt like myself again, and began to despise the powers of cold and winter. The parlour seemed to be in the heart of the house. There were windows on one side only, and they were deep and heavily curtained. Behind the stove were two doors, which seemed to open on bed-rooms. In one corner stood a sewing-machine, which I had not observed before, and a work-basket, well filled, beside it. The pictures were those to be seen everywhere in the country,—a large wood-cut of "Faith, Hope and Charity" in a gilt frame, which had been given as a premium with some newspaper or other; the "Meeting of Wellington and Blücher at Waterloo;" two bright companion chromos—"Wide Awake" and "Fast Asleep." The other decorations were some mottoes in Berlin wool, and a wreath of wax flowers in a deep square frame. The piano was a good one, of native manufacture, and must have cost a pretty penny. Some sheet music was lying about—"Silvery Waves," "The Maiden's Prayer," "Home, Sweet Home," with variations; a couple of "Song Folios," and a number of "Liederschatz." The carpet was new and everything as tidy as it could be. It was the snuggest cosy corner I had found in my wanderings for many a long day. Presently the girls came back into the room, and made no secret of the fact that they had been washing the dishes and "clearing up" generally. They immediately proceeded "to entertain the company" in the orthodox way. Miss Black Eyes showed me the family photograph album: "poppa" and "me when I was little," and a long array of uncles, aunts and cousins. This custom of showing the visitor the album is a good one. It serves as an introduction to the family history, appeals to and gratifies your love of anecdote, humanity and the picturesque. In this way I learned a great deal about the generations of the Schmidts. Their mother was dead, and although they did not need to do so, they kept house for their father and did nearly all the work. They did not like living in a tavern, and had long been coaxing him to give the business up. "Poppa" did not need to keep a hotel for a living, they told me with a touch of pride. It came out that they understood German, but did not speak it among themselves. They had attended the country high school and had been taught music, as the presence of the piano testified. Once or twice their father had taken them, in fair time, to that centre of civilization, Toronto. They were fond of dancing, like all German girls, and chatted eagerly about the "balls" and "parties" that were always going on in the winter. They were so bright and lively and thoroughly unaffected, it was hard to think of them as daughters of taciturn, smoky old Jacob and his Cardigan jacket.

They had brought in with them another member of the family, namely, a shaggy brown dog, who forthwith curled himself up on the mat behind the stove. He was not allowed to enjoy himself very long, for Miss Pale Face, who was evidently much petted by her elder sisters, and accustomed to have her own way in the house, roused him from his lair and proceeded to put him through his tricks. He was old, stiff in the joints, and in no pleasant humour at having his nap disturbed; but his mistress bullied him into showing off his various accomplishments. He "begged" and "spoke" and "said his prayers" with his nose between his paws on the back of a chair. He would not touch a bone that was "bought on trust," but worried it when told that it was "paid for." He really was a very accomplished dog, and his disgust at it all and air of performing under protest kept us laughing. At last he was released and went back to his mat, growling over the unreasonableness of human beings.

Then it was Miss Pale Face's turn to be put through her pacings. After much persuasion, her sisters got her to play and sing. She played

203

well enough, not in concert style to be sure, but none of us were critical or hard to please. I asked for something from the "Liedeschatz," and she gave us "Der Tyroler und sein Kind" in fair style.

"She's been taking lessons two years and that's the only tune she knows," said Miss Brown Hair teasingly.

But this was a libel on the fair pianiste, and she showed it to be without foundation by singing several others, which was probably what that artful minx, Brown Hair, intended. At last, she declared that it was somebody else's turn, and I tried to induce Brown Hair to take her place. No, she couldn't and wouldn't sing.

"Then you play, don't you?"

"I play in the kitchen," said the pert thing.

And so the evening went. It was half past ten before I knew where I was. I got up and apologized for keeping them up so late, for they were not city girls who can afford to turn day into night; they must be astir long before daylight next morning. After many protests that it was early, and so on, Pale Face brought Jacob. We said good-night and I followed my guide to my chamber in the second storey. It was tidy and clean like the rest of the inn, but cold as Greenland. There was no fire, and the lamp showed the window panes all furry with frost. But after toasting by that coal stove all evening, I was almost impervious to the cold. In a few moments I was between the blankets and sound asleep.

Next morning I resumed my journey. Early as it was, I was the only one at breakfast; the other boarders had finished their meal and dispersed. Miss Pale Face waited on me, but I did not see the others. When I came to settle with Jacob, I was surprised at the smallness of my bill. I am ashamed to say how little I paid for my entertainment, but he would not take more. Then the stage lumbered up to the door and I embarked again. All the day in the cold I kept pondering, by very force of contrast, the incidents of my pleasant evening, and wished in vain that such another hostelry would greet me at the day's end. Since that day I have never seen Krahwinkel, though it is much easier of access now. The stage no longer runs and a spur of railway connects the little village with the rest of the great iron net-work of the province. Sometimes I have wished to go back and find out how Jacob and his pretty daughters flourished; discover if they ever succeeded in coaxing him to give up the tavern; and, if so, what has become of it and them? Is it kept as of yore? Or has some one taken it off Schmidt's hands and allowed him to retire? At any rate, I have never found harbourage like it anywhere, and I note it as a curious survival of old-fashioned comfort and hospitality. Again, I was afraid to return, lest what I saw might spoil my recollections of that pleasant winter's evening long ago. Sometimes I have doubts as to whether Krahwinkel or its hostelry every really existed. It is my "Schloss Boncourt." Every detail of the room and every feature of my entertainers' fresh faces is plain before me at this moment, and yet I have a desolate sort of conviction that there is not a stone of it remaining, and that the plough scores long furrows over the site of that old-time, wayside inn.

ARCHIBALD MCKELLAR MACMECHAN was born in 1862 in Berlin (now Kitchener), Canada West, and died in 1935 in Halifax. A graduate of the University of Toronto and Johns Hopkins University, he was Professor of English at Dalhousie University from 1889 until shortly before his death. His numerous publications include works of poetry, biography, history, description, and scholarship. His most important contribution to Canadian literature, *Headwaters of Canadian Literature* (1924), is a critical survey of writing in English and French Canada. MacMechan wrote a collection of essays, *The Porter of Bagdad and Other Fantasies* (1901), and *The Life of a Little College, and Other Papers* (1914) in the familiar essay style. His knowledge of local Maritime history is evident in such works as *Storied Halifax* (1922), *Old Province Tales* (1924), *The Book of Ultima Thule* (1927), *There Go The Ships* (1928), and *Red Snow on Grand Pré* (1931).

The Medicine Man of 1790

Pauline Johnson

"Indian Medicine Men and Their Magic"*

WITCHCRAFT HAS ALWAYS BEEN a predominant superstition among
the North American Indians. It is one of the most impregnable bar-
riers to be overthrown on the doorstep of civilization, for a deep-
rooted belief that generates suspicion and terror in the nature of an
otherwise grandly courageous manhood, is as difficult to expunge as
an hereditary physical blemish.

The faith in things supernatural is, among the Iroquois, a strange
admixture of hideousness and beauty, and few are the legends, and
little the folklore, that has not been constructed upon some reasonable basis. Religiously, the native belief is a poem, practically savour-
ing too strongly of the magician's wand to be plausible in theory. But
the secret of all things marvellous and miraculous lies within the hollow of the "Medicine Man's" hand.

He it is who commands the invisible forces of this world and the
next, whose voice can charm anything from a plenteous harvest to a
fell disease, he is prophet, avenger and conjurer combined; witches
are servile to him, evil spirits are his playthings, and wisdom in all
things is his, beyond dispute.

Whatever his power may be, or however he exercise it, whether
nefariously or philanthropically, — it most assuredly *is* a power beyond

The Dominion Illustrated Monthly, April 1892, pp. 140-43.

the understanding of greater men than he, whether his success in healing the sick or foretelling events is due to the fact that he may be a naturally born scientist, or, indeed, as his people believe, in touch and tune with witches his craft is one of undoubted acquirement, which even the most sceptical must acknowledge.

Years ago when, as a little child, I sat at my grandfather's feet, listening, with wide-eyed curiosity, and a shrinking, timid awe, to his wondrous tales of still more wondrous witchcraft, I conceived an overpowering desire to see the "Medicine Men," or, as he called them, "Witch Doctors," but the first one I saw was monstrous enough to satisfy this longing for many years to come. He was a huge man, wrapped from head to foot in a buffalo skin, and wearing an alligator's head atop of his own. He moved about the room with a slow, shuffling tread, dancing occasionally, first on one foot then on the other, chanting the while with a peculiar nasal intonation never used in religious festivals. In his hand he carried a shovel filled with ashes, which he tossed through the room, up to the rafters, about the walls, over the patient, — everywhere. Then he turned us all out, closed the door, and parleyed with the witches over the unfortunate invalid for an hour. It was a fever case, and the man recovered.

My grandfather used to tell of a very marvellous "doctor" who visited the Grand River Reserve (which district this article refers exclusively to). He came from the St. Clair River, and was an eminent "practitioner" in his own tribe.

The first person to employ him was a woman, who was "bewitched" and bed-ridden for months. She declared he used no mightier means of effecting a cure than the magical bone of a loon's leg, which was hollowed, and polished very highly. Through this he extracted, from the back of her neck, a coarse horse hair, that had a wampum bead fastened at either end, and in the centre. After that she got well, and the fame of the St. Clair medicine man went abroad.

Any morning, at dawn, the early fisherman could see this strange miracle worker, flitting like a shadow through the heavy fogs on the river shore, chanting softly his uncanny songs, and invoking supernatural aid from the spirits he seemed so familiar with.

But he and his kind have long ceased to exist among the Six Nations of Brant County. The "medicine man"of to-day works more on the faith cure plan and imposes less upon his patient's credulity, inasmuch as he has long since abandoned the practice of extracting ill-shaped bones, beads, and all manner of impossible things from the witchworried invalid.

Sometimes he sets out with three or four of his associates to tramp across the Reserve—on miraculous cures intent. They seldom take the roadway, but cut through the heart of the bush, walking slowly and in Indian file. Far through the loneliness of the sparsely settled forest and swamp land, their strange hollow voices float in a weird cry that plays an intonation of two half notes in a high key. Few people even get a glimpse of the odd-looking group going their rounds, each carrying a staff, and wearing the most atrocious masks, made of wood, painted, chiseled into hideous human features, and fringed with lengths of grey and black hair. On they go, their figures bent forward, almost to a right angle, striking the earth periodically with their staffs, with always that evil call, and a peculiar slight motion of the feet, that is both a dance and a shuffle.

By-and-by a woman opens the door of a distant log house; with an inverted broom handle she strikes the door-step a number of times; it is a signal for the "medicine men" to visit the house; there is a sick person there.

Their song ceases then, and, entering, they strew ashes about the room, which signifies a cleansing of the house from evil spirits that have brought the disease.

The chief "doctor" then goes into a room by himself to mix the medicine, which is a concoction that he alone knows the ingredients of. They always assert that they can tell by the appearance of the medicine, and the manner in which it compounds, whether the patient will recover or die. "The witch" within the medicine speaks to them, they say, and its decree is infallible.

The head "medicine man" then enters the sick room, turns out all the relatives and visitors, shuts himself up with the patient, in silence administers his "witch herbs," chants a little, scatters ashes over the sick bed, and then leaves the house, having given instructions that none but three elderly persons in the tribe are to see or speak to the patient for ten days.

He goes to his home,—perhaps five miles distant,—puts on his false face, and sits up alone all night in a darkened room, chanting to himself and taking no food whatever until the following morning; for ten nights he does this, and at the same time the members of his household and his neighbours keep up a constant dancing in another part of the house.

Sometimes at midnight he bids the entire company into the darkened chamber, and while still wearing the painted wooden mask he gives them a "witch powder," which they eat in silence, then they leave him again to resume their dance outside, while he chants once more to himself the long night through.

After the allotted time — generally ten days — he starts forth to his patient's house, who, needless to state, is by that time dead or convascelescent.

The practise of employing these men is not by any means confined to the Pagans; the belief in charms and witchcraft is prevalent among many of the educated, as well as the civilized Indians. Love charms, spirit charms, medicine charms — they all exist in the faith and imagination of a people whose own greatest charm lies in their exquisite beliefs, their seeing of the unseen, and their touch of the poetic in nature, which is, of all things, the most beautiful.

EMILY PAULINE JOHNSON was born in 1861 on the Six Nations Reserve near Brantford, Canada West, and died in 1913 in Vancouver, British Columbia. The Indian heritage of her father, a Mohawk chief, furnished the main themes for her poetry, while the specialized education she received as the daughter of an Englishwoman provided the skills to write in the accepted forms of the day. Today Johnson is not considered a "great" poet, yet she enjoyed a large following during her lifetime, partly because of her appealing public readings and partly because of the popularly romantic way she presented Indian culture. When she retired from public performances in 1909 and moved to Vancouver, she turned to writing tales and sketches of Indian legends. The pieces in her first book of prose, *Legends of Vancouver* (1911), were originally published in the Vancouver *Province*. Johnson's two later collections of tales were *The Shagganappi* (1912) and *The Moccasin Maker* (1913). The major collections of her poems are *The White Wampum* (1895), *Canadian Born* (1903), and *Flint and Feather* (1912).

Medicine Men of to-day.

211

TEEPEE AND RED RIVER CARTS.

George B. Brooks

"A Horrible Night. An Historical Sketch of the North-West Rebellion"*

IN THAT LAND OF CLEAR SKIES and magnificent distances which is bounded on the south by the north branch of the Saskatchewan river, and which stretches northward to the region of eternal ice and snow, there is, perhaps, no lovelier spot than that known at one time as the Frog Lake Settlement. Beautiful as the landscape generally is in that particular portion of the Dominion, nature seems to have redoubled her efforts in some localities, and to have made one supreme exertion to excel herself about the lake and settlement with the somewhat uneuphonious name. Grander scenery, more magnificent views, can be seen in hundreds of places in Canada, but it is doubtful if anywhere else — even in beautiful Prince Edward Island — can be seen more pastoral loveliness, more of that charming landscape which so reminds the traveller of rural England. There is the same hill and dale, the same refreshing greenness of leaf and blade, the same park-like beauty, the same wealth of fern, bracken and wild flowers: all that is wanting to make the visitor believe himself in Devonshire or Kent is the villages with their ivy covered churches and thatched cottages.

Frog Lake is a sheet of water about ten or twelve miles in length and from three to four miles in width, clear as crystal, full of fish and studded with islands. It is connected with the Saskatchewan river by

*The Lake Magazine, Oct. 1892, pp. 165-68.

Frog Creek, and it is on the bank of that creek, five miles from the lake, and thirty from Fort Pitt, that the settlement was planted, some ten or twelve years ago with every prospect of a flourishing future, by sturdy pioneers from Ontario. Seven years ago the place was in ashes; its inhabitants — those who had not been cruelly tortured and murdered — had been driven away, and where once all was industry, hope, happiness and contentment, there was desolation and ruin.

The events which led up to the North-West Rebellion of 1885 are too well known to need recapitulation, but during the month of March in that year rumors of a very ugly kind reached Winnipeg from Fort Pitt, Edmonton and Battleford districts, and were forwarded on over the rest of the Dominion. Among them was one to the effect that the Cree Indians in the Fort Pitt district, after driving Inspector Dickens and his force of Mounted Police from the Fort, and taking the Hudson Bay factor and his family prisoners, had raided the settlement of Frog Lake and had massacred its people. The excitement in Winnipeg and throughout Canada was intense, and was rendered doubly so by the impossibility of obtaining any trustworthy news. Time brought no details of the affair, for the Indians and Halfbreeds were in rebellion, the telegraph wires had been cut near Battleford and there was no communication to be had with that place, Fort Pitt, Edmonton, or Frog Lake.

The Dominion Government issued a call to arms — a call responded to with alacrity, from the Atlantic to the Pacific — and it was the lot of the writer, as a commissioned officer in the 91st Regiment or Manitoba Light Infantry, to be one in the first party of white men who reached Frog Lake settlement after the rumor of massacre had been received.

Without going into any description of the plan of campaign that General Sir Fred. Middleton saw fit to carry out, it is necessary to state that a column under the command of General Strange, and consisting of the Alberta Mounted Rifles, the 91st Winnipeg Light Infantry, the 65th Mount Royal Rifles, 25 Mounted Police, with a 12 pounder field piece, and about 80 Mounted Scouts under Inspector Steele — a total force of about 800 — congregated at Calgary early during the month of April, 1885, the object being a rapid march to Edmonton, which was supposed then to be in a state of siege, and the relief of that place. The excitement at Calgary when the troops from the east arrived there was intense. The wildest rumors were flying about regarding the uprising of Indians and the dreadful danger of the settlers in the north. Applications for military help and assistance poured in on General Strange, and that thorough soldier, as brave a man as ever wore British uniform or was snubbed by a self-conceited Commander-in-Chief, had to yield to the pressure, and a company of the 91st, under command of Captain Vallancey, was sent south to Fort McLeod, while another company of the same regiment, under command of Major John Lewis, was sent to the Blackfoot Reserve at Gleichen, and a third company of the same regiment was left at Calgary, together with a company of the 65th Mount Royal Rifles. The remainder of the force, some 500 men, started for Edmonton, which place was reached late on Sunday afternoon, after a rapid march of eleven days, two of which were spent in crossing the Red Deer river, at the time considerably swollen by melted snow and rain.

Everything at Edmonton was quiet. There had been uneasiness and the settlers had crowded into the fort for protection, but had returned to their farms, the Indians having given no trouble. Leaving a company of the 65th to garrison the fort, and sending another company of the same regiment to the Indian farm near Edmonton, the remainder of the force proceeded eastward towards Fort Pitt, the mounted men by land and the infantry in flat boats down the Saskatchewan as far as Fort Victoria. At Fort Victoria the four companies of the 91st rejoined the Scouts and Mounted Police and proceeded with them by land to Fort Pitt; the companies of the 65th continuing their journey to the same destination in the flat boats.

The scenery along the north shore of the Saskatchewan was exceedingly lovely, but neither Indians, half breeds nor whites were met after Fort Victoria had been left. That place had been looted about ten days before the troops arrived there, and bags of flour, sides of bacon, etc., stolen from the fort, had been cached along the banks of the river, together with several thousand dollars worth of furs. All this property was secured and appropriated to the use of Her Majesty. The march towards Fort Pitt was slow, owing to the swollen condition of the creeks and the time it took to get the baggage waggons across, and also to the care which had to be exercised to avoid falling into an Indian ambuscade. No one knew where the Red Skins and their allies, the Half Breeds, were. Not a soul was met to give any information; it was the march of a column into an enemy's country without any knowledge of the number of that enemy or his whereabouts, only that he was somewhere near. The Queen's Birthday, 1885, fell on a Sunday, and is a day never to be forgotten by the members of General

Strange's Edmonton column. The day broke with heavy rain, thunder and lightning, and as the troops turned out at 4 o'clock a.m. and folded away the dripping tents, humped their backs in their dripping overcoats and swallowed their morning coffee, it dawned upon most of them that soldiering in earnest is somewhat different from what soldiering is on the streets of a city. The constant marching, day after day, the lack of any comfort, the hard ground every night for a mattress, the hot days and cold mornings and nights, the suspense, and, above all, the inability to catch up to the Indians or even find out anything about them, were having their effect. When after the troops fell in that Queen's Birthday morning, reeking wet, and the chaplain had offered prayer and the Old Hundred had been sung, General Strange addressed the column, stating that during the night the scouts had brought him trustworthy information that the Indians were in the neighborhood of Fort Pitt and we should probably be up with them in a day or two, a mighty shout of gladness went up from those 500 and odd men. And when the brave old soldier further called upon his soldiers to remember it was the Queen's Birthday and to give her Majesty three cheers, there went up three cheers and a tiger that neither the thunder, lightning, rain or wind could drown. The despondency vanished in a moment, and, in spite of the heavy walking and dripping clothes, no 500 men ever stepped out for their day's march of 25 miles with more spirit, and more determination to take it out of the Indians when they got the chance, than did our brave men in that far nothern portion of the Dominion.

About noon the rain ceased and the clouds rolled away, and by evening the column halted for the night one mile from Frog Lake Settlement, posted double sentries and sent out a strong picket. As already stated no trustworthy news had been received from the settlement for weeks. The fate of the people there was still in doubt, and naturally General Strange was anxious to ascertain the worst. It was a glorious spring evening. After supper the order came for a troop of scouts and a company of the 91st well armed, to proceed to the settlement and reconnoitre, and should any rebels be seen, to fall back on the main body without risking any engagement. Cautiously the order was carried out, those engaged in doing so passing a night which will never be forgotten as long as memory lasts.

With the exception of a half-starved dog, a number of hawks, eagles and other birds of prey, there was no living creature to be seen about the place. The settlement itself was in ashes. The walls of the little

Roman Catholic Church were standing but the roof was gone, and the bell was broken and lying in the churchyard. The mill was an utter ruin and every house and cabin in the settlement had been fired and either totally or partially consumed. It was a sorrowful sight — so much ruin and destruction in the midst of so much natural beauty. But what about the settlers? Were they lying dead among the ruins, and were the rumours that had reached Winnipeg and shocked all Canada true, or had the settlers escaped? The doubt had to be settled, and the only way to settle it was by searching the ruins.

It was about seven o'clock when the troops commenced the search. What a horrible discovery there was! About the ruins of the little church there was a strong, fetid, disgusting smell; and attracted by this unnatural odor, and by the fat sleek-looking birds of prey that were perched on the walls of the building, a party of the 91st made an inspection — one never to be forgotten. In the basement of the church, and evidently thrown there after death, were the bodies of four white men very far gone in decomposition. Words fail to express the horror of the sight. In every case the features of the deceased were unrecognizable, having been rubbed with coal oil and then set fire to. Every head had been scalped; the hands and feet in every case had been cut off; and the leg and arm bones protruded. The hearts of the dead victims had been cut out and other indignities which cannot be mentioned here had been practised — it is to be hoped after, and not before, death. It was a sickening sight, arousing in the hearts of those who witnessed it, feelings of indignation and a desire for swift, terrible vengeance. Strong men — men who had faced death in the trenches before Sebastopol, who had stormed the walls of Delhi, and had fought in Zululand and Egypt; men who wore Crimean, Indian Mutiny, Egyptian and South African medals — broke down and blubbered like babes. There was not a man in all that little company of red coats who was not deeply affected, and not one who did not echo the remark of an old Indian Mutiny soldier that the devils who had perpetrated the foul deed must be wiped out without mercy or quarter.

Word of the state of affairs was sent back to the camp, and in a short time a fatigue party with lanterns, shovels, picks, etc., was at work. It was no easy matter getting the bodies from the basement of the church to the surface, they were so much decomposed. With great trouble, and after long working in a sickening atmosphere, it was at last accomplished by getting tarpaulins under each body. By midnight the remains of the four dead men — two of whom were the Roman

Catholic priests in charge of the mission, as was evident by the fragments of dress they wore—were lying side by side amid the wild roses in the little churchyard. While one party had been engaged getting the bodies to the surface, another had made four rude coffins and four large crosses, and another had dug four graves. Just at break of day—about 3 a.m.—the bodies of the murdered men were reverently lowered into the graves, the Litany for the Dead of the Roman Catholic church being read over those containing the two priests by Captain Frank Clarke, a Roman Catholic officer of the 91st, and the burial service of the Church of England being read by Lieutenant-Colonel Osborne Smith of the same regiment over the graves of the two laymen. The soldiers stood around bare-headed, and simple as the ceremony was, no four men were ever buried by strangers with more reverence and devotion than were these Frog Lake victims. The service over, the graves were filled in, a rude cross was planted at the head of each and wild roses and other wild flowers were gathered and twisted into wreaths and were hung on the crosses, and there in that beautiful scene of desolation, with nature at its brightest, and the birds carrolling their morning hymns, were left to slumber their long sleep the poor victims of Indian treachery, cunning and cruelty.

At 5 a.m. that morning the column continued its march towards Fort Pitt, arriving there the same evening to find the place in flames, and a strong force of Indians in the neighborhood.

CANOE LAKE, Muskoka R., Ont.

Thomas C. Birnie

"A Trip After Bark in Northern Ontario"*

AS MANY KNOW, birch-bark is a very important thing among Indians and hunters; especially in a country that abounds in lakes and streams. With it they make many useful things, but above all, their canoes, which are as useful to the hunter of the woods as the horse is to the hunter of the plains.

The bark of the birch, like the bark of most trees, peels best in June. But the Indians, when they want a supply, generally put off getting it until July, on account of the bears. June is the month in which the bears mate, and though the Indian, at most times of the year, is only too glad to meet with bears, yet he knows that both bears and wolves, in places where they are numerous and have collected in large numbers, are dangerous at their time of mating. This is especially so with bears. They go tearing about the woods, often fighting with each other, and, absorbed as they are, neglect seeking their food, and often get very hungry. The she one, too, feels very important, attended by so many rugged gallants, and will attack indiscriminately everything she meets; and the he ones, anxious to secure her favor, eagerly back her up, making it very dangerous to meet with a herd at such a time, and the Indians are careful to avoid their haunts at this season of the year.

*The Canadian Magazine, May 1893, pp. 206-15.

But June had passed, and we hoped the bears had become less savage, and as our two Indian friends, Wig-e-maw-way and Nan-e-bo-tho, were about starting for a supply of bark, Ned and I thought we would join them, for we wished to see the part of the country they were to visit, having some thoughts of starting a hunting and trading station there the following fall. It must not be thought that the right kind of bark can be got any where about the forest: sometimes the Indians go hundreds of miles for it, and the place to which we intended to go was very distant. It could have been got nearer, but getting it nearer would require an overland journey, and the longer distance was the easiest, as it was by water, with the exception of a few portages we would have to pass.

Our route lay up a river—the Maw-e-net-e-che-mon, the name signifying, "They chased him with a canoe." And here our Indian friends told us one of their lingering traditions of the terrible Iroquois. And it is very pleasant to travel up a wild river with an Indian, whose confidence you have gained, and who is well acquainted with the traditions of his tribe, and the past and present history of the place. The language of the Indians is very expressive, and enables them to give a concise name to a place, describing its character, or any incident connected with it; and many a place is marked with a name which makes it a Gettysburg or Waterloo to them. This makes a trip up their wild routes, with an intelligent Indian for a companion, a very enjoyable one.

Now you come to a falls: it is "The place where Big Otter sleeps." Big Otter was an Indian hunter, who, in the excitement of the chase, ventured too far, and was swept over these falls, and, as is the Indians' custom in such cases, when they find the body, they bury it near the place. You go and take a look at the lone grave. It is a lonely spot, but when you think of the human bones you have seen tossed about by rude and careless workmen, or carted away from some cemetery that has become too valuable to let the dead rest there in peace, you think Big Otter sleeps well beneath the pine trees, with the wild, free winds singing a requiem in their tops.

Or you come to a wild, rocky lake, amidst whose yawning chasms the storm wind shrieks and howls, while the echoing thunder reverberates from rock to rock. It is "Lake Ween-daw-goo" — "the dwelling-place of the spirit of the thunder-storm." You must pass it reverently, or the spirit will come, enveloped in dark clouds, lashing the waters into fury, and roaring and shooting fire at you.

Or, as you paddle along, you come to a creek of dark, polluted water slowly oozing out into the river from a small lake of a very dreary and desolate appearance. Some grim rocks and bare sandhills are seen, but the Indians tell you no living thing is found in its waters, or anything verdant seen about its shores. It is "The place of death." Whatever we may think of the Indian from the degraded specimens we have seen of him, it is literally true that he "sees God in clouds and hears Him in the wind." To him "millions of spirits walk the earth both while we wake and while we sleep," and though they may not be spirits that correspond with our ideas, to him they are realities, surrounding him on every hand. Left to his own communings in his lonely wanderings amidst the mysteries of nature, everything around him is alive with the invisible and every odd-looking thing he sees is the home of some spirit, ready to do him good or do him harm. It is no wonder, then, that such a place as this excites his superstition and becomes the abode of an evil spirit, or that his fancy has supplied it with one coming down in the traditions from long ago.

They tell you that long ago this part of the country was the residence of a celebrated pow-wow (medicine man), noted for his skill, and feared and hated for the way in which he used it. A number of the Indians, at different times, had suffered through his influence with the evil one. At last, Shaw-wun-e-ge-lihik, a much-loved chief, sickened and died of a disease mysterious to the Indians. Suspicion was at once fastened on Wah-wun, the pow-wow, and in a secret council the Indians resolved to put him to death. Stealthily they crept up to him in the dead of night, and, pouncing on him, secured him before he could get his medicine bag (they think the potent spell lies hidden in it), and brought him before the chiefs and old men of the nation, who condemned him to be burnt to death for sorcery. Poor Wah-wun, naturally bitter and vindictive, had his evil passions aroused by such barbarous treatment, and while the flames were gathering around him, true to his character, he bequeathed to them his curse. He said: "May the evil spirit curse you. May your hearts be faint in time of battle, and your scalps ornaments in the wigwams of your enemies. May the evil mind that dwells in the marsh light on you and blast your corn, blight your children and kill your game," and then Wah-wun's spirit went off in a black cloud and settled down here, lived here and has ever since remained, trying to put his curse into execution.

Thus we journeyed on, sometimes passing through lakes wild and rugged-looking, while others were beautiful as fairy-land, crowned with lovely islands, the shores lined with park-line plains, beneath which lay smooth, sandy beaches, and where, in the distance, might be seen the stately moose, or the lonely bear, as it paced its solitary way in search of some new feeding-ground.

Then, again, we would pass up some quiet stretch of the river, where the water animals attending to the wants of their young, would enliven the scene. Thousands of birds along the banks made the woods vocal with their joyous songs; and it seemed very strange to meet with the companions of your childhood's home in such a place as this. You expected to see wild savage creatures. It is nothing to see the bear or the wolf. But to see the darling little humming bird that flitted about the honey-suckle that entwined your mother's door, or hear the sweet song of the robin that gladdened your childhood's days, seemed strange indeed; but it was all very pleasant. And so was the paddle against the swift-flowing rapid, and the camp by the waterfall, whose never-ceasing murmur soothed you to rest.

Passing on, we came to a great wild rice marsh, where thousands and hundreds of thousands of wild geese and ducks were congregated, many of them with broods of young ones. Some of these marshes are of vast extent, and are the favorite resort of innumerable water-fowl. It is well known how anxious the migratory birds are to return to the north, and, no sooner does the spring open up a spot of water, than geese and ducks begin flocking to it, and before the ice and snow are all gone, thousands may be seen together in flocks, presenting a scene of life and joy greatly in contrast with the dreary aspect of the place a few weeks before. Here they breed and multiply, luxuriating in the plenty and security of their wild northern home, at first living on the old rice still lying in the water, and the succulent grasses which soon start to grow in it. But it is not until the rice begins to ripen that they revel in the abundance which is spread around them. Then the young ones have learnt they have wings, and seem delighted to use them; the old ones, too, seem to know the necessity of their young being prac- tised for their long coming flight, and morning and evening flocks numbering thousands and tens of thousands may be seen flying from one part of the marsh to another. But, though they are preparing for their long journey, they are in no hurry to leave, and it is only when the ice begins to close in the rice-fields, they show uneasiness, which is a sign they are about to depart. And after marshalling their hosts — sometimes a number of broods together, sometimes only a single one

—they rise up above the obstructing trees and hills, and wing their way to the sunny south.

Nor alone to the wild geese and ducks is the wild rice marsh a prize. The Indians, too, value it very highly, not only as a game preserve, but also for the rice, of which they are very fond, and often gather it and store it away for winter's use. We read of the inhabitants of the Nile sowing their crops from boats, but here we may see the harvesting done in canoes. The rice grows in the water and the Indians sail through it, bending the heads of the rice over their canoe, and threshing it out with their paddles, the grain falling into their canoe.

They have two methods of preparing it. One is to simply dry and winnow it; in the other, which involves a great deal more labor, they roast it in their kettles, and then pound it in a mortar. The last method makes it much the better, as it takes the black skin off and makes it a very palatable dish, not only relished by the Indians, but in places not too distant where it is sometimes brought, the whites readily buy it for three dollars a bushel.

The rice-gathering is often a time of merry-making, and makes a pic-nic which others than Indians would greatly enjoy. Happening at a time of the year when the forest is thoroughly enjoyable, men, women and children have a happy time. The "lords of creation" go off shooting geese and ducks, while the women are busy attending to the rice. The boys and girls do pretty much as they please, and, like white boys and girls, some of them are too lazy to do more than lounge around, while the more industrious ones either help their mothers or go with their fathers and take their first lesson in the hunter's art, while some few of the boys, who are yet to become the noted hunters of the tribe, strike out for themselves, and if they are lucky enough to return at night with a wild goose hanging at their girdle, which they have captured with their bow and arrow, they become the heroes of the hour, and rightly so, for they have achieved a difficult task. But all seem very happy, feasting on ducks and geese, and enjoying their "outing" quite as much as their pale-faced brethren could do.

After a rather tiresome paddle over the torturous course of the river in its windings through the marsh, we came to a falls, which the Indians call "Re-che-wa-saw-qua-sing—The place that can be seen from afar." Here the river tumbles over a ledge of rocks, one may say, right into the marsh. A swell in the ledge of rocks divides the river, and causes it to flow over in two channels. On the little island thus formed, an immense pine tree towers aloft and makes a very prominent land-mark that can be seen from afar. And, probably, what has impressed these lone travellers more deeply, you come within a few miles of this tree hours before you reach it. Indeed, at one place you are nearer to it than you are an hour later, though you may have paddled hard all the time, a bend of the river sending you very far out of your way.

Leaving here after a short day's paddle, we reached a beautiful basin, a little below a lake. Here we camped, and, as it was Saturday night, and we intended to remain until Monday, we made a little extra preparation for our comfort. Our two Indian friends had left us and gone on to the lake, where they had an uncle by the name of Me-no-ma-na living, and where they intended spending the next day. They gave us an invitation to go with them, assuring us of a hearty welcome, but we said we would rather remain where we were, but would call up and see their uncle the next day; and they, knowing the next day was one we held in respect, importuned us no further.

After they had gone and we had made preparations for our stay, we took a stroll about the place. It was a lovely evening and a lovely spot to enjoy it. The basin is a very pretty one. The land on the side upon which we were encamped ran back for a quarter of a mile or more, nearly level. No fallen trees or brush lay on the ground, and there was very little undergrowth, but enough of small pine trees grew scattering about to make a grateful shade. The ground was covered with a carpet of many-colored mosses, which gave the whole place the appearance of a fine park. The other side was high; hill after hill rose up till the last was lost in the blue distance. At the lower end of the basin, a curiously-formed cliff of rocks rose up, garlanded with twining plants. It was a place one might expect to find associated with a legend, and the Indians tell a story very much like one we have all heard about other places, of a beautiful maiden who threw herself from this rock. Sometime after dark we saw a light coming down the river a little distance from the shore. It was a son of Me-no-ma-na hunting deer with a light.

When the weather becomes hot and the water warm, deer often flock to it to paddle about in it, and feed on the water-plants, especially in places where the flies are bad; and the Indians then often slaughter them in great numbers. They attach two clapboards, eight or ten inches long, to a staff, one in a horizontal, the other in a perpendicular position, and then fasten the staff, like a little mast, in their canoe. They place the torch—a cotton rag twisted and saturated with turpentine,—or, if not able to get that, a piece of very resinous pine wood—on the horizontal board, thus making a kind of dark lantern, which enables them to see anything ahead of them, while they and their canoe are hidden in the darkness. A dark night is best, and it must be calm, not only to keep the light from blowing out, but to prevent the scent of the boatman being carried to the deer. Then, a person can approach very near a deer standing on the water's edge, so near that I have known the animal, when fired at, in its sudden consternation to spring right on the canoe. Before you get used to it, it seems very strange to see a wild deer standing in open view, gazing at you without offering to move, while you sail up to within a few feet of it.

This is an easy method of hunting deer, but one that does not bring much credit to the hunter. When the Indians wish to speak contemptuously of one, they say "he hunts with a light."

The next day we went to see our friends' uncle. We found him located on a beautiful lake, and living in a snug little log house, with potatoes and other vegetables growing around him. We thought it a hunter's paradise. Here he was surrounded with game, and when he wanted a deer, all he had to do was to put a torch in his canoe, or call out his dogs, when one would soon be got; or, if he wanted a partridge, or a duck, it was to be found at his very door; or fish, the lake was full of them. In the trapping time, the surrounding country was full of fur, and we could not help wondering why so few Indians adopted his plan of life. The red men, like ourselves and the "gulls and crows" like to flock together and gather into settlements, where necessarily the game becomes scarce for miles around.

Poor Me-no-ma-na was in trouble. He was a pow-wow, and we found him with a hawk's skin fastened to the wall, busy chanting and beating his drum to it, invoking its aid to save his son, a young man of seventeen or eighteen, who lay on a mat near by, apparently far gone in consumption. When we came in, he ceased his weird music, and knowing how these things appeared to us, with natural good breeding he apologized, telling us not to mind, but he had to do something to try and save his son. To some the scene might have appeared absurd, if not ludicrous; to us it did not, for we felt he only voiced the wail and weakness common to humanity in the presence of death, and the hawk's skin to the Indians is no more than the images and pictures in some of our churches are to us, and to which some of us bow down;

for hawk skins to them, as the images and pictures to us, only represent the unseen spirit which lies beyond our ken.

It may be thought their pow-wows are a set of impostors who deceive their brethren, but this is not so. The pow-wows and other Indians believe it a gift from their mun-e-doos, or gods; or rather that some god has taken them into its special favor, and when that god has made itself known by appearing to them in their dreams in the shape of some beast, or bird, or reptile, they procure the skin of that creature, and drying it, put it in their medicine bag, and ever afterwards, when they seek their protector's help, they hang the skin up, and appeal to it.

Out of respect to poor old Me-no-ma-na and his trouble, we did not stay long, but, promising to meet our friends there early next morning, we returned to our camp.

The Indians have a burying-ground here, to which the different hunting parties, from far and near, bring any of their number who happen to die when out on their hunting trips. Towards evening we paid it a visit. Their manner of making their graves is very tasteful, considering their rude means, and looks quite picturesque in the lovely places they often choose for the last resting-place of their friends. They heap up the ground over the grave as we do, then place four small logs of wood around the border, and roof it over with clap-boards split from the cedar tree; and then enclose the whole with a fence formed from logs of wood of about an equal size, standing end-wise and made even at the top. At the head of the grave they drive down a stake, hewn smooth on the inside, and on it paint figures descriptive of the person who lies beneath. Some of these figures are very striking and beautiful. We noticed one tiny grave, and on the stake a blossom, broken and hanging down, was painted—a most appropriate emblem of the dusky little darling who lay beneath.

After our walk, we sat down on the bank of the river to enjoy the fine prospect before us. Before long a large buck, which had taken to the river to escape the wolves, came swimming past. As he floated by he was a tempting sight, with his large, spreading horns, and had it been another day our hunting instincts might have been aroused, but as it was we let him go in peace.

After the sun went down, the water animals of different kinds came from their hiding-places and commenced their gambols and their search for food. We watched them till it became too dark to see; then we repaired to our camp, spent a while in conversation, and retired to our humble but sweet bed of cedar boughs to sleep.

The next morning the wind threatened to be ahead, and, as we wished to get across the lake before it blew hard, we started shortly after day-break.

When we reached the old pow-wow's, we found our friends ready and waiting for us. After two hours' paddling we reached the other side of the lake, with appetites sharpened for our breakfast.

After breakfast we entered a large creek which ran through a low, rich flat, covered with rank ferns and umbrageous elms and soft maples. Deer frequented these flats in large numbers and had well-beaten paths running in different directions. And along with the tracks of deer were the tracks of wolves. For in any place, especially attractive to deer, there, too, are sure to be wolves. And as we passed along, more than once our ears were assailed with the low, mournful howl of a wolf strayed from the pack, or the more dismal yells they make when banded together. But we did not wonder to find wolves plentiful, for not only the paths told us deer were numerous, but every little while, as we passed round a bend of the winding stream, a deer would bound off with a snort, perhaps not twenty feet away. We nearly ran on top of one which was lying in the water hiding from the wolves.

When one looked into this wild flat with so thick a covering of wide spreading trees and dense undergrowth, he felt it was a perfect lair for wild beasts, and as he listened to the dismal yell of wolves he was ready to wonder how deer could willingly frequent such a place. But, strange as it may appear, deer are not disturbed at the voice of their enemy; when a little distance off, in fact, they do not seem to know what it is, and men may shout and wolves howl within thirty or forty rods of them without giving them much concern. Yet deer are quick, remarkably quick, to distinguish between the falling of a branch or the noise of the trees shaken by the wind, and the breaking of a stick by being trodden on. To the first sounds they pay no attention, while the last sound puts them on the alert at once, and yet the report of a gun or the sharp shout of a man, at equally close distances, gives them no alarm. It is true it attracts them, and is often used by the hunter to stop them when they are passing on the run, but it is their curiosity, not their fear, that is aroused. It would seem that nature provides them with an instinct that helps to secure them from immediate danger, while it leaves them free from the distressing fears a real knowledge of their situation would inspire. This is a merciful provision, and it enables them to enjoy their life while it lasts. Then, nature has taught them that water is a refuge from their great enemy the wolf; and, when they are pursued, to it they run, and if a lake is within reach they are safe. A river, unless a large one, affords them less security, for the wolves, if hard by, will follow down the stream on both sides and often get them in the end; though sometimes they catch a tartar in so doing, for if the deer is a large one, and it comes to a shoal, it will remain there, and if the wolves come out to it and the water is not too shallow, the deer will defend itself so dexterously with both hind and fore feet that the would-be destroyer often becomes the destroyed. They will also flee to a creek when hard pressed, though that is not often of much avail. Yet even here they sometimes baffle their pursuers; for nature has endowed them with a good deal of cunning, and they use many devices to hide their scent, not only lying under water with their noses alone sticking out, but sometimes finding their way under an overhanging bank, in order to reach which they must have wholly submerged themselves; and, last of all, if they are annoyed too much, they entirely desert the place, and seek another where they can find more peace. So, we see, the yell of the wolf as it resounds in some dismal swamp, is not as terrible to them as might be supposed.

These flats extended for eight or ten miles, and were the resort not only of bears, deer and wolves, but, what pleased us more, we saw numerous signs of beaver, otter and mink as we passed along, and as we were nearing our destination, we hoped to have some fun as well as profit among them at some future time.

Farther on, the land turned higher, and soon evergreens lined the banks of the stream. Here we saw numerous signs of bears, some of them of very recent origin. The signs grew more and more plentiful as we passed along, showing that the bears had had a high time here a few weeks before, and our Indian friends congratulated themselves on having put off their trip as long as they had.

Bears have a curious habit in their mating season, of reaching up and biting the evergreen trees along their line of march, and tearing off the bark. Some of the Indians call it their "blaze," or mark. They say the he-bears, now and again, as they march along, stand on their hind legs, and, reaching up as high as they can, bite the tree, as a sign to any bears that may follow, as much as to say, "If you can reach that, it may be safe for you to follow, but if not, you had better stay behind." Others, not quite so imaginative, say it is to clean their teeth; but as they only do it at this time of the year, I think it is because they like the taste of the sap, which flows copiously under the bark at this season. Or it may be from some propensity such as makes a cat scratch a chair or table leg, or a dog, at certain times, scratch up the ground — the cause of which nobody seems to know.

But now a break in the trees showed us a lake was near, at which we all rejoiced, for we were weary after our day's paddle, and now were nearing our journey's end. We soon entered the lake, and, passing over to an island, camped for the night.

We were all in good humor, and after feasting on a beaver the Indians had shot during the day, our conversation gradually turned upon bears and bear-hunting. This led to stories about them in their mating season, and as the Indians have a genuine dread of them then, it has led to many traditional tales, many of which would eclipse the adventures of Sinbad the Sailor. The Indian is so accustomed to fall back on legends to answer the many questions which suggest themselves to his circumstantial mind, that he is prone to the marvellous, and when on the mythical, nothing is too extravagant to exceed his belief. When conversing with you on a subject within his reach, he shows himself an observant being, and traces cause and effect with a great deal of accuracy, but question him on something beyond his knowledge, and he at once flies to the supernatural, and will tell you the wildest tales in support of his views. He will relate a personal adventure without exaggeration, in a calm, rational way, but let him turn to a traditional one, and nothing is too strange or impossible for him to narrate as fact. Our friend, Wig-e-maw-way, for instance, bore deep scars received from a bear in an encounter in which he nearly lost his life. Yet he would tell this story in a simple, truthful way, but let him get to a story of "long time ago," and he would become excited at once, and his flashing eye, impassioned manner, and wild gesticulation, in the dim, shadowy light of a camp-fire, made a picture any artist might covet.

The next morning the Indians went after their birch-bark, while we launched forth to take a survey of the lake and pick out a location for our future home.

There is something very fascinating in coasting around a wild lake which the eye of the white man has never seen before. A strange thrill passes through you as you look on waters which have danced and played in the sunlight for thousands of years, and now seem to leap with a fresh joy as they meet you for the first time. And these solemn old hills, which were old when Adam was young, seem to stare at you and wonder at the new thing which now comes to disturb their repose. And could they speak, what a tale they could tell!

But aside from the interest we take in looking at the work nature has done when she was young, and which has only now been revealed to us, there is a pleasure which none but the rover knows, in exploring a wild lake. Not only are new sights and scenes presenting themselves as you round every bend in the shore, but here its wild denizens, unaccustomed to the presence of man, are often abroad in daytime, and in the security of their wild home, act out their native moods. It is one thing to see a wild animal in its native wilds, and another to see it the pet or prisoner of man, where it soon loses the characteristics so necessary to its existence in its wild habitat regions. It was a very pleasing thing to me—and I think would be to many of my readers— to see the beaver working at its dam, or busy bringing in its winter stores, or, what might be of more interest, to see young deer or wolves on the beach skipping about like playful lambs or happy dogs. It looks so strange and different from what you expect, that it is hard to think they are the wild and savage creatures that they are. But let your presence become known, and all is changed. One wild stare, and away they fly into the thicket.

Or, if you want to leave this world, and dwell among goblins and ghosts, coast around some wild, lonely lake, alone in your little dug-out, as night is coming on and the wild creatures of these wild places are leaving their lairs. As the gloom thickens, the fierce yells of wolves ring out from the top of a neighbouring hill, or the scream of a lynx is heard from an adjacent thicket. Silence is hardly restored before strange, unearthly sounds come from a marsh, accompanied by the splashings of uncanny creatures at play. Then the lone, weird cry of the loon, in answer to the ghostly hootings of the great horned owl, breaks the stillness of the night, and you find your way to the camp, ceasing to wonder that the Indian lives in a world of spirits.

We returned from our cruise well pleased with all we saw, and could easily believe what our friends told us, that the country, far and near, abounded in game. And as the place was well situated to catch the hunters who passed on beyond, and as these passages would be before and after the hunting season, we expected to be able to do a little trading without interfering much with our own hunt.

The lake, too, was a beautiful one; dotted with pretty islands, and in

232

every way adapted to make a pleasant forest home. The only thing against it was its name. The Indians called it Min-e-gob-e-shing, "the place of the big eyes." The name did not suggest pleasant memories, for the "big eyes" were the frozen, swollen eyes of an unfortunate hunter, who perished here from exhaustion and cold; and as the lake hereafter would be "our lake," and as it was a bright, cheerful one, we called it Pretty Lake.

When we returned to our camp, we found our friends had already arrived with their bark, ready for a start homeward the following morning. So, after a good night's sleep, we started down the creek on our return journey.

When we drew near the old pow-wow's he appeared with his face blackened, and then Wig-e-maw-way said, "Pe-na-she, the pow-wow's son, is dead." And so it was. He had passed away the night after we had left, and now lay arrayed for his burial. The old man had put away his drum and his hawk's skin, as now of no avail, and he sat with a heavy heart mourning for his first-born son. But no outward manifestations bespoke the struggle within, and he calmly spoke to us about his son's death. He said he had seen Ne-wak-e, a distant and unfriendly pow-wow, prowling around there in the shape of a black dog. Soon afterward his son fell sick, and in spite of all he could do, grew worse and worse; for Ne-wak-e's god was stronger than his own, and his son's body grew so full of pain and weakness that he was glad to leave it, much as he loved chasing the wild deer, or hunting the moose and the beaver.

A number of the friends had collected and we felt they would rather be alone than have strangers among them at such a time as this, so we told our two friends we would go on to the burying ground and camp there, and help them to lay Pe-na-she away the next day. Taking the old man by the hand, we silently bade him good-bye, and proceeded on our way to our old camping-ground.

On visiting the burying-ground next morning, we found a deep grave had been dug, to hide Pe-na-she's body, as the Indians said, from the wolves and the fishers, for they are very careful of their dead, and the reputation of our "resurrectionists," has travelled far and near among them, and fills them with horror. They say "the wolf, the fisher and the white man's doctor are the only brutes that rob the grave."

About ten o'clock we saw the canoes coming on their solemn journey with the dead to its last home on earth. It was a simple sight, but to us one more impressive than would be the grandest pageant made

233

at the burial of a monarch. There was no sham or display here. All was sincere; for whatever the Indians lack, they have faith, and they were now with their loved one on the first stage of his last and lonely journey. They knew Pe-na-she hated to leave his friends and his hunting grounds. The song of the birds was still pleasant to him. And as the fawn lingers about the place where its mother has been killed, so his spirit would linger about the grave for six moons, hating to leave his body, and fearful of starting on the unknown journey to the spirit land. But at last his body would waste away, and he would have to go; and then they could see him travelling day after day and week after week towards the setting sun. And would he be able to walk the slippery pole that lies across the dreadful river that separates this world from the one beyond? Or would he fall off and be carried by the rushing torrent into the dreadful abyss? They hoped it would be well with their son and brother, but their hearts were sad.

The canoes soon arrived; and the dead hunter, lying in his birch-bark coffin, was carried to the grave. He was dressed in all his finery, his hunting belt strapped around him, with his tomahawk and knife fastened to it and his gun laid by his side.

Soon he was lowered into his grave, and the last solemn "feast with the dead" commenced. A little fire was made at the head of the grave, and all sat down around it. The food was passed around and eaten in silence, for Pe-na-she was now in the land of silence; and why should we disturb his spirit with our noisy talk.

A way down to the coffin had been dug out at the side of the grave. After the feast was finished, the old pow-wow went down and carefully adjusting the things lying beside the young hunter left some medicine, in case he might need it before he reached the spirit land. Then the old mother went down with some food and a pair of moccassins, and with a mother's tenderness placed them with her dead son. But, less stoical than the father, as she left she gave a dismal howl, which probably sounded better to savage than civilized ears. Last of all, a young maiden timidly stepped down and placed a wild rose on his breast, which eloquently told the story so well-known to all human hearts. Now a birch-bark cover was placed over the coffin, some slabs placed over it, and the grave filled in. When all was done, a pole was stuck in the ground leaning over the head of the grave, and some food left hanging to it, that Pe-na-she's spirit might not want while it hovered about the grave.

234

It is hard for us to sympathize with those who have been trained into a different way of thinking from ourselves, and, perhaps, some of my white friends will laugh at the story I have told. But to me it was deeply interesting. It was simple nature's grappling with the mystery of life and death, and if they have solved the great problem to their satisfaction, why should we laugh at them? Do we not try to solve it ourselves? And, perhaps the Great Father smiles at our attempts as we do at theirs, and in the end it may be found that they were as near the truth as the wise ones among ourselves, who tell us we shall "float as airy nothings in the illimitable void." Be that as it may, I left the old pow-wow with feelings more akin to all mankind, and I hoped that he and I might find our way through the darkness, and, at last, meet in the happy hunting country that lies beyond the grave.

AUNT JANE, AE: 92

William Wilfred Campbell

" 'General' Bain, of Sandy Beach"*

THE INHABITANTS OF SANDY BEACH had a strong and enduring interest in General Bain, he being the most fascinating and mercurial character in that vicinity. The "General" (how he ever got the title no one knew) was all in all the most reprobate of reprobate characters who had arrived in that region.

If a bundle of negative virtues and positive vices make up a character, he certainly was one. He had arrived one season from that vague and unsatisfying region called "down below," whence all the inhabitants had come at some time or other, and which designated one of the older settled districts. On his arrival, he had taken up his residence on a deserted apology for a farm, composed of seven dry and bald conical sandhills, with a certain amount of slightly arable land between. Here, in a small hut built by the former owner, he established his home and proceeded also to establish his claims to the title of farmer, by methods which, if not the most solid and painstaking, were certainly the most unique ever practised in that region. The General, as he said himself, was Irish and Protestant to the backbone. He was from the North, that home of Orangemen and flaxen fabrics, but he had, in common with the rest of his race, a perpetual thirst, which was only

*The Canadian Magazine, Oct. 1894, pp. 527-30.

237

satisfied by the contents of a black bottle. To add that he was a mixture of braggart and coward, that he was well on to eighty, and yet, as he said of himself, as "frisky as a kitten," would be to enumerate some of his characteristics. He was of a tall and bony figure, with a prominent nose which had a purplish terminus, and, when well dressed and not drunk, the General had a seductive and engaging manner which had deceived many a parson.

He had come suddenly, and had certainly brought enough money, however he had got it, to furnish his rude home, and to be able to buy a yoke of oxen, and a cart and sleigh, things indispensable even to a pretence of farming in that or any other region. His first arrival had been celebrated by a series of debauches, and this, coupled with his conduct at the nearest village, and a certain rumor as to his past that was as much surmisal as fact, did not add much to the General's character as a saint. And, even in that rude region, the inhabitants were doubtful as to his admission to society, until he conquered them all by an act that settled his claim to respectability for ever after. Once a month, a wandering parson would come and hold forth in the log school house, and there was a large attendance, and, when made aware of the occurrence, the General said "Sartinly" he would "attind" the "sarvice" as "become" a "rispictable" man. He always spoke of himself in this way, and never seemed to have lost confidence in his own personality, however much the world might doubt it. He had bragged in a vague way of his former greatness of estate down "below," but only in a general way, and beyond this and the fact that he was a man of family, and had been through the trials of wedlock three times—a fact of which he seemed to be very proud—they got nothing more out of him. Sometimes, when in a maudlin state, he would bemoan his late deceased spouse in a manner certainly not to her credit. "Poor baste of a woman, she was a great thrial to me, that she was; divilish great thrial," he would say: but what her name was, or where she had lived, or whether or not he had had any children by her, the General never stated.

At last, the Sunday on which there would be service had arrived. The General had been sobering all the previous day, and had kept to himself, and on Sunday morning the group of young and old, who had already arrived, were amazed and dumbfounded by the sight of the General coming round the bend of the road, seated on a board in his oxcart, and dressed in a grandeur of fashion never before seen in that community. His body was encased in an old and well worn but neat dress suit of black broadcloth, and on his head he wore an equally old and well worn beaver hat, that showed signs, to the close observer, of having been slightly battered in places, and to complete his attire he had on the remnants of a once respectable shirt collar, that much washing and want of washing had wasted and marred. In a more particular community, the General would have been regarded as decidedly seedy, if not dilapidated, as to his outward apparel, but, at Sandy Beach, where even a paper collar was scarcely known, and black clothes rarely came, even with the parson, this was a sign of dignity and grandeur that was not to be slighted. There was also a sort of compliment to the inhabitants in this tribute to their feelings that made them all bound to honor the man who so added to their respectability. So those who had but the day before called him a drunken beast, approached the General to-day with a sense of respect. Mooring his cart by the nearest stump, the General alighted with a certain stiff dignity, which might have been overdone, but which impressed the bystanders, and, going forward, he began a series of handshakes with those he knew.

"D——, ef the Gineral ain't most a gintleman," said one old man to a neighbor. "He's the rale stuff in him; it's easy seein' he's lived below," whimpered an old crone to another. The General, evidently greatly pleased in a stiff way with all this notice, moved to the centre of the door, and, with an old battered silver watch displayed in his hand, gravely awaited the parson. That person, when he arrived, was so dumbfounded at the General's dignity and patronage that he could hardly preach, with observing him, and, in his confusion, gave the plate to the General to take up the collection, passing over the leading Deacon, who, in his wonder at the General's style, forgot to notice the omission. The next day, when he had discarded the dignities with his clothes, on being complimented on his success, he answered: "Ah! didn't I, though; wer'nt I the divil of a churchwarden in me day?" But there was no doubt, that with all the General's peccadilloes, there was a certain link between him and society which he asserted in this much valued suit of clothes, as, when he wore them, he was always a more respectable man.

Next in order to his wonderful dress and unique character, the General was chiefly attractive to the community as a marriageable man, and when, in referring to the "poor baste" of a woman, "who was such a thrial," he hinted that he was on the look out for another to take her place, there was quite a sensation in the settlement. "The

239

Gineral's goin' to get married," was the general talk; "wonder who he'll take."

But, after quite a little flirting and coquetry in an ancient way of his own, he finally singled out a strapping young maiden (one of a large family), who had just turned fourteen, which was the marriageable age in the settlement; and dressed out in his resplendent apparel, he took her in the oxcart to the nearest town, where they were married. When remonstrated with as to their great disparity of ages, he merely remarked: "O, shure, she'll grow, and as for me, why I'm jist one of the bys."

But, successful as he was as a man of society, the General proved a failure as a husband. Whether owing to the disparity of their ages, or to the General's eccentric habits and extreme distaste for work, is not known, but the result was a series of domestic storms at the Seven Hills farm, in which there was a good deal of give and take on both sides, for, if the General was a man of remarkable parts, the young woman was endowed with a certain muscle as well as determination. So, if the young woman appeared with a black eye, the General matched it with a scored nose, the hostilities being well equalized.

But the climax came when the General, who, egged on by some waggish admirers, attempted to conquer a woman, was ruined in the attempt.

He had a habit of periodically going to the nearest village and getting gloriously drunk, and, while in this uncertain state, he would brag of his great prowess as a fighter. "Form a ring, bys: Gineral Bain's going to fight," he would say, and then, when, contrary to his expectations, a ring was accommodatingly formed, he would commence weeping for some one to "hould" him, for fear he would hurt somebody. So far, in their broils, his young wife had respected his person, when he came home drunk and quarrelsome, for the sake of the clothes he wore; but when he was in other attire, she gave no quarter. He soon began to perceive this, and, thinking to take advantage of her weakness in this respect, and his vanity being touched at the many stories of her prowess, he said: "Bys, if there's a man av matremonyal expayrience, it's me's the man. Just come home with me, bys, and see me conquer a wiman;" and they went. The General had on his elfin attire, so he thought he was infallible. "She'd niver spile these, no matter what I did," he said to himself, as he went under the darkness, followed by the others, who had come to see "the Gineral conquer a wiman."

But the General was out his calculation for once, for who can speculate on a woman, and in this case there were other conditions involved. She met him at the door, so there was a pitched battle in the yard. But to the General's horror, the conquering was all on the other side. She went for him with a vengeance, did that young woman he had essayed to conquer. She jammed his darling beaver on a stump, and then sat him so heavily on it that its symmetry was destroyed forever. She slit his elfin coat from the tail to the collar, and then ripped it from his astonished back. The crowd who came to see her conquered, were even too astonished to laugh at this surprising out-bursting of feminine energy, but she kept on till the General and his darling wardrobe were in two separate heaps, and each in a state of ruin.

"'Thar," she said to the young men, as she flung the final rag on the heap of clothes. "'Thar; I don't feel married a bit. I married that thar suit of clothes, I did, and now it's gone I fell as single as ever;" and, with a defiant laugh, she disappeared into the house. That night she left for parts unknown with a younger man.

From that night the General was a doomed being. The settlement was much excited over the conjugal rupture, and some tried to com-miserate with him on her unfaithfulness. But it was the clothes he lamented and not the young woman. "Wimmen is plinty," he would say, "but if she'd only lift thim clothes — It's kilt entirely that I am." It was soon seen that the General was broken-hearted: he took to his bed and complained for the first time of being old. He had a man with slight claims to being a tailor come and try to fix up his wrecked wardrobe, but it was no use — she had done her work too well: the tailor did his best to fix them together, but they were not the garments of yore. The General took this circumstance more and more to heart; he had them placed on his bed, where he could see and feel them. "If she'd only a lift me them" he would mourn.

A kindred spirit with similar tastes came to stay with him, and they took more and more to drink. At last the General sent for a doctor.

"You had better sober up, General," said the doctor, "it's your only chance." "The divil, docther," said the General; "it's a quare, unheal-thy counthry where a man can't have his wee drop; it's better to be out of it. O, thim's happy as is under the sthones. If she'd only a lift me thim clothes, docther, I might a stood it."

It soon became more and more evident that the General was about to depart to another country, and this being made clear to him, with the suggestion that a parson be sent for, he said: "It's nary use, Tim, it's too fer—an' then it's too late; but just put on me clothes, Tim, and I'll feel as I'm in churrch. I'll die rispictable at laste." By dint of a great deal of work, Tim managed to get the poor, weak, old man into his dilapidated garments, and though sinking fast, his eyes brightened when they were on; he tried to fondle the tattered sleeve with his emaciated hand; then he lay for a long time very quiet, when suddenly starting up, he said: "Indade, it's about time for the collection;" and then he rolled over—the collection was at last taken up, and so was the General.

But it was afterwards known that the General with all his shiftless ways, had been mindful of his latter end, for Tim had found a small wooden slab in an old outhouse, which he put over the grave, and on it had been carved the following legend by the General himself, in rude capitals:—

HERE LIES
GENERAL BAIN,
WHO DIED IN HIS BIST
CLOTHES, A RISPICTABLE
MAN—A RAYL OULD
IRISH PROTESTANT.

WILLIAM WILFRED CAMPBELL was born in Berlin, Canada West (now Kitchener), in 1858 and died in 1918 near Ottawa. His childhood was spent largely on the Bruce Peninsula of Georgian Bay—a setting that was to have a profound influence on the lyric poetry of his adulthood. Campbell was ordained in 1886, fulfilling the duties of his priesthood in New Hampshire, New Brunswick, and Ontario before leaving the ministry in 1891 due to a crisis of faith. He then joined the civil service in Ottawa. There, having met Archibald Lampman and Duncan Campbell Scott, he collaborated with them on "At the Mermaid Inn." In 1893 he was admitted to the Royal Society of Canada. Campbell also wrote a weekly column, "Life and Letters," for the Ottawa *Evening Journal* from 1903 to 1905.

His poetry includes *Snowflakes and Sunbeams* (1888), *Lake Lyrics* (1889), *The Dread Voyage* (1893), *Beyond the Hills of Dream* (1899),

The Lyre Degenerate (1903), *Collected Poems* (1906), *Sagas of Vaster Britain* (1914), *War Lyrics* (1915), *Lyrics of Iron and Mist* (1916), and *Lyrics of the Dread Redoubt* (1917). He also wrote several plays, and two novels. Always seeking to promote Canadian literature and nationalism, he published descriptive books about Canada and edited *The Oxford Book of Canadian Verse* (1913).

CARIBOO MINERS AND INDIANS.

John C. Werner

"Buried Under an Avalanche:
An Experience in British Columbia"*

IN THE SPRING of the year 1881 a great excitement prevailed in British Columbia and Washington Territory over the alleged discovery of rich deposits of gold in the mountains at the head of the Skeena and Stikeen rivers. A party of old prospectors had made the find during the previous year, and, although they tried to keep it quiet during the winter they spent in Victoria, the secret leaked out, and in the spring a rush was made to the new El Dorado. All sorts and conditions of men, Jews and Gentiles, miners and gamblers, shopkeepers and sailors, flocked thither, bent on making their fortune. A few miles up the Skeena river was soon founded a town, to which was given the imposing name of Shakespeare, and from thence a constant stream of fortune-hunters flowed towards the "diggins," which were situated fifty miles up the mountains. I was, at the time, second mate of a bark, which I left to join the heterogeneous crowd on board the steamer bound for Shakespeare. I had about three hundred dollars in cash with me, and soon procured a "fit out," and in a short time was on my way to the mountains.

How we toiled and struggled for a bare existence that summer, how disappointment followed upon disappointment, with seldom a gleam of encouragement, has nothing to do with this story. In the fall of the

*The Canadian Magazine, March 1895, pp. 453-57.

year, the crowd had greatly diminished; most of them returning broken and dispirited; while a few, very few though, were richer than when they arrived. I had, like others, staked out a claim, which I had worked with varying success for some time, when I became acquainted with a young fellow who had, for several years, followed up every rush, and who, if he had not made much money, had gained a great deal of experience, and together we were doing fairly well, when the exodus set in. The owners of some of the adjoining claims then proposed that we should club together and lay in a good stock of provisions and stay over the winter. As our new partners were men who had spent the best part of their lives in the mountains, and were seemingly "passing honest," I accepted their proposal, and instead of returning to Victoria, as I had intended, I remained in the fastnesses of the Baldheaded mountains.

Lumber was plentiful, and before the snow had covered the ground we built a roomy and comfortable log house and laid in a goodly supply of firewood. We could not do much gold-digging during the winter, and our time was spent in interchanging visits, playing poker for small stakes, and spinning yarns. Occasionally some one would sally out with his rifle and bring in a deer or a bear, and in this way our larder was kept well stocked. As all my partners and neighbors were old hunters and miners, and I was the only "tenderfoot" among them, I had at first to figure as a butt for their rather coarse witticisms, until one day, over some trouble about a poker game, I made a demonstration that rather surprised them, and from that time forward I had a considerable amount of respect shown to me.

We were now getting well on into February, 1882, and had had for nearly two months no communication with the outside world: the weather had been terrible, even for this region; snow fell almost every day, and all the passes and trails were impassible. But, for the last two days the weather had changed, and it was now freezing hard, so that the crust of the snow was as solid as ice. Our life, after our isolation was complete, had been to me rather dull, and I was willing to engage in any adventure that promised to break the monotony. Hearing one of the old stagers declare his intention to start down to the town the next day, and if possible return with letters and papers for the boys, I volunteered to accompany him. The expostulations of my partners only strengthened my purpose, and I prepared for my journey in hot haste. But, during the night, a thaw set in, and in the morning the other man refused to proceed, as it was no longer safe, he said. After vainly attempting to make the old fellow alter his mind, I concluded to start alone, principally because I thought everybody would laugh at me if I hung back after all my eager preparations. As the road was nearly all down hill, I calculated that I would be able to accomplish the journey in a day, if no accident happened, for I had made a pair of snowshoes, on which I was a good performer. I received a great deal of advice about the course I should take, and was especially admonished not to make any noise going down the mountains, for the slightest concussion in the air might start the snow, and I would be buried by an avalanche before I had time to escape. No objections were made or any difficulties put in my way when they saw that I was in earnest; and when I left at seven o'clock in the morning they gave me three hearty cheers.

I carried a swag containing two blankets, a change of clothing, and two days' provisions, so that I was not burdened with a heavy load. I had also a short Winchester rifle, with the chamber full of cartridges. For the first two hours I glided along at a good pace, for the snow was still hard and it was all down hill. At 3.30 p.m., I had got as far as the river, but had still fifteen miles before me. The mountains on the bank of the river ended here abruptly in a high peak called the Devil's Toe. This peak was at least 150 feet in height, and very steep; and in the narrow space intervening between it and the river, a log house had been built under the lee of a low precipice which nearly overhung the cabin, and which was separated from it by a space of 15 feet or a little more. It contained only one room, and had a fire-place at one end. The door was in the middle of the side fronting the river, with a small enclosed stoop or shed outside: the window, consisting of an aperture a foot square, and closed with a shutter, was opposite the door and towards the mountain. The house was substantially built of heavy logs, and boarded over on the outside. It had a ceiling, and a fixed ladder leading to the loft over it. I determined to stay here over night, for I had the worst part of the road before me, and I did not care about risking life and limbs in the darkness. I found nobody living in the cabin, but, as the door only closed with a wooden hasp, I made free to enter. The outside shed was full of fire-wood. I found a quantity of straw in one corner inside, several barrels and an iron bucket in another; and half a dozen pieces of bacon were hanging near the fire-place. I opened the shutter to let in some fresh air, for the room had a damp and unwholesome smell, and then made a fire. Taking the bucket and filling it with snow, I put it over the fire to melt, for it would be too difficult to procure any water from the river.

A fox now approached the door, and was watching my proceedings, and, without thinking on what I was doing, I raised my rifle and knocked him over. As I stepped forward to pick him up, I heard a dull, rumbling sound overhead, and, looking up, it seemed to me that the whole mountain was toppling over and tumbling down on me, sweeping everything before it, snow, rocks and trees, in one immense mass. I had just time to throw myself inside the cabin and shut the door when the hut was overwhelmed and all was darkness. I expected to see the cabin collapse under the terrible weight that must have been on it, but it withstood the pressure. After the first shock all was still as death. I had thrown myself on the ground inside the door, and the stillness was so intense that I could hear my heart thumping.

It took some time before I could collect my scattered senses and examine my position. I had escaped with my life for the present—that was one thing to be thankful for,—but, if I had to endure a lingering death, the present respite was no boon. I had seen a rude lamp standing on a cask when I first entered the house, and this I lighted, but it gave only a faint light. A lot of snow had come down the chimney and extinguished the fire, and more of it had come in through the open window, which was now closed with a solid bank of snow. I went to the door, and tried to open it, but I could not move it, although I used my whole strength; but, as it opened outwards, no doubt an immense mass of snow, which defied my puny efforts, was pressing against it. I thrust my rifle up the chimney, but it struck against something hard a short distance up, and I supposed the chimney above the roof was broken off and part of it had fallen inwards.

The air was still pure; but how long would it remain so? Buried alive! The thought maddened me! I could not expect any relief for a month at least, and by that time it would, in all likelihood, be too late. Even if I had provisions enough to sustain me, the air would give out, and I would die a slow and lingering death. I searched round the room, but found no tool or anything with which I could dig myself out. The door I could not open, and the window presented a wall of snow. I overhauled the stores, and found one barrel containing some flour; another had some cornmeal in it; evidently there was enough food to last me a considerable time.

I lighted the fire again. At first it would not burn, though the smoke filled the room: but after a while it began to flicker up. The smoke disappeared gradually, and, to my great relief, I saw that it had an outlet somewhere up the chimney, and consequently I would not be deprived of fresh air. This put new life and hope into me.

I looked at my watch, and found it was 9 o'clock. I had some cold venison and some hard bread in my bag, and made a good supper, and immediately afterwards fell asleep. But I awoke shivering with cold, and the dead silence and the darkness were appalling. I tried to sleep again and imagined that my situation was only a horrid dream; but I could not do it; it was too real, and I had to get up and face it. I struck a match—I had only one block, and I had to be careful of them—and saw it was 7.40—in the morning, I supposed. I kindled a fire, and saw that it would burn if I did not put too much wood on at a time. Then I scraped some snow from the window and melted it, and took some flour and made a few dampers. I had a pouch full of tobacco; so I lighted my pipe and calmed my overwrought feelings. I was not in such a bad predicament after all. If the house held together—and I could not see why it should not, for it had stood the first shock—I had only to husband my resources until I was relieved, which I was sure to be, sooner or later. I was in a disagreeable position, true enough: but I was safe and sound; I was young and healthy, and could stand a lot of hardship.

I began to whistle, but somehow the whistling died out ignominiously, and I fell into the other extreme, and was in a fair way to having a good cry. The worst of it was the continued darkness. I could not afford to keep the fire going all the time, but had it banked up with ashes during the day, and it went out almost every night. The oil had given out in a few days, and after that it was constant night. To mark the flight of time, I made a notch in a log for every twenty-four hours, and I was careful to keep my watch going. After the first ten days, I slept fourteen hours out of the twenty-four, and the rest of the time employed myself with my culinary affairs, and in walking up and down the cabin singing and reciting to myself. Day after day passed, but whether it snowed or rained, whether or not the sun was shining, or whether or not it was blowing a gale, was entirely unknown to me, I knew the air was getting milder, and the snowbank outside the window was melting, and that was all.

Twenty-nine days had passed, and I had food for only about two days more; the firewood was finished also. I had made up all the flour and meal into damper before the firewood gave out, and this was now my only fare. The food and the confinement were beginning to tell upon me, and I was becoming feverish and listless. Many times I would start up suddenly in my sleep, imagining that somebody was calling me, and my disappointment was fearful when I awoke in the tomb-like silence. Another day passed, and I remained prostrate on my blankets, too sick to sit up; the snow melted of itself in the bucket now, and this was the only nourishment I took. Two more days of suffering elapsed, and I had given up all hope. I could not sleep now, and the most horrible fantasies hovered constantly before me; I could see figures dancing in the dark, grotesque, but dreadful to behold, beings all eyes and no legs, and others all legs and nothing else, and I shrank beneath the blankets. How I suffered during these days!

All at once, during one of my spells—night or day, I did not know which for my watch had run down—I heard voices. Thinking they were the goblins, I had buried myself under the blankets, when suddenly the door was flung open, and the blessed sunlight streamed through the aperture. Several persons entered, and, seeing me, started back in astonishment. "Halloa! what have we here?" said one. I could not speak at first. They soon saw what a state I was in, and, holding me up, poured some whiskey into my mouth. This revived me, and I began to thank them in extravagant terms for my delivery. They looked at each other with some surprise.

"What have we delivered you from, pard?" asked the one who had first spoken. "What have you been doing, and how did you get here?"

"Goodness," I cried, "can't you see that I was buried here by an avalanche, and that but for your timely help in digging me out, I would have perished."

They looked at each other again, and finally broke out in a loud laugh.

"Some mistake here, I guess," said the former speaker, after their mirth was exhausted. "You may have had an avalanche here, but you have surely not been buried in it, and we did not dig you out, either. I passed by here a couple of weeks ago, and the place was as free of snow then as now, except at the back of the house: if I had supposed that anybody had been living here, I would have called in."

I looked at him incredulously. I thought he was making fun of me and my distress.

"Look here," said he, and, taking me by the arm, he led me outside the house.

No snow was to be seen, except on the more distant mountains, and the sun was shining brightly on the ground, which was already dressing for summer. The daylight hurt my eyes and made me dizzy, and I had to return to the cabin to get accustomed to the light. The rough but kindly miners gave me food, and boiled some coffee, while I related to them my vicissitudes, at which they were highly amused.

The avalanche that I had seen in its rapid descent had shot over the cabin into the river, and only the loose snow had tumbled on the roof, and from there slid down into the space between the cabin and the rock, and filled it up. The branch of a tree had lodged outside the door, which it had jammed so hard that I could not open it in my hasty attempt to do so; if I had kept on trying, no doubt I would have loosened the obstacle and opened the door. Instead of thoroughly ascertaining my position, I had taken it for granted that I had been overwhelmed by the avalanche, and been buried under it; and thus had suffered incarceration for 35 days, the actual time I spent inside the hut, for nothing.

After I had recovered myself a little, I continued my way to Shakespeare. The story had got ahead of me, however, and wherever I went, I had to hear about "the tenderfoot and the avalanche"—exaggerated, of course, in the telling—and as I could not silence a multitude, I concluded that mining was not my forte, and so left in disgust for Puget Sound, where I shipped for Callao.

YOKOHAMA.

DRAWN SPECIALLY BY H. W. MURCHISON.

A COUREUR-DE-BOIS.

William McLennan

"The Coureur-de-Bois: A Sketch"*

THE GUARD HOUSE at the Porte du Port of the old town of Montreal was comparatively empty that cool May evening of 1701. There had been a week of almost stifling heat, and every one was exhausted by the sudden change from the temperature of winter into that of mid-summer. Most of the men had turned in early, glad of the prospect of a refreshing night's rest. In the guard-room a couple of non-commissioned officers were chatting and smoking, three or four soldiers were playing passe dix on a long bench which served as a table; the officer in command was walking to and fro in the empty Place du Marché with his his friend Jacques Bizard, the Town Major, and the sentry yawned sleepily in the refreshing coolness as he slowly paced up and down before the gate.

From the windows of the Ancien Seminaire opposite, a few lights twinkled, but the town itself was as dark and as silent as the grave.

Outside the wall, beyond the "Little River," the new mansion of Monsieur Louis Hector de Callière, Chevalier of the Order of St. Louis and Governor of Canada, loomed up imposingly with its heavy bastions. Before the main entrance a sentry paced up and down, for the Governor had come up from Quebec to spend a few days with his friend François Dollier de Casson, the Curé of Montreal.

*The Canadian Magazine, Aug. 1898, pp. 321-25.

253

Within the new dining-room the two friends sate in earnest converse. The Governor grey-haired, worn with years and service, rested with his gouty leg pillowed on a chair, talking as cheerfully as a man might under such circumstances. There was at times a strong sympathy in his voice and an affectionate light in his eyes as he marked with regret the failing of that herculean strength which had so long distinguished Dollier de Casson.

Both men were evidently nearing the end of their careers and both had much in common. They were equal in birth; in youth their profession was the same,—for the priest had ridden far on the highway to fame under the great Turenne before he had donned the cassock; and for years the object of their common labour and devotion had been the success of the struggling colony.

The windows at the lower end of the room giving on the river were wide open and the night wind swept pleasantly in. Suddenly a shrill, high-pitched cry, broken into sharp, short jerks, burst upon them from the outer darkness.

The Curé started to his feet, while the Governor sat bolt upright in amazement. "Mordieu! Les Iroquois!" he exclaimed; for the quick jerk of the Iroquois war-whoop once heard can never be forgotten.

The challenge of the sentries both at the Governor's and at the town gate rang out simultaneously as the priest hastened to the window. For answer, the same sharp, evil cry arose from the blackness of

Note.—Dobosq was one of the most notorious Coureurs-de-bois of his day, and though he does not figure so prominently as La Taupine in the reports of the Intendant, he peeps out here and there in contemporary records, especially in the letter of the Franciscan, transcribed at length by the Abbé Tanguay in that interesting common-place book, "A Travers les Registres," which forms so happy a supplement to his exhaustive work on Canadian genealogy.

Dobosq inherited a strong strain of Indian blood, for his grandfather, Laurent Dubosq, a native of St. Maclou (Rouen), married, in 1662, the daughter of Joachim Arontio, the first Huron chief baptized by Braboeuf; his mother, however, was a Frenchwoman and the family might have reverted in time to the original type, but in Dubosq the wild blood was uppermost and sent him wandering amongst his savage kinsmen. The main facts of the above sketch are true, as may be seen upon reference to the letter above cited, which will be found under the date 1703.—W. M.

the river, and without further hestitation the sentry before the Governor's levelled his piece and fired in the direction whence it came. At the gate quick command was followed by instantaneous commotion as the whole guard turned out; and lights flashed across the square, when from the river came a wild chorus of shouts, and laughter, and jeering cries of mock reproach and welcome, as a large canoe was faintly seen to sweep round the Point and up to the beach opposite the Porte du Port.

"The devil takes care of his own! It is that vaurien Dubosq back again," reported the Curé from his post at the window.

From the canoe sprang six men, followed by two women, who made their way up to the gate, but to their surprise it was still fast closed and remained so in spite of their clamourous demands for entrance. As they paused for a moment for some response, they heard within the commands of the officer and the tramp of retreating footsteps as the guard was dismissed and returned to quarters. Whereupon one of their number drew a short axe from his belt and began to batter on the stout oaken gates. His performance was cut short by a commanding voice overhead:

"Here! Below there! Rest where you have lit, ye thieves, until morning. If I open, you shall all go under lock and key, and if one of you dare so much as lay a hand on that gate again or speak above his breath I'll open fire!"

There was no mistaking that voice; each one of the riotous crew sullenly cursed the unlucky chance by which the Town Mayor happened to be at the gate to spoil their triumphant entry; but they knew he was quite capable of carrying out his threats and retired in silence, consigning him to everlasting tortures for a "maudit suisse," as he was. After watching them until they disappeared in the darkness the corpulent Major withdrew to rejoin his companion, laughing and pleased at this tribute to his authority.

Meanwhile there was angry discussion, and hot reproach bandied back and forth between the discomfited and mortified arrivals; at length he who had plied his axe to such disappointing effect said in a low tone of savage authority, "Hold your tongues, fools! Get that canoe and set me across at the Point and we'll see if the Governor will refuse to receive a man who returns as I do!" As he awaited the fulfilment of his orders he turned toward the gate, and, patting his axe with an angry gesture, growled slowly, "You pack of hounds! Would you have me come to your beggarly town on my hands and knees

255

because I am without a load of furs behind me? You'll have another song to sing by the morning."

He never raised his voice or made other gesture than that sinister patting of his axe, and he quietly ordered, "Put me across!" as he stepped into the canoe.

A few strokes were sufficient to reach the farther side, where their leader, followed by the two women, scrambled up the steep bank. He answered the challenge of the sentry who had advanced from his post before the main door of the chateau, and civilly demanded permission to see the Governor.

However lightly the authorities might hold him, he was well known and highly admired by the soldiery, most of whom looked with longing towards the freedom of his roving life; so he and his two companions were readily admitted into the entrance hall and bidden await the Governor's pleasure.

Under the light of the smoking oil-lamp he stood the ideal half-breed Coureur-de-bois. He was rather under-sized, but his lithe, graceful figure was perfect in its proportions and his olive face strikingly handsome, with its thin, regular features framed by his jet black hair, which fell in two long braids on each breast. He was dressed in complete buckskin, and notwithstanding the season, his blanket, which hung over his left shoulder, was wound closely round his waist in approved Indian fashion.

The two women were squaws, clearly Iroquois in feature and dress; one middle-aged and ordinary enough, but the other was a girl of not more than fifteen, with the soft eyes and fawnlike timidity of face which constitute the charm of Indian beauty.

The Governor was annoyed at the bravado of the intruders' approach, but amused at the predicament into which they had fallen, and after a few words with the Curé ordered the trio to be admitted.

As the Coureur-de-bois entered, followed by the two squaws, the Governor eyed him with no friendly glance, for he represented the worst type of that lawless class which had outgrown its first usefulness, and had now developed into the most disturbing element in the internal government of the colony.

The Coureur-de-bois advanced into the room with a natural dignity and assumed deference of manner, for he fully realized the delicacy of his position; and, after bowing low before the Governor, turned towards the Curé, to whom he extended his hand with easy assurance.

"All in good time, Master Dubosq," said Dollier dryly, waiving aside the proffered greeting, "Let us first hear what you have to say to His Excellency."

Dubosq smiled as his name was mentioned, dropped his hand palm upwards on the table, and bending forward said, with scarcely hidden insolence, "Is he necessary?" indicating the soldier standing armed and motionless at the door.

The Governor frowned impatiently, but signed to the soldier, who withdrew. Dubosq on his part turned to the squaws, who at his bidding backed over to the wall, where, crouching on the floor, they remained immovable throughout the interview, silently following every gesture and expression of the actors with their tireless eyes.

"Now then," said the Governor impatiently, "no lies and no boasting more than you can help! I am sick of you and all your tribe! What new deviltry have you been up to that you must needs carry your impudence into my presence at this hour! I care nothing about your idiocy before the gate; you shall answer to the Major for that to-morrow! Now then, begin!"

An angry blush burned redly under Dubosq's dusky skin, but his low voice, with its trace of Indian sweetness, betrayed no resentment as he spoke, "Yes, mon gouverneur, I have something to tell, and something to show, or I would not have disturbed you and Monsieur le Curé at this hour.

"It is not two weeks since I left with La Taupine to trade; and my congé was in proper order," he added quickly. "We had fine weather, two good canoes and four men; we had attended to all our duties, as you know, Monsieur le Curé," glancing at the priest, who, however, gave no sign of acknowledgement to this adroit feeling for support. "We owed no man anything but our regular accounts; so nothing could promise better.

"But see how things fall out! No sooner had we entered Les Mille Iles than we heard La Mouche was in camp at a place we knew of. Good! I was not too well; so La Taupine, taking all the men, set off in the big canoe, and I was left with the smaller and most of the goods to await for their return till evening.

"To kill time I unloaded the canoe, lifted it up under the bushes, and piled the stuff beside it. Then I set to work to wait, and, with nothing to do and no one to talk to, waiting is the devil. So during the morning, somehow, I fell asleep, and I slept until I was awakened by a fly tickling my nose."

"Get on with your story, fellow!" said the Governor sharply.

257

"Pardon me, mon Gouverneur, but that fly has much to do with my story, and I can only tell it my own way. I shook my head, but the fly returned. I tried to hit it, but hit my nose instead, and, half asleep, I started up and began: 'Ah! mon....' but the fly was gone, and, instead, there sate an Iroquois with a twig in his hand and seven other devils like himself, in full war paint, squatting close round with a grin on every face.

"There I was! This was the end of our beautiful journey for which we had paid so many masses! The canoe was gone, every Indian had a pile of goods on the ground before him, and I without so much as a musk-rat skin to show for it all.

"'Well, my children!'" I said, "'You have only caught me asleep, so don't boast too loudly! If you had been men you would have wakened me. Any squaw could have done as much,' but no one answered me a word. At last I said, 'Now, if you want to move I am ready!' and so we started.

"Such a march! We went through the bush at a half run, only stopping once that evening when we reached their camp, where we picked up these two squaws; but half an hour later we were astir again. All that night we marched without halt until daylight, and it was the next afternoon before they dared make a regular camp. They knew La Taupine was with me, and that they were not safe within any reasonable distance.

"No doubt we would have moved on the next day as well, only one of the Iroquois insisted he had carried his plunder far enough, and now would taste it." Dubosq caught the Governor's angry start at this admission of his carrying the forbidden spirits, but, like the fly on his nose, it was too important a point to be passed over, and he continued with a well-assumed innocence: "So they tapped one of the kegs, and when I awoke — for I was so done out that I slept like the dead as soon as I could throw myself down — they were all pretty reasonably drunk, and they had begun on a second.

"We were all friends together now; they boasted of how they would be received in their bourgade when they walked in with Dubosq, Dubosq le Coureur tied between two squaws — and they laughed, those painted devils, and struck me on the back, and I laughed with them. Why not? Were we not all friends together? They said my standing quarrel with their people was an old affair, something that had passed, and I let them say on. So we drank, but all the time I was keeping my head clear by planning how I would take that same quarrel up before long.

"A third keg was opened, and then a fourth; which was sheer waste, for before it was touched, and long before the moon was an hour up, the two squaws and I were the only ones sober in the camp.

"They had tried to fasten me in their usual way, but only one arm was really tied to a sapling, and the Indian on my right was so drunk that as soon as I determined upon my plan I drew my arm with the unfastened cords from under him, and with his own knife cut myself free. I was sure of him, but was not quite so certain of the one on my left.

"The two squaws were asleep, as far as I could tell; but I dared not make any noise for fear they should scream out or escape, so I raised myself slowly on my elbow, and, after just touching my Indian over the body with the tips of my fingers to make sure of how he was lying, I struck with all my strength, and at the same time threw myself across his body, covering his mouth and nose with my hand. I might have spared myself the trouble, for my knife had found its way to the right place, so he only drew himself up together and trembled a little and then lay quite still.

"I raised my head, and listened with both ears. Nothing moved but the wind in the trees. There was no sound but the moving of the leaves and the snoring of the drunken Indians. I sat up, took my cords, and, tying them together, crept softly over towards the two squaws, and before they were well awake they were so tied that I was safe from any move on their part, and I easily showed them it would not be well to make any noise. Now I had only to finish my work.

"I walked back to my first man, and with his own cassetête I sent him, and after him his six fellow thieves, one after another, down to Hell in such quick following that they were treading on each other's heels.

"In three days I was back at the River again, for I had all the trading I wanted this journey; but I have not come empty-handed."

Here the vanity of the half-breed could not be controlled, the Indian blood asserting itself. He drew himself up to his full height, and his voice swelled into a triumphant boast, as he repeated: "No, I have not come empty-handed! I have brought no furs, I have come back in a strange canoe! I have brought back no goods, nor have I a pound of beaver to show for them! I will not trade on the Place du Marché to-morrow, but there is a proper man in Montreal who would not give ten years of his life for my butin! I travel light, mon gouverneur. I travel light, but I carry the lives of eight men! There!"

At the word he threw back his blanket, and slipping a belt from his waist hurled on the table before the two gentlemen eight Iroquois scalps, with their long locks twisted and plaited with coloured porcupine and beads in the highest refinement of savage skill. They both started involuntarily. Dubosq stood with his arms crossed on his heaving chest and his gaze fixed on the Governor's face, while the eyes of the two squaws sparkled and danced in admiration of the successful warrior.

The Governor, with an exclamation of disgust, pushed the belt with its horrible trophies from him, and he and the Curé looked sternly into each other's eyes before he spake:

"Take up your devil's necklace, you scoundrel! The law allows you a reward; but, had I my way, it would take a different shape. It is to you, and such as you, we owe the stain that is gathering on our name. You are worse than the savages whom you disgrace by your presence; and, if you come before us for praise, you have brought your suit to the wrong court. I have nothing to say to you! Tomorrow you may bring your tale before the Governor of the town, and if I have any influence with him, be assured you shall meet with your full reward."

Dubosq calmly replaced his belt, and gathered his blanket about him; but the angry flush on his cheeks burned still redder as he signed to the two squaws, who arose and stood in their places.

"We will go?" he enquired softly.

"Non, mordieu! You shall not go!" thundered the Governor, striking his stick fiercely on the table.

At his signal the doors swung open, and a sergeant with four men entered.

"Here! Take this fellow and keep him and the women safe till morning. See they are comfortable, though, and have enough to eat."

The sergeant saluted, and crossed over to Dubosq, who, bowing quietly to the Governor and the priest, passed out of the room, followed by the squaws and the soldiers.

*　*　*

In the early morning there was a commotion in the courtyard of the Governor's residence there was much running to and fro, and indignant reproach and answer.

One thing alone was clear. Dubosq had escaped in some mysterious manner in spite of his guards, for the elder squaw was the only occupant of the outhouse in which they had been confined over night.

Later on, a piece of coarse paper was discovered fastened high on the main door of the Château on which was scrawled in red chalk, "ETIENNE DUBOSQ, SA MARQUE," and in the centre was one of the ghastly trophies, an Iroquois scalp, pinned fast by the blade of his hunting knife.

WILLIAM MCLENNAN was born in Montreal in 1856 and died in the same city in 1904. A graduate of McGill, he practised as a notary in Montreal but is now chiefly remembered for his contribution to the late nineteenth-century popularization of Quebec life and history. His first publication, *Songs of Old Canada* (1886), is a volume of translations of French-Canadian popular songs. He contributed several short stories and sketches to various magazines, including a series of sketches of French-Canadian life to *Harper's Magazine*. McLennan was a friend of Archibald Lampman, and a member of the Royal Society of Canada. His books include *As Told to His Grace, and Other Stories* (1891), *Montreal and Some of the Makers Thereof* (1893), *Spanish John* (1898), *In Old France and New* (1899), and in conjunction with J. N. McIlwaith, *The Span O'Life. A Tale of Louisbourg and Quebec* (1899).